Peace and Justice Studies: Critical Pedagogy

This book explores the interdisciplinary arena of peace studies and shows how the field has evolved and continues to grow and change. Dedicated to bringing students face to face with the grave injustices and violence in the contemporary world, it equips them with the tools to work for transformational change. Informed by an intersectional perspective, scholar-activist authors probe contested terrain, including teaching social justice from a place of privilege, decolonializing pedagogies, and community organizing. Games and simulations, storytelling, experiential integrated learning, and pedagogical approaches are employed to encourage critical thinking, empathy, optimism, and activism.

Margaret Groarke is Associate Professor of Political Science at Manhattan College. She was Director of Peace Studies there for 11 years, and Co-Chair of the Peace and Justice Studies Association for 4 years. She is co-author, with Frances Fox Piven and Lorraine C. Minnite, of *Keeping Down the Black Vote* (New Press, 2009), and articles on community organizing and American electoral politics.

Emily Welty is Director of Peace and Justice Studies, and Associate Professor of Women's and Gender Studies, at Pace University. Her previous publications include *Occupying Political Science: Occupy Wall Street from New York City to the World* (Palgrave, 2013) and *Unity in Diversity: Interfaith Dialogue in the Middle East* (United States Institute of Peace, 2007).

Peace and Justice Studies

Critical Pedagogy

Edited by Margaret Groarke and Emily Welty

Routledge
Taylor & Francis Group
NEW YORK AND LONDON

First published
by Routledge
711 Third Avenue, New York, NY 10017

and by Routledge
2 Park Square, Milton Park, Abingdon, Oxon OX14 4RN

Routledge is an imprint of the Taylor & Francis Group, an informa business

Published 2019

Library of Congress Cataloging-in-Publication Data
Names: Groarke, Margaret, editor. | Welty, Emily, editor.
Title: Peace and justice studies : critical pedagogy / [edited by] Margaret Groarke, Manhattan College; Emily Welty, Pace University.
Description: New York, NY : Routledge, 2019. | Includes bibliographical references.
Identifiers: LCCN 2018029315| ISBN 9780815346340 (hbk) | ISBN 9780815346357 (pbk) | ISBN 9781351170604 (ebk)
Subjects: LCSH: Peace--Study and teaching (Higher) | Peace-building--Study and teaching (Higher) | Social justice--Study and teaching (Higher)
Classification: LCC JZ5534 .P423 2019 | DDC 303.6/60711--dc23
LC record available at https://lccn.loc.gov/2018029315

ISBN: 978-0-815-34634-0 (hbk)
ISBN: 978-0-815-34635-7 (pbk)
ISBN: 978-1-351-17060-4 (ebk)

Typeset in Sabon
by Taylor & Francis Books

Contents

Contributors

Geoffrey W. Bateman, PhD, is Associate Dean for Student Support and Experiential Learning in Regis College and Associate Professor and Chair in the Department of Peace and Justice Studies at Regis University in Denver, Colorado. His current research examines the queering of non-violence in the work of activists like Bayard Rustin and Barbara Deming. Previous publications include *Don't Ask, Don't Tell: Debating the Gay Ban in the Military* (Lynne Rienner, 2003).

Amanda Smith Byron, Ed.D, is a social justice educator with over 25 years of experience working with diverse communities to heal trauma and transform conflict. Dr. Byron is an Assistant Professor in Conflict Resolution at Portland State University, where she directs the Holocaust and Genocide Studies Project, and focuses teaching and research on unsettling the role of identity in conflict, understanding enmification and hatred as root causes of violence, and developing peacebuilding strategies to effectively address ethnoreligious conflict.

G. Michelle Collins-Sibley, PhD, is Professor of English and Chair of the Department of Interdisciplinary & Liberal Studies at the University of Mount Union. Her recent publications include, "'Becoming the Bear': A Meditation on Racial Battle Fatigue, Resistance & Grace in Academia," *Racial Battle Fatigue: Insights from the Front Lines of Social Justice Advocacy*, Jennifer L. Martin, ed. (Prager, 2015) and *What Does It Mean to Tweet #Black Lives Matter: Reflections on Black History Month 2015* (Alliance Review, Feb 2015).

Margaret Groarke, PhD, is Associate Professor of Government at Manhattan College. She was Director of Peace Studies at Manhattan College for 11 years, and Co-Chair of the Peace and Justice Studies Association for 4 years. She is co-author, with Frances Fox Piven and Lorraine C. Minnite, of *Keeping Down the Black Vote* (New Press, 2009), and articles on community organizing and American electoral politics.

Randy Janzen, PhD, is a past Chair of the Mir Centre for Peace at Selkirk College in British Columbia, Canada, and teaches Peace and Justice

Studies to undergraduate students. Randy has also been involved in a number of different community education initiatives, including mediation, conflict transformation and nonviolent action. Randy's research focus is unarmed civilian peacekeeping/protection and he is a founding member of the global Unarmed Civilian Peacekeeping/Protection Research Network.

Amal I. Khoury, PhD, is Assistant Professor in the Global, International and Area Studies Department at the University of North Carolina-Charlotte. Dr. Khoury specializes in peace and conflict studies, with an area focus on the Middle East. She also has an active research agenda that focuses on peacebuilding and post-conflict reconciliation. She has co-authored a book on interfaith dialogue in the Middle East (*Unity in Diversity: Interfaith Dialogue in the Middle East,* United States Institute for Peace Press, 2007).

Mark Lance, PhD, is Professor of Philosophy, and Professor and former Director in Justice and Peace Studies, at Georgetown University. His work spans philosophy of language, logic, moral theory, and activist strategy. He was a board member of the Peace and Justice Studies Association, and is currently on the steering committee and chair of the advisory board of the Truth Telling Project. His activist work over 35 years encompasses a wide range of peace and justice movements.

Joy A. Meeker, PhD, leads the Peace and Justice Specialization in Saybrook University's Transformative Social Change Doctoral Program. Dr. Meeker has taught peace and conflict studies for two decades, and serves on the Peace and Justice Studies Association's board. As a conflict practitioner, she serves diverse communities including students, organizations, and people who are incarcerated. Joy's work seeks to contribute to a more just world, a place where it's even more possible to love.

Edmund Pries, PhD, is Assistant Professor of Global Studies, Social Entrepreneurship, Religion and Culture, and Community Engagement at Wilfrid Laurier University where his teaching is centered in the area of Peace and Conflict Studies. His research focuses on religion and peace/conflict and on social contracts derived from citizenship and military oaths. He also researches and writes on pedagogy. Edmund is the recipient of three awards for teaching excellence. He is the former co-chair of the Peace and Justice Studies Association (Canada & US) and continues on the board of the Peace and Conflict Studies Association of Canada. He recently co-edited the book *Peace Studies between Tradition and Innovation* (Cambridge Scholars Publishing, 2015).

Karen Lynn Ridd, MA, teaches Conflict Resolution and International Development Studies at Menno Simons College of the Canadian Mennonite University, an affiliate of the University of Winnipeg. Her work has been honoured with the 1992 Governor-General's Award: 125th Confederation of Canada Anniversary Medal, the 1990 Canada YM/YWCA Peace Medal and the 1989 Manitoba Human Rights International Achievement Award. Karen excels in alternative pedagogy, and has worked in Latin America, South East Asia and First Nations Territories. In 2013, the Peace and Justice Studies Association awarded Karen "Peace Educator of the Year." Her most recent publication is "Teaching Peace, Being Peace" in *Voices of Harmony and Dissent: How Peacebuilders Are Transforming Their Worlds*, eds Richard McCutcheon, Jarem Sawatsky and Valerie Smith (Canadian University Press, 2015).

Sara Shroff is a PhD candidate at The New School. She teaches across various disciplines including global studies, peace and justice studies, gender and sexuality studies and economics at The New School, Pace University and NYU. Her research broadly revolves around feminist, queer and trans interventions in economics and philanthropy studies. She previously worked in global philanthropy and development for over 18 years.

Emily Welty, PhD, is Director of Peace and Justice Studies, and Associate Professor of Women's and Gender Studies at Pace University. Her previous publications include *Occupying Political Science: Occupy Wall Street from New York City to the World* (Palgrave, 2013) and *Unity in Diversity: Interfaith Dialogue in the Middle East* (United States Institute of Peace, 2007).

Introduction

Margaret Groarke and Emily Welty

This book explores the different strategies, philosophies and methodologies that guide the pedagogy of professors teaching Peace and Justice Studies (PJS) at the university level. It aims to both challenge and support faculty teaching as well as to inspire both faculty and students exploring the field. As in many interdisciplinary academic fields, faculty and students in PJS may have academic training in a different academic disciplines and are looking to broaden and deepen their own training as interdisciplinary scholars.

The authors in this volume grapple with the challenges of promoting a critical perspective in our students and reflexively explore both the strengths and shortcomings of their individual practices in the classroom. In bringing together the particular authors in this book, we have sought out both senior and emerging scholars, and highlighted writers who offer the insights of critical pedagogy, queer theory, postcolonial studies and experiential education. The chapters in this book center around four central questions:

- How do we promote the particular habits of mind and heart we consider critical for PJS students – critical thinking, an ethos of solidarity, optimism, activism – while recognizing that some of these qualities may be in tension?
- How do we guide students in recognizing their positionality in the midst of the issues we study?
- How might experiential learning be used to encourage the development of important qualities in our students?
- Finally, are we continually re-evaluating the field of Peace and Justice Studies itself? What do "peace" and "justice" mean to us, and how can different approaches – among them, critical pedagogy, queer theory, postcolonial studies and experiential education – help inform our understanding, our research agendas, and our teaching? What is the role of Peace and Justice Studies in the university?

What is Peace and Justice Studies?

Peace and Justice Studies (PJS) is an interdisciplinary field that seeks to understand the causes of violent conflict, develop new ways to transform conflict and address the root social causes that lead to conflict. These root social causes are described by PJS scholars as structural violence (sometimes also called institutional or cultural violence) and include racism, classism, sexism, heterosexism, and other forms of injustice. Peace is not defined simply as the absence of war or the absence of conflict; in fact, most scholars agree that conflict can actually be a productive, healthy way of exposing societal or personal grievances. This orientation can be seen in the ways that PJS scholars and practitioners describe their work as conflict management, conflict resolution or conflict transformation. The latter designation, "conflict transformation" is often used to signify the way that conflict is not an inherently destructive force to be avoided but rather can act as a transformative agent that promotes needed social change.

The relationship between peace and justice is therefore critical. Without justice, peace is false – a way of describing the privilege of some, at the expense of others. Without peace, justice can be destructive, concentrating solely on revenge, evening the score without regard to relationship. The earliest academic programs were focused on the perils of war, and took the name Peace Studies; these programs came to realize that the mere absence of open hostilities was not peace, but that true peace, what Galtung (1996) called positive peace, required "right relationships and harmonious relations," (Earth Charter; Wood, 2016, p. 2) or what many would call justice. Today, many universities embrace the interconnected nature of both peace and justice by using both in the title of the program.

It is also true that in Peace and Justice Studies, both of these concepts are problematized, as one clearly sees in several of the chapters in this volume. Our research, study and activism is not only a pursuit of solutions to violence and injustice, but also a continual reconsideration of what our goals really are – what really constitutes peace and justice?

One of the foundational claims of PJS is that problems such as war are too complex to be completely understood by any one discipline. Therefore, an interdisciplinary or transdisciplinary approach encapsulating many disciplines is required. For example, an understanding of war should take into account the insights of political science (seeking to understand power and ideology), economics (scarcity, resources, markets), history (previous examples of conflict, trends), sociology/anthropology (social movements, globalization, identity), psychology (aggression, fear, competition), communication (image-making, messages), computer science (technology, weaponry), literature (war narratives, symbolism/discourse of heroism), religious studies/philosophy (ethics of violence, utilitarian vs. normative theories), environmental studies (ecological costs of war), gender studies (militarism and gender), the arts (creative expressions of or critique of conflict), and others.

Peace and Justice Studies first emerged as an academic discipline in the US in the aftermath of World War II with the establishment of the first program at Manchester College in 1948. In the late 1960s, four more programs were founded in the United States, and in 1977, Conrad Grebel University

College's Peace and Conflict Studies program (PACS) at the University of Waterloo became the first peace studies program in Canada. In the 1980s, the field expanded rapidly in both the United States and Canada. Today there are more than 400 undergraduate programs in Peace and Justice Studies worldwide, more than 30 MA programs and several PhD programs. At the undergraduate level, Peace and Justice Studies programs tend to be a part of a four-year liberal arts curriculum, though a growing number of community colleges and two-year degree programs are beginning to also offer PJS certifications. Programs building on the key themes in PJS are beginning to be offered in elementary, middle and high schools – often focused on anti-bullying initiatives, peer mediation and tolerance work.

The interdisciplinary nature of PJS programs reflects the wider move in academia to go beyond a "silo approach" that sees texts, methods and theories as solely based in one particular discipline. Peace and Justice Studies classes tend to reflect an intersectional approach to knowledge that focuses on the ways that issues of race, class, gender, sexual orientation, nationality, etc. affect both our research and our teaching.

There are multiple career paths that students with degrees in PJS pursue including advocacy, human rights work, nonprofits, restorative justice, mediation, negotiation, facilitation, humanitarianism, poverty alleviation, education, counseling, trauma work, social entrepreneurship, public health, government, economic development, research and environmental protection (Smith, 2016). Of course, a liberal arts education is not only about preparing students for a career, but shaping the kind of person they will be.

Rejecting the Canon, Embracing Habits of the Mind and Heart

Every academic program defines kinds of knowledge that a student is expected to master. Can one earn a degree in Economics without reading Adam Smith? Or study American Politics without reading the Federalist Papers? Defining the canon for any field is necessarily an endeavor fraught with controversy, but the interdisciplinary and wide-ranging nature of Peace Studies makes it especially difficult (Archer, 2016). Many scholars of PJS reject the idea of the canon entirely, seeing it as a disciplinary tool that inappropriately elevates some and silences others. The very idea of a canon suggests that some particular voices capture an idea with wide-ranging applications across all contexts. This concept is viewed with suspicion by many who have found themselves written out of history by the same process of canonization of often white, male, English-speaking, upper middle-class voices. It is nearly impossible to find a single text that is taught in all PJS programs. However, this doesn't mean that PJS lacks coherence as a discipline. Beyond sharing an emphasis on particular themes, this field has emphasized the habits of mind and heart we want to cultivate in our students, in our colleagues and in our own research.

Who do we want our students to become? Peace and Justice Studies programs want to educate our students to be advocates for peace and justice.

We want them to be good citizens of their own nations and good global citizens as well. What is a good citizen? Not a docile subject, but a person who actively participates in creating the kind of society she wishes to live in, and demands justice from institutional structures, both for herself and for others. Such a person, we think, needs some important habits of mind and heart: critical thinking, an ethos of solidarity, optimism, activism.

Critical Thinking

Every discipline in every university claims to build "critical thinking" skills. The term itself is so overused that it has nearly become a useless cliché. If we are to espouse critical thinking as a core value of PJS then we need to articulate the particularity of its value to our field and body of knowledge.

One of the key challenges to an intelligent and careful analysis of conflict and violence is the tendency to oversimplify the complexity and specificity of individual contexts, histories, and populations. If we are to truly begin to build peace in a meaningful sense, we need to understand the root causes of conflict and those are rarely able to be understood in simple tropes or fixed narrative paths. When asked what they want to learn in a PJS classroom, undergraduate students often request to talk more about "the news" or "current events". On the surface, this seems like an eminently reasonable request. However, PJS programs need to go beyond just teaching students to be conversant in the crisis of the day. If we are to produce critical thinkers who can respond intelligently to conflict, we need to teach not only current events but also how to unpack the complexity within any given outbreak of violence.

One of the uphill battles in training students to think critically about justice and peace is that culture and language is rife with slogans and clichés about conflict. Part of the process of training critical thinkers is to engage in an unlearning process where students accept that it doesn't make one sound clever to blithely say "history repeats itself" or "violence is never the answer". Even the challenge to "be the change you want to see in the world" is nothing but an easy motto if it isn't undergirded by analysis about what that might mean structurally/institutionally/politically. So as educators we are faced with the dual challenge of inspiring students but also urging them beyond inspirational quotes in order to engage in the real work of thinking.

An Ethos of Solidarity

One hallmark of Peace and Justice Studies programs is the goal of building a radical sense of solidarity with suffering, marginalized and oppressed people. Programs often aim to do this in a variety of ways including careful exposure, often in the form of service learning programs or other community service organizations and through a pedagogical lens of accompaniment rather than pity or charity.

The starting point for the work of solidarity is not to try to identify problems in some Other place and try to imagine and offer solutions to a remote group of people elsewhere. Nor is it to turn entirely inward and pretend that we only have an ethical obligation to our own communities. The work of solidarity is to teach students to work at multiple levels of self and Other, home and away. This echoes the words of community organizer Grace Lee Boggs who wrote, "To make a revolution, people must not only struggle against existing institutions. They must make a philosophical/spiritual leap and become more 'human' human beings. In order to change/transform the world, they must change/transform themselves" (Boggs, 2016, p. 153). There is a danger in a program orienting itself exclusively towards either inner or outer transformation. The best PJS programs manage the fine line between teaching students to examine the self but also to understand the Other.

One of the ways this balance between inner and outer transformation manifests is in training students to recognize and critique privilege. For white students (and faculty) this means a willingness to look at the ways that their own achievement has been scaffolded by a world that sees them as inherently valuable. In a final paper, one senior PJS student reflected, "I am so privileged in so many ways, and feel that because of this and because I am in a position where I have mobility and security, I have a responsibility and an obligation to use my privilege and to make it functional. Otherwise it is simply a selfish and self-serving privilege." This demonstrates an understanding that the student is not going to suddenly stop benefiting from white privilege just because she is aware of it but that she has learned to ask how this privilege might be used to strengthen the voices of other people do not have it.

The commitment to an ethic of solidarity not only drives the choice of classroom materials and course topics but also affects the way that students are trained to conduct research. Academic programs often aim to develop a sense of reflexivity in their students that enable the students as researchers to think critically about their own identities and the way it affects the politics of knowledge production. This inward reflection organically builds a sense of empathy for other positionalities. As we begin to imagine and name the way that our own story and identity has shaped us politically, socially and intellectually, we can also begin to imagine and define how others have been shaped in different ways.

In the methodology section of a senior capstone paper, one student reflected:

> While conducting qualitative interviews, I had to reflect quite often throughout the process. Reflexivity is the process of examining myself as a researcher and my relationship to the research I was conducting… Being reflexive throughout the process has made me aware as an interviewer of my own conceptions and experiences as well as the knowledge I gained through the literature review.

Optimism

The seriousness of the problems we confront in our classes – war, injustice, racial oppression, entrenched poverty – can lead to pessimism and paralysis. The grim cost of war, in human lives, and in the money devoted to armaments instead of human needs, does not seem to discourage its continuation; as of this writing, there are more than 40 active conflicts across the globe (IRIN, 2018). Knowledge of the brutal inhumanity of the Holocaust did not prevent the genocide of hundreds of thousands in Rwanda, or the numerous atrocities of the war in the former Yugoslavia.

For some students, the most challenging thing is to learn that our own countries are far from blameless in the injustices of the world. As we recognize that our countries – or our religious communities, for that matter – have often failed to live up to the ideals they espouse, it can be tempting to reject entirely those ideals or those institutions.

We don't want our students to become cynical critics of a world so terrible it cannot be improved, but optimistic creators of a better future. Optimism is a necessary ingredient of positive social change. Elise Boulding, an important early scholar in peace and conflict studies, often talked about the concept of a 200-year present. She explained it thus:

> The 200-year present began 100 years ago, with the year of birth of the people who reach their hundredth birthday today. The other boundary of the 200-year present, 100 years from now, is the 100th birthday of the babies born today. If you take that span, you and I have a lot of contact with a lot of people from different parts of that span.
>
> (Boulding, 2003)

Boulding used this concept to encourage people to imagine the future they wanted to create. But she also, in talking about the 200-year present, encouraged us to reflect on the social progress made in the previous hundred years. One hundred years before the publication of this book, women in most parts of the United States and Canada had not yet won the franchise. Much of the world was directly ruled by colonial powers in 1918. Recognizing what humankind has been able to achieve in the last one hundred years can balance out our sorrow and rage at the injustice and violence that has so colored human history, with a recognition that people have, in every era, banded together to stand up for justice, to improve the human condition, to invent, cure disease, and work for the common good. Even in the most difficult of times, there is the hope of change. Such optimism is empowering.

Activism

Peace and Justice Studies is by its nature a field that encourages activism. As professors, we are not content for our students to merely recognize injustice;

we want them to take action to end that injustice, as we do ourselves. We want our students to develop both the inclination to respond to an injustice by considering what action they might take to draw attention to it, correct it, and organize others to participate in stopping it. We want them to learn the skills necessary to be effective activists.

Activism makes use of many conventional academic skills, common to many disciplines. The ability to research a topic and write coherently about it, so central to academia, is also a skill that activists can use to educate others and build a constituency for a cause. The ability to structure a coherent argument, to be persuasive, so central to academia, is a skill useful to mobilizing a constituency or lobbying government officials to take action.

However, activism also requires skills that academia does not always value highly or effectively impart. Activists must be skilled at working with others, and finding ways to include the interests and abilities of a wide range of individuals in a common effort. They must recognize that there are times and reasons to hold firmly to one's position, and to be willing to compromise, and that both humility and wisdom are needed to determine which is which. In a space like academia that has been governed by rule-following, activism requires an ability to be disobedient, to be willing to break the rules and suffer the consequences in service to a higher ideal.

We want our students to not simply copy the strategies they see used by the movements they admire, but to be aware of the theory of change that underlies that strategy, and able to critically evaluate it. Effective activists have learned how to analyze the dynamics of power in a situation, and to identify the opportunities to shift power and decisions.

We work to develop these habits of mind and heart in our students, although others in our universities may find them beside the point, or impossible to measure. We cultivate these values in ourselves and in our students, although the process may be uncomfortable, for us and for our students, and may require us to question long-held assumptions. We struggle to understand the complex problems of our world, imagine a more peaceful and just world, and develop the abilities to contribute to making it so. We hope this book serves as one way that we share with each other our efforts towards this goal.

Summary of Chapters

This book is organized into four sections. The authors in Part One, "Intersectional Identities and Peace and Justice Studies," encourage us to reflect on our identities as professors and students in Peace Studies, and how those identities structure our perspective on the world around us. The authors in this section present ways they encourage students to do the difficult but important work of recognizing their own positionality.

Part Two, "Experiential Learning in Peace and Justice Studies" offers three examples of professors reflecting on their use of experiential learning to promote the habits of mind and heart we think are so crucial to Peace and Justice Studies. All three examples present case studies of how the classroom might be transformed into a place of deeper learning by shifting the power from the instructor to the students or the larger community. These practices draw upon the wisdom that learning is more deeply-seated when it is drawn from experience rather than mere knowledge-transfer.

The authors in Part Three address the power of story in our classrooms, discussing the ways that stories – both personal narratives and fictional narratives – can be a tool for deeper exploration of difficult questions, and opportunities to build an ethos of solidarity among our students. This is not without its challenges – the authors in this section are sensitive to the way that we read or hear stories from our own social position, and that the dynamics of who is a part of the conversation in our particular classroom will necessarily shape how we interpret those stories.

As is so often true in education, we are constantly engaged in a balancing act – between encouraging and evaluating, between sharing knowledge and co-creating knowledge. In the final section of this book, three authors address the important but delicate balance between hope and critical thinking and offer challenges for how we might continue to critique and deepen our commitments to both justice and peace.

References

Archer, Douglas. 2016. *A Peace Studies Canon*. South Bend, Indiana: Notre Dame University, Hesburgh Libraries.

Boggs, Grace Lee. 2016. *Living for Change: An Autobiography*. Minneapolis: University of Minnesota Press.

Boulding, Elise. 2003. Interview by Julian Portilla. Beyond Intractability. Accessed at www.beyondintractability.org/audiodisplay/boulding-e.

Earth Charter. 2012. What is the Earth Charter? Accessed at http://earthcharter.org/discover/.

Galtung, Johan. 1996. *Peace by Peaceful Means: Peace and Conflict, Development and Civilization*. London: SAGE Publications.

IRIN. 2018. UPDATED: Mapped – A World at War. IRIN. Accessed at www.irinnews.org/maps-and-graphics/2017/04/04/updated-mapped-world-war.

Smith, David. 2016. *Peace Jobs: A Student's Guide to Starting a Career Working for Peace*. Charlotte, NC: Information Age Publishing.

Wood, Houston. 2016. *Invitation to Peace Studies*. New York: Oxford University Press.

Part I

Intersectional Identities and Peace and Justice Studies

1 Creative Discomfort

Dilemmas of Teaching Toward Social Justice

Joy A. Meeker

Emotions in the classroom are invaluable guides for educators—while their role is often devalued, particularly in higher education. Feminist educators highlight how creative interpretations of emotions can raise consciousness that is personal and political. In other words, our *felt senses* can signal opportunities for learning toward personal–social change (Boler 1999). This chapter explores how peace and social justice educators can renew their attention to emotion in their pedagogy in ways that can animate learning and change.

As a peace educator and feminist, I have long recognized that the emotionally charged moments can instigate learning, while they are challenging to navigate. This led me to develop a qualitative inquiry where I interviewed 14 seasoned peace educators who hold feminist orientations, asking each to reflect on their tangible experiences of engaging emotion in their pedagogy.[1] In this chapter, I focus on the dilemmas of teaching that emerged as significant for the participants as they reflected on encountering emotions in their classrooms. My hope is to make their insights available to a larger audience of educators, expanding the concrete possibilities available for peace educators to respond creatively to emotions in ways that activate learning toward social justice.

The Role of Emotions in Teaching toward Social Change

Emotions can signal an engagement with oneself, with one's relationship to others, and one's relationship to the social political world. Yet as the peace educators I interviewed testified, emotions are tricky to address in classrooms. Not only are educators and students often unprepared to respond to emotions in fruitful ways, but they also are constrained by the common interpretations of emotions in Western contexts, which consider emotions as natural, internal, and private forces.

While a review of emotions is beyond the scope of this chapter, I join those who reject the Western assumptions that emotions are dichotomous and inferior to cognition and instead consider emotions as having a mutual relationship to thought and as indispensable for interpretation (Demasio

1994). Feminists have reworked the meaning of emotions by considering them as "social cultural practices" instead of private, psychological experiences (Ahmed 2004, 9). I also join feminists who are less interested in what emotions are, but what they can do (Boler 1999). This chapter considers how emotions work in pedagogical practice, suggesting that the concrete circulation of emotion can open a charged social space in our classrooms that offers possibilities for nourishing change.

Dilemmas of Engaging Emotions in the Classroom

While all the educators I interviewed agree that "positive" emotions such as love and empathy are crucial forces to build a learning community, I will instead focus on the moments when emotions were uncomfortable and opened the possibility of difficult knowledge (Ahmed 2017). Three dilemmas that emerged as particularly significant for the participants relating to emotions in the classroom were: (1) responding to emotions that accompany conflict; (2) challenging an inheritance of teaching toward privilege; and (3) responding to loss. After introducing each dilemma, I will share examples of how participants responded to these challenges.

My intent is not to offer replicable prescriptions for educators but to harness the energy from the tensions of these dilemmas. Clearly, the dilemmas raised in this chapter are not exhaustive: A different group of educators might emphasize a distinct set of challenges. Yet the dilemmas suggest that bringing attention to emotions in pedagogy can help prepare educators to open spaces for deeper learning toward social change.

(1) The Dilemma of Responding to Emotions that Accompany Conflict

One educator who I interviewed, who I will call Nathan,[2] describes how his students are often comfortable with structural analysis of conflicts, but when structures become enlivened—when "this happens in a real personal and direct way," it presents a challenge:

> I think it's a difficult jump for people … The jump from the sort of structural level to the individual level. It's a big leap, and people have a lot of difficulty making that leap. I mean a lot of people feel comfortable with the structural analysis at a societal level, realizing that there is a lot of oppression or injustice has occurred. When this happens in a real personal and direct way, how should it be handled, that's a real hard jump for people.

To support the "hard jump" that Nathan speaks of, participant educators spoke of the need to anticipate and respond creatively to the discomfort that accompanies conflict. Specifically, they suggested four strategies: Aiming toward creative discomfort; utilizing emotions to discern when to intervene;

harnessing the force of emotions to consider injustice; and using emotions to destabilize Othering.

Aim toward Creative Discomfort

Participant educators often discussed how they work to sustain a "learning edge" with their students—what educator Ramiro names "creative discomfort." As Ramiro states, "people learn when they are uncomfortable." However, he also argues that if students are too uncomfortable and change seems beyond their reach, they are likely to retreat from the challenge.

Ramiro stresses the need to first establishing some "caring connection in the room" before working on the "hard stuff" of conflict:

> People hear the hard stuff better if there is some caring connection in the room. If you try and teach too much too fast, either their racism or their defensiveness or their fear comes out. So what you want to do is you want to minimize their fear ... of each other, of you, of the content. And so you layer it in such a way ... you don't teach about institutionalized oppression and the legacy of colonization until you've clarified that the purpose of multiculturalism is to create mutuality.

Ramiro seeks to sustain a creative discomfort where "students are uncomfortable enough that they want to learn," but not to the point where they are no longer able to respond creatively:

> People change and grow when they are uncomfortable. But if they are too uncomfortable, they just retrench. So they have to be uncomfortable enough to want to learn. So if the concept is too raw, like polarized, that's not creative ... It may even be on the verge of polarization, but your job is to pull it back to the middle of community. And so you're using conflict creatively to nourish growth.

Aiming toward creative discomfort makes it more likely that a learning community can respond creatively to the emotions that accompany conflict, increasingly the possibility of learning and growth.

Notice Emotions to Inform When to Intervene

A second strategy recommended by the participant educators is to look for embodied discomfort, which can reveal unarticulated dynamics in the classroom and inform an educator to respond. Educators reflected that they often raise the unstated discomfort of students to the surface by responding to body signs including coughing, the shuffling of chairs, or the rolling of eyes.

For example, Alice spoke of a student who presented a research project in her class that relied on racial stereotyping. Alice said she was in the process of deciding whether she should interrupt the problematic presentation when another student started coughing, attuning her to a palpable but unstated "discomfort in the room." This discomfort provided the impetus and a point of entry for Alice to intervene and stop the presentation. Alice decided that not responding to the discomfort risked inadvertently reinforcing a felt undercurrent of racism.

While Alice's example illustrates how educators can bring attention to discomfort that is present but unnamed in classes, educators also spoke of introducing discomfort into their classes in order to instigate learning moments. For example, Hanna recounted her spontaneous decision to introduce race during a go-around of introductions on the first day of her course by stating, "My name is Hanna and I am white." As she described below, the class quickly became alert:

> I didn't tell them how to introduce themselves, but there was a pattern which began which seems very common and familiar. And when I introduced [myself] I said, 'My name is Hanna and I'm white.' ... There was a reaction. It felt palpable, you could hear a pin drop ... But I'd just say you could feel that there was a shift in the room. A pregnant pause so to speak. And that to me—that moment and what followed felt creative.

Hanna spoke of how bringing attention to her racial identity led to a palpable "shift in the room," which created an entryway to creative dialogue. She was able to connect her embodied racial identity to the course material, discussing why "naming race felt so unusual," and how it matters when learning about racial injustice. As Alice and Hanna's reflections illustrate, naming or instigating discomfort raises the attention of students.

Harness the Power of Emotions to Consider Structured Injustice

Educators highlighted how asking students to consider social structures often requires destabilizing students who have adapted to a status quo that "feels right" because it is comfortable, familiar. Ramiro describes how the dominant culture in United States socializes us to adapt to structures of domination, what he articulates as "socialization into dominance." Ramiro suggests that social justice educators need to actively disrupt the common notion that injustice is exceptional, and that injustice emerges from an individual intent to cause harm—in contrast to being woven into the fabric of social relations in an unjust society.

As an example highlighting the emotional dimension of recognizing structures, Sage discussed an embodied activity she learned from anti-racism work in South Africa:

> I was doing some anti-racism work when I was at a sabbatical in South Africa and there was an exercise there that I find very helpful which was to have students share, to have everyone share a time when they were victimized ... You have them share one on one, they each share a story. And the amount of talking in the room is deafening. It's like a buzzing noise. And then you ask them, five minutes later, 'Now tell the story of the time that you victimized someone else.' And the room is just silent. Nobody talks.

After this exercise, Sage creates the space for students to make sense of the contrast between the energetic "buzzing noise" that accompanied stories of being victimized, and the silence when students were asked to speak of times they have victimized others. Interpreting the experience of this audible difference gives students the chance to analyze how they have been taught to not speak of the harm they enact on others. Further, doing so in a social space gives students the chance to consider how this reticence is a socialized inheritance, not merely an individual deficit. Experiencing and analyzing this shared hesitancy can lead students to question what blocks us from acknowledging harm to others, and to consider how challenging suffering often involves unearthing structured harm.

Use the Force of Emotions to Challenge Generalizations of the Other

Participant educators commonly spoke of heated moments when a student expressed a negative stereotype about an "Other," particularly when a member of that group was present in the class. Because polarization is a particularly alive in our current landscape, intervening in response to disrespectful generalizations is useful for students to practice in a supportive space.

For example, Nadia described how a student in her class "made a generalized comment about the laziness of people on welfare and the tendency of women to bear children in order to continue to abuse the system." Nadia recounted the experience:

> When I asked the student what evidence was she basing her generalized statements on, she detailed the story of relative's neighbors. As I was searching for a way to use the problematic comment as the spark of a teachable moment, another student raised her hand and with tears in her eyes, recounted her life story growing up on welfare in a nearby trailer park. She then turned to the student who made the initial comment and said, "I was really hurt by your comments. You shouldn't make such generalizations."
>
> I looked around at the other students. A few had tears in their eyes. Others were making eye contact with the two women who became the protagonists of the teachable moment. The empathy and ability to look at the world through another person's eyes or experience—that were

> missing from the comment which sparked the teachable moment—were now present in abundance in the classroom. I set aside the text and my original lesson plan and instead facilitated a discussion on what had happened in the classroom.
>
> I was conscious of the need to not only support the two women who were the catalysts of the teachable moment and to re-create the safety of our learning community but also to relate the teachable moment to our course objectives. I have no doubt that such experiences remain as vivid in my students' memories as they are in mine.

This account highlights two significant ways emotions can destabilize damaging generalizations. First, I notice that Nadia "set aside" her previous plans for the class and "facilitated a discussion on what had happened," demonstrating her commitment to make collaborative sense of emotional moments as they emerge between students. Nadia then built upon the courage of the targeted student who challenged how her identity and life experiences were being generalized and marginalized. This gave the students a taste of how staying with uncomfortable exchanges—instead of closing or avoiding them—can offer learning that, as Nadia stated, is likely to "remain (s) vivid in students' memories."

Second, the students and Nadia seemed to recognize through their empathetic eye contact that the student whose troubling comment catalyzed the teaching moment faced different risks as her assumptions became publicly exposed and contested. This suggests the need for educators to develop the challenging art of balancing the complex, uneven needs of students which is the second dilemma I discuss.

(2) The Dilemma of Teaching toward Privilege

A second dilemma raised by the social justice educators relates to unintentionally prioritizing the learning of the privileged. As educator Grace succinctly states, a core question for social justice educators is, "Who benefits?" The participant educators stressed the importance of considering who benefits during the process of their teaching, particularly when emotions arise.

Most of the educators I interviewed discussed the dilemma of how to address uneven learning needs when teaching toward social justice. They highlighted two aspects of teaching that can disrupt a tendency to teach toward privilege: A strategic attention to the pace of learning; and a caution against using the stories of those aligned with marginalized subjectivities as content for other students' learning.

The Pace of Teaching: Using Multiple Paces and "Slowing Up"

When discussing the significance of attending to the pace of teaching, Hanna described the "default" mode as working at the pace of the privileged:

> I feel like the default in the field of social justice ed ... is to move at the pace of the privileged. That's problematic, I think. I think that what I'm learning is I'm trying to translate that into teaching people how to conflict intervene is that there is no way that we'll be universally meeting everyone's needs.

Alice told an evocative story that illustrates how the uneven needs of students can make establishing a pace of learning challenging. When Alice, who is white, taught a unit on race in the United States, she described a tension between a group of African American students who were "being very stimulated by the material ...who needed to talk it out, and needed sometimes to jump in," and a larger group of white students who wanted to "move on."

Alice's response was to create room for the African American students who wanted to talk more about race and white supremacy. Yet because the class was getting behind, Alice also tried to respectfully move the class forward:

> I was looking to the students who wanted to talk more and I was saying, 'We kind of need to move on, we're getting behind in the material ... you have some great ideas, and we just don't have time for everyone to talk on every topic.'
>
> And so [an African American] student said, 'Well wait a sec,' and [a white student] just turned around and said, 'Just get on with it.' ... It's like, 'We just need to move on with it! We just have to move forward, move on with the material'... For her, I think I would say, because she was white, this was something interesting to study. But for the other students this was ... opening doors, explaining about their life and why they saw themselves in the struggles that they did.

Alice noted that for the white students in her class, racial inequalities were just something "interesting to study," while in contrast it was "opening doors" for the students of color who were deepening their understanding of the sources of their struggles. Teaching toward privilege offers a predictable solution to this tension, bolstered by a rehearsed norm of following the pace of the syllabus—which prioritizes "moving on" to efficiently cover the material.

Those with dominant subjectivities are often less experienced with their learning needs not taking center stage. Thus, they are likely to be less practiced in facing the emotional tension involved in witnessing or engaging in learning where they are not the center actors. To challenge relying on a default pace, I discuss two creative strategies participants suggest: moving at multiple paces, and slowing up.

One strategy Hanna put forth to avoid teaching toward privilege is to structure courses in ways that allow people to move at multiple paces: "So we need to think of structures that allow people to move at a different pace. And look at the risks and the drawbacks of asking people to move at the same pace. And make sure that we make a conscious decision about who that's geared toward."

In order to support an awareness of the importance of pace to the learning process, Hanna explicitly names her practice of moving at multiple paces during her courses:

> So it's to normalize that, and again to say, 'I might not be leading it at the pace that works for everyone. Right now, we're going to work at the pace of the group that's zooming along. And next class, or next activity, we're going to work at this pace.' So have them expect that it's normal to have this happen.

Further, Hanna proposes that class members might practice together considering whose needs are being met—and whose are not—by moving at particular speeds. She suggests, "That's something that even the class as a group could discuss."

Ramiro speaks of a structural dimension related to moving at the pace of privilege which he describes as the "time oppression" of a "too speeded up society." He notes that prioritizing what can be done quickly is typical, but that this often side steps tensions that could otherwise be mobilized to foster deeper learning and change. Ramiro goes on to argue that "short time frames favor dominance," reminding educators that accepting a default pace is likely to reaffirm current power relationships.

In response Ramiro stresses the need to "slow up"—to pay attention to where the group is in contrast to sticking to a preconceived teaching agenda or timeline. For example, he reflected on a similar situation to the incident Alice faced when her students were expressing distinct desires to "move on" or to stay with a discussion on race that was "opening doors" for some students:

> I think this is where creative intercultural facilitation comes in. Let's say you get a room full of people… And so and so says, 'Man my eyes are opened' and so and so says, 'Man, whatever identity I had I just lost it.' …One thing you can do, again, depending on circumstances … what I do is I slow up.

For Ramiro at the heart of slowing up is listening—following the energy of the students and creating the space to hear and take seriously diverse interpretations of what is happening—which helps open the possibility of creative responses.

Avoid Using the Stories of Others: "Watching Other People Learn"

Along with reconsidering pace, participants suggest alternatives to teaching toward privilege by not asking students who are socially marginalized to educate those more aligned with privilege. Critical dialogue to analyze the concrete lives of students is a centerpiece to critical pedagogy. Yet participants note that unreflexively relying on the stories of students raises pedagogical concerns.

For example, in her graduate research, Ellen analyzed the experiences of peace and conflict practitioners of color who facilitate intercultural dialogues. She became aware that students of color were often asked to be vulnerable and express their life experiences related to race, which prioritized the learning needs of the white students. Ellen, who identifies as a person of color, named this awareness as an "awakening for her":

> One of the participants said something at the end that was really profound for me, that again sparked this desire to do more research on the paradigms that we use and the assumptions we make about the model of dialogue. She felt that the dialogue process had asked her to kind of parade around her pain for the benefit of the white students. And that she didn't mind doing it, because she realized how important it was for the white students, but she didn't really gain anything from it, and in fact it kind of re-traumatized her.

While Ellen's participant stated she was willing to "parade around her pain for the benefit of the white students," Ellen remains troubled by the ethics of placing students of color in a position where they are either the content for other students' learning or, as Hanna stated, are "just watching other people learn about them."

As another example, Hanna reflected on an activity she facilitated surrounding environmental justice and poverty which intended to illustrate how industrial pollution disproportionately impacts people of color and the poor. Hanna recognizes that this activity can lead to an "aha moment" for upper middle class and white students—"but it is not an aha" for students from communities who are more likely to be poisoned. This contrast led Hanna to raise a question:

> So how do I design the curriculum so there is learning for [those targeted by oppression] instead of just watching other people learn about them? And in effect discuss them. And then they're in a place—just like queer people who have to decide if they want to be out—do I engage in this discussion as if I'm one of them? [Who] are being talked about? Or [as] I'm one of the people studying people like me?

Hanna's question deserves ongoing attention from educators who seek to offer learning opportunities for all of their students. In terms of alternatives to teaching toward privilege, many of the participant educators stress that they invite but do not require students to share their life stories related to the course material.

Also, educators spoke of infusing their curriculum with first person narratives to highlight diverse and under-represented perspectives, often in the form of films or speakers. The usefulness of these narratives further confirms the need for an increased availability of literature from the perspective of marginalized subjectivities in Peace and Justice Studies.

Create Separate Spaces: A Pedagogy of Coalition

When considering the dilemma of teaching toward privilege, Ellen recommends that temporary separate spaces can be useful when discussing emotionally charged issues related to intersectional injustice:

> I feel like having the separate groups first for people to work though that destabilizing process in a space where others are experiencing something similar can be very helpful. Because then it's a process ... they have that moment and there are other things that have to happen for behavior to shift or for thinking to shift. And I think that a lot of that has to start before getting into a mixed race dialogue. Because otherwise I really think it's unfair, and really unbalanced.

Anna, who teaches Peace Studies at an all women's college, described an experience where separate spaces were useful to complicate women's experiences of violence. She reflected on a dialogue about gender in her class when her male co-teacher, who is supportive of feminist goals, was absent. Anna reflected that her students "felt freer to express certain ideas about gender without men there."

Anna mused that the difference of not having her male colleague present provided a "different kind of space" for the women to discuss the differences among them. Significantly, the students' discussion centered on making sense of their intersectional identities, specifically providing room to discuss how the agency of Muslim women is often negated when they are positioned as "oppressed" by white women or by Western assumptions:

> It's a very diverse class. So we also ended up talking about the differences among women, and the frustrations for example of women of color, or Muslim women especially, when they're used—or infantilized or objectified by white women or by the West. And the relationship between the idea of the Muslim woman as oppressed and the negation of their own agency.

Building on the suggestions from participants above, educators can borrow strategies from social movements who use coalitions in their organizing and who consider separate affinity groups as temporary home spaces. Typically, a coalition model eventually brings affinity groups together—without requiring shared experiences or affectional solidarity, but rather requiring a willingness to learn and/or to do politics together (Sasaki 2002).

The members of affinity groups need not share identities of marginalization. Educators might construct groups based on students' felt resonance or their pressing questions in relationship to the text. For example, one could divide students into separate groups based on their interest in discussing the issue from distinct perspectives ranging from "Why does this matter?" to "What options might it open or inspire?" In this way, using separate spaces need not cast students into preconceived identity-based groups, but instead can acknowledge the complexity of overlapping subjectivities and diverse levels of consciousness.

Destabilize Students as a Whole

A second strategy participants put forward to avoid asking the marginalized to educate others is to create moments in class where *all* students are destabilized. For example, Ramiro creates opportunities for students to consider how all students have experienced marginalization. Ramiro gives all his participants the chance to speak of ways that they have been harmed:

> I do have people reflect on their hurt—how they were hurt by no fault of their own. … Because I want to make some point—I want to make one point that everyone in this room without exception has been oppressed and hurt. And by the time I take them through the exercise, nobody argues with me. And so I learned to combine exercises with reflection and content. And not teach some content until I felt they were ready to hear it, with the most chance of understanding it.

Sage extends Ramiro's suggestion by using a storytelling exercise to "theorize and problematize" how student come to consciousness of their subject positions and privileges:

> Far enough into the semester where students feel a little bit safe—I'll often ask them to tell one story [about] the moment they knew their race, class, or gender. And use that to theorize and problematize the material. Usually what they'll tell you is a story of de-privilege. You know, [instead of] "I thought I was a male when I had all this privilege," [they'll say] "Well I'll tell you I thought I was a girl the day that I couldn't do x." That is always the types of stories they tell. And then you can work with that.

Through Sage's activity, students share a felt knowledge of how it is often easier to recognize—and to not assume—the parts of one's identity that are not structurally affirmed. Being aware of a tendency to attend to de-privilege when considering uneven distribution of power may guide students to consider how their multiple positions affect the stories they tell and the stories they avoid which impacts the knowledge they are likely to consider credible.

Ellen creatively stretches Sage's exercise by asking participants to "draw an image" of their "first reaction or interaction or realization of their racial background." In response, students create images ranging from abstract to very detailed images based on what they are moved to share, and they are not required to add a narrative explanation. Afterwards, Ellen asks students to do an "art walk, just to look at what people created," and she subsequently facilitates a dialogue based on their observations. In this way, all students are likely to be a bit destabilized, and students of color are not required to retell their stories for the benefit of others.

(3) The Dilemma of Supporting Loss: The Loss of Innocence and Positive Identities

A third dilemma the participants raise related to responding to emotions in the classroom is how to support students who face loss when learning about social justice. For example, Anna articulates how students from more privileged positions may experience a "loss of innocence" as they complicate their interpretation of violence:

> Because [most in Anna's university] are very privileged. Mostly, not all of them ... The ones that come from privileged background come to Intro to Peace Studies as 'la la land.' Peace, love, and we all get along. So the things that are wrong in the world are because there are bad people. They have no idea of structural violence, cultural violence. The difficulty of day-to-day living in poverty... struggling to get through a day of school let alone a degree. So the idea is that this class transforms them ... it's a loss of innocence. A loss of the secure world that they inhabited before, where everything was clear, black and white.

For most of Anna's students, losing the perception of a "clear, black and white" world is destabilizing, and yet it may also open students to transformation. However, the transformation comes only after the "secure world that they had inhabited before" is shaken, lost.

While Anna describes how students who are more buffered by privilege experience loss, a sense of loss can extend to all students regardless of their life experiences and access to privilege. For example, Ramiro suggests students may experience a "limbo of identity" as they realize what they have given up in response to the pull of assimilation. Yet participants note this loss is particularly acute when students are invested in worldviews that provide them a clear sense of "to whom they belong," but which clash with ideas engaged in the course. Educators reflected on the challenge of respecting students' expressed identities, particularly when these identities provide the student with rehearsed foundational assumptions that makes change frightening.

For example, Sage discusses a student who described himself as the "white red neck" and who often disrupted the dialogue in her class by challenging the importance of the issues the class was exploring:

> I do catch him paying attention in lectures. He'll never admit it. His persona is, 'I'm the white red neck and I'm going to push every one of your buttons.' He's not really obnoxious about it, but just obnoxious enough to get attention. So sometimes I try to engage him on it, like 'Why do you care about these issues so much?' And he often deflects ... I sometimes feel like, 'You are that person but you're not only that person.'

I appreciate that Sage did not require her student to disavow his "persona" or performed identity, but instead invites him to speak more of what leads him to care about the issues he raises. Also, her comment that "You are that person but you're not only that person" recognizes the multiplicity of his identity, inviting an expansion of identity without first requiring a rejection of previous commitments.

Another place that many participant educators notice a sense of loss for their students is in students' positive identification with the United States, specifically when learning that current injustice is not exceptional and builds on long-standing patterns of domination. For example, Alice suggested her students face loss and grief as their previous conception of the United States as benevolent—or that the particular injustice enacted by the current administration is exceptional—is destabilized:

> So I think a sense of loss [relates to coming to] terms with what role the United States has played in the world socially, politically, and environmentally... in the sense of loss, of losing themselves, but also about grieving about their culture ... And that's very difficult. But at the same time, there's loss but there are also some students for whom it's very liberating ... it also opens new perspectives.

Alice spoke of her students as "losing themselves" when they come to terms with their country's role in the world as well confronting their larger grief for the limits of their culture. I also note that Alice stated that while facing loss is painful, what is on the other side after loss can be liberating, opening "new perspectives."

The educators I interviewed suggested three strategies to support students who face loss. These include preparing students to anticipate loss; acknowledging the pain evoked by change; and activating critical hope.

Anticipate Loss before Transformation

Many participant educators recommend preparing students to anticipate loss to help students expect that transformation requires leaving a familiar place.

Offering an evocative example, Anna discusses how her co-teacher helped students anticipate loss at the beginning of their *Introduction to Peace Studies* course:

> He was telling [the students] about how the goal is transformation. There is going to be some destabilizing. He told them right at the beginning ... You know, how to deal with loss and trauma ... [Later in the class the students] expressed the sense that they didn't know, they were confused. They expressed a sense of confusion ... And I sent them this piece, 'The Fear of Transformation.'
>
> It talks about how when we are in life transitions you are in that moment, in a moment similar to a flying trapeze. When you have to let go of the old bar, and take a leap, and go to the new bar in order to get to the other side. And it's terrifying. Because you leave something that you are hanging on to for dear life!

Forefronting the expectation that students will face "letting go" of what they hold onto in order to invite transformation may help students recognize that their confusion or fear may be a signal that change is afoot. In other words, their confusion when facing an awareness of the enormity of the problems in the world can be understood as creating an enlivened space—a space in-between—where learning and transformation can occur as students prepare to leave what they have known so they may think and become otherwise.

Acknowledge Fear and Offer Support

A second way participants support students is to acknowledge the fear involved in facing loss. As Parry (1994) argues in the article that Anna gives her students, the transitional space that opens before students "is a scary, disorienting confusing nowhere" that our culture encourages us to move through as quickly as possible (n. p.). Anna suggests asking students to remain awake to the possibilities of this place in-between requires supporting students as they lose the comfort of the familiar and face the ambiguity of the unknown.

Participants discussed the usefulness of students receiving and offering support to each other in social spaces of dyads, in small groups, or with the full class. For example, Hanna stated that "having a chance to have a public conversation is useful," particularly as students become aware of how their positions of privilege may have buffered them from recognizing the harm they placed on others:

> And there's a mixture of getting support from other people. Let's say a man says 'I didn't know there was this much violence against women, I didn't realize sexism still plays out, I didn't realize I had privilege, I

> knew that there was sexism, but I didn't realize about privilege.' Or a white women going, 'I've been concentrating so much on you know gender subordination that I haven't thought about intersectionality and the fact that I'm white, or that I'm Christian and not Jewish American and not experiencing Anti-Semitism.' And so I think that getting support from people, 'You too? Wow.' Having a chance to have a public conversation is useful.

Creating social spaces of support can help students to realize that "they are not alone" as they awaken to the complexity of injustice, and to recognize that they can face change together.

Activate Critical Hope

A third way participants support students who face loss in their classes is by emphasizing critical hope. Grace expressed a concern that was echoed by many participants when she worries that she may "overwhelm" or "depress" her students:

> Sometimes I worry that I make them depressed and they have less agency. I overwhelm them. And I don't necessarily give them good outs, or good places to go. I want them to have agency but maybe I make them feel powerless, and overwhelmed and helpless.

Participants recognize that reclaiming the power of emotions can also be risky at our current historical moment when injustices can appear unsurmountable. Students often desire comforting stories that reiterate an assurance that all is well (or eventually will be), or that affirm a sense of habituated numbness that change is beyond students' reach. Thus, engaging emotions in relationship to injustice risks overwhelming students, which can lead to strategies of disengagement in the forms of denial, despair, cynicism, individualism, or apathy (Kumashiro 2009).

In response, educators suggest balancing an attention to discomforting knowledge with critical hope (Bozakek, Liebowtiz, Corolissen & Boler 2014). In particular, participant educators seek to inspire critical hope by stirring students' imagination for a different future, discussing how others have organized for change, and sharing their own struggles with hope with students to normalize an ongoing struggle.

Conclusion

The peace and justice educators I interviewed agree that students need guidance and support to consider the relational and social force of emotions in the classroom. In response to the first dilemma—how to respond to the emotions that accompany conflict—participants advocate taking the time to build a learning community to prepare the ground for keeping discomfort creative. Further, they offer practices that can assist students in using discomfort as a starting point for a collaborative consideration of how to engage the limits of students' ideas, their relationships, and the wider world.

The participant educators also acknowledge that welcoming emotions into classrooms that hold uneven power relationships is difficult work, and raises the risk of "teaching toward privilege." Without careful attention to the maldistribution of comfort, educators may prioritize the needs of those most immediately destabilized when addressing injustice—inadvertently focusing on students who are most buffered by privilege or who are most invested in supporting current distributions of power. By recognizing this dilemma, educators are better positioned to attend to the diverse learning needs of students—meeting each of them where they are while inviting the learning community to stretch beyond what they already feel and know.

Finally, the educators introduced a third dilemma of how to support students who experience loss as they recognize the distance between their current realities and a more just world. The space in-between the present world and a desired world is unsettling. Emotions can signal the presence of this space, and peace educators can be significant guardians of these spaces in-between where students navigate the distance between their present reality and more just realities.

Anna spoke above of a liminal or borderline space where transformation can occur. She aligns with Gloria Anzaldua (2002) who suggests that transformation occurs in a vulnerable space—a "liminal zone":

> Transformation occur in this in-between space, an unstable, unpredictable, precarious always in transition space lacking clear boundaries … and living in liminal zones means being in a constant state of displacement—an uncomfortable, even alarming feeling (1).

I consider this place in-between that extends beyond comfort zones as akin to a classroom that seeks to nourish critical consciousness. Peace educators can anticipate this dissonance and support students to stay with these discomforting emotions long enough for new interpretations and responses to become available. Educators can enrich their pedagogy by attending to its troubling dimensions, and I am grateful for the participant educators who generously shared their stories of dilemmas in their teaching. I hope their insights help inform social justice educators to engage students' emotions as critical and transformational forces that can help build a more just, loving world.

Notes

1 This chapter relies on interviews from a longer inquiry that addressed the role of conflict and emotion in social justice pedagogy (Meeker 2012).

2 I use pseudonyms for all 14 participant educators. For more details on the participant educators and the qualitative methodology utilized, see Meeker, 2012.

References

Ahmed, Sara. 2004. *The Cultural Politics of Emotion*. Edinburgh, Scotland: Edinburgh University Press.

Ahmed, Sara. 2017. *Living a Feminist Life*. Durham: Duke University Press.

Anzaldua, Gloria. 2002. Preface: (Un) Natural Spaces, (Un) Safe Spaces. In G. Anzaldua & M. Keating (Eds.), *The Bridge we Call Home: Radical Visions for Transformation,* 1–5. *New York: Routledge.*

Boler, Megan. 1999. *Feeling Power: Emotions and Education*. New York: Routledge.

Bozakek, Vivienne, Brenda Liebowtiz, Ronelle Corolissen & Megan Boler (Eds.). 2014. *Discerning Critical Hope in Educational Practices*. New York: Routledge.

Demasio. Antonio. 1994. *Descartes' Error: Emotion, Reason, and the Human Brain*. New York: Putnam's Sons.

Kumishiro, Kevin. 2009. *Against Common Sense: Teaching and Learning toward Social Justice*. New York: Routledge.

Meeker, Joy. 2012. *Engaging Emotions and Practicing Conflict: Emotions and Teaching toward Social Justice* (Doctoral dissertation). https://pqdtopen.proquest.com/doc/1017702941.html?FMT=ABS

Parry, Danaan. 1994. "The Parable of the Trapeze: Turning the Fear of Transformation into the Transformation of Fear", *Earthstewards*. www.earthstewards.org/ESN-Trapeze.asp.

Sasaki, Betty. 2002. Toward a Pedagogy of Coalition. In A. A. Macdonald & S. Sanchez-Casal (Eds.). *Twenty-first Century Feminist Classrooms: Pedagogies of Identity and Difference*, 31–57. New York: Palgrave Macmillan.

2 The Tyranny of Good Intentions

Critical Reflexivity and Peace and Justice Pedagogy

Emily Welty

As a new Peace and Justice Studies program in an ever-expanding field, Pace University had to think carefully about what frameworks to use to guide the development of our program. Intellectually, our program is situated around the importance of critical reflexivity and the importance of identifying positionality in our teaching, learning, service in the community and research.

Many of my students assume that simply because they want to change the world and work for "progressive" causes, the work that they do will be good and helpful. This is not simply a self-centered desire – most students are inclined to assume that any non-profit, any new initiative for social change is basically good. As the field of Peace and Justice Studies continues to develop, our students, our professional associations and our universities must go beyond the simple struggle to gain recognition in academia and must also rigorously interrogate our own good intentions. Using critical reflexivity is one way to understand whether our interventions in conflict transformation and peacebuilding are reflecting the needs of the world or simply mirroring and reproducing our own belief systems.

Encountering Peace and Justice Studies

Most of the students who first encounter the Peace and Justice Studies program at my university are there for one of two reasons. The first is that the class may fit their schedule, provide a chance to take a class with a friend or fulfill the graduation requirement for service learning. (The *Introduction to Peace and Justice Studies* class requires that each student complete twenty hours of service learning in a New York City nonprofit organization which means that it fills the university requirement for a civic engagement course.) The second reason that students end up in the Peace and Justice Studies classroom is that they have a vague notion that "peace" and "justice" is something that they believe in and want to know more about.

It can be a challenge to teach those students who enter the classroom for the first reason – they are not as deeply incentivized by their own curiosity and finding a way to captivate them can be difficult. However, the second group of students presents another unique challenge. Their openness and support for "peace and justice" broadly defined means that they see themselves as advocates and activists. The community of undergraduate activists is small at my university and the students that self-define in this way find themselves in the minority. This means that they come into the classroom eager to be in a space where their passion for changing the world moves from the fringe to the mainstream.

Enter the danger of good intentions. Precisely because they are not surrounded with other students who share their engagement in world-changing, they are often unaccustomed to rigorously interrogating the issues that they care most deeply about. I sometimes find that for the budding human rights activist, the first scholarly contact that questions the universality of human rights norms feels less like liberation than attack. I find the earnest positivity of my students both endearing and difficult to navigate. Indeed, the first few weeks of teaching about the complexities of international aid often feel like an ongoing lesson in disenchantment. I feel guilty as I watch the faces of some students slowly crumble as the class begins to debate the merits of child sponsorship and I realize that particular students are beginning to question the cheerful photographs of a foreign child hanging on their refrigerators at home.

In a sense, this theme is nothing new for undergraduate education. The very process of engaging in non-compulsory, university education has typically created a space and a time in which young adults question the received truths of their family, faith group and community. What I believe is particular to the study of Peace and Justice is the need to deconstruct good intentions even while continuing to believe in the need for social change. For students who find joy and meaning in defining themselves as social justice activists, questions that cross-examine the effectiveness or unintended consequences of interventions often feel invasive and threatening.

Critical Reflexivity and Positionality

I am aware that "reflexivity" means something different in different disciplines. I use it in its anthropological sense to denote a mode of thinking in which the thinker is aware of the ways in which her own sense of Self impacts the content of what she knows. That is to say, our many ways of being in the world including our gender, race, class, sexual orientation, age and ability affect the way that we perceive the world, what we believe and what we know. This challenges the positivist view of the world in which facts are static and removed from the influence of the researcher.

I encourage students to identify their own positionality and to ask how their unique social location (including power and privilege – or lack thereof) affects what they know. For many students, identifying the way that their gender identity affects their knowing is an easy place to begin. Students from dominant cultures (white, English speaking, heterosexual) often struggle to see these identities as shaping their ways of knowing; their own deeply ingrained privilege conditions them to see their own identities as normative or "the way things really are". Thus, asking how a white student's race affects what they believe about the world, often feels like an absurd question to them whereas a Latinx student may readily see how their ethnicity affects their knowledge because they've been forced to identify this by a dominant culture that demands assimilation. Identifying positionality as important and challenging the idea that knowledge is neutral is a critical challenge for this course and once I became aware of how difficult and important this was, I began to infuse this into the Peace and Justice Studies program as a whole.

Teaching Reflexivity in the Classroom

I first began using the idea of "critical reflexivity" to teach about power and privilege in the context of international aid in a class called *Humanitarianism and International Aid*. Beyond just helping students to understand the types of agencies and forms of work that humanitarianism and aid encompass, the course focuses heavily on ethics and power. Typically, most of the students in the class are interested in working overseas and in careers based on helping "the Other". The class requires that they think carefully about their own motivations for this kind of work in order to avoid engaging in practices that empower the aid worker but ultimately quash the agency of the beneficiary community.

When I first began teaching the course, it was evident that students were not accustomed to identifying their own ways of knowing. One section of the course is called "Epistemology of Place, Self and Others" and explores how we come to know what we think we know about helping. I ask students to practice observing their own reactions and beliefs and differentiating them from "facts" about new situations they encounter.

The week that we first discuss critical reflexivity, I assign two readings to guide the students' thinking: Jane Gilbert's article (2005) "Self-knowledge is the pre-requisite of humanity: personal development and self awareness for aid workers" and Ann Cunliffe's (2004) "On Becoming a Critically Reflexive Practitioner". Gilbert argues that aid workers need to develop the capacity to listen and reflect on their own thoughts and reactions in a way that is very difficult to teach. She emphasizes the need to develop the capacity to listen accurately and actively to another person coupled with the ability to reflect on our own feelings without fear. In the context of aid work, there is an overwhelming need to be able to listen to the intended beneficiaries even when (especially when) they are offering a critique of the help being offered.

Gilbert writes:

> Are we prepared to address our own vulnerability and fears when we become the pupil rather than the teacher? Do we actually *want* the person to whom we are listening to become more confident and to assume more power? ... It can feel much 'safer' to hold on tightly to

> our image of ourselves as being the person who 'knows'. Can we care enough to empower the other person, if that means letting go of our own power?
>
> (67)

De-centering the classroom at this moment and unsettling the line between professor and student is helpful. We discuss situations in which it is difficult to listen; I ask them to recall instances in which it was unbearable for them to listen rather than speak. We talk about how honesty about our uncomfortability in listening is a radical step towards both humility and better humanitarian practices.

Cunliffe's article directly names "critical reflexivity" as "examining critically the assumptions underlying our actions, [and] the impact of those actions" (407). She frames three types of questions that arise from this reflexivity: existential (who am I and what kind of person do I want to be?), relational (how do I relate to the world around me?) and praxis (what did I do in the past and what should I do in the future?) (408). These questions seem to be at the heart of the type of education we are aiming for not only in Peace and Justice Studies but in liberal arts as a whole. If my students leave our program with a strong ability to answer these questions authentically, then I care very little about whether I am placing them in the best graduate schools in the country (an instrumental marker of success) or whether they all become committed pacifists (a normative marker of success). I trust that a student who can honestly scrutinize their own identity, longings, behavior, relationships and intentions will become a human being that will work for a vision of peace or justice in the world. In order for me to also be critically reflexive about my role in the classroom, I need to be frank and consistent about my desire not to create younger versions of my own idealized self. My students may choose careers that don't reflect the way that I define peace and social justice. They may make choices that I strongly disagree with. But if they can act from a place of critical reflexivity, I believe they will be making the choices that are both ethically grounded and best for them as human beings.

Writing from the perspective of environmentalism, Derrick Jensen (2005) puts the question slightly differently:

> Who are you? Who are you really? Beneath the trappings and traumas that clutter and characterize our lives, who are you, and what do you want to do with the so-short life you've been given? We could not live the way we do unless we avoided that question, trained ourselves and others to avoid that question, forced others to avoid placing that question in front of us, and in fact attempted to destroy those who do.
>
> (42)

Sometimes I wonder if pushing students to go inward and examine the self is a fundamentally indulgent practice, somehow inappropriate in a moment in which so much seems to be at stake for both the planet as well as other human beings. But Jensen seems to suggest that avoiding asking questions about desire is also destructive, perhaps because by not directly articulating what it is that we want, we risk manipulating those around us into providing it for us.

Nonetheless, the Peace and Justice Studies classroom must be more than a space to muse about a student's identity and write private ruminations on their past experiences. The scholar in me demands that this sort of reflection must be paired with theory, case studies, data. (However, a strong argument could be made that we are losing the open space to dream together in unstructured ways about who we want to be and how we want to live.)

Teaching Positionality

Students who have taken classes in Women's and Gender Studies, Queer Studies, Sociology or Critical Race Studies may already be aware that their identities affect knowledge. For students coming from a scientific background, this is a more difficult concept to grasp. Standpoint theory, intersectionality and feminist epistemologies provide a rich place from which to begin to examine how our lived experiences affect our ways of knowing, being and acting.

I want students to understand how our identities affect what we know for two reasons: I believe that naming the way that our own stories have shaped us ends up de-centering our certainty. For me, this is one of the ways in which my activism clashes with my academic identity. As an activist, clear, unambiguous messages are important: violence is wrong, occupation is morally repugnant, etc. The daily online petitions and consciousness-raising emails that often flood our inboxes seem to specialize in framing the opposition as ignorant, evil or stupid. Activism often favors the bumper sticker message – clear, unambiguous, declarative. But the facts are more complex and our opponents are usually not evil, but they may be motivated by an entirely different set of concerns, desires and fears than we are. Understanding myself and why I believe what I believe is a bridge towards understanding that my opponent is also driven by her own positionality.

The Forbidden "I"

Invariably in the first few weeks of class, my students and I end up talking about the word "I". Specifically, they want to know, "am I allowed to use the word 'I' in my papers?" This question always surprises me and my answer always seems to surprise them. Yes. Absolutely.

As an academic, I am well-aware that the conventions of many scholarly journals and other publications dictates that the author quash her personal voice, that such a personal approach is inappropriate for intellectual ventures. I know that I need to train my students to write outstanding research papers, to compete in the shrinking marketplace with the ability to write well. If academic publication will demand the stripping of the "I" from a text and the steely objectivity of "the author", why ask students to name themselves? Have I just created another barrier between my students and the realization of seeing their work in print?

I allow my students to use the first person because I need to train them to think carefully and to not become so certain about their own opinions that they forget that their positions are not universally held, that it was a complex Self, shaped by numerous experiences that led them to what they believe today. And so, I encourage them to name the thinker, to be clear about who is thinking – in the same way that I require them to properly cite their sources, I also urge them to name themselves as thinkers. It is easier to teach them to remove the "I" from a paper later than it is to teach them how to add their own analysis. I find it difficult to encourage undergraduates to move beyond description of a text into analysis. Most of them are initially confused by the idea that they are expected to bring something additional to the text beyond describing what the text was about. To tell them that they must draw something additional out of the text but also write in such a way that the extrication is anonymous seems to be both confusing and a mixed message.

So part of my emphasis on positionality and reflexivity means that I ask students to insert themselves – into, under, around and above the text and to engage with it from all of who they are. How do you hear this text as a millennial? As a woman? As a white person? As a transgendered person? How does this text resonate with your experience?

As we begin to engage with the text from multiple positions, we sometimes venture into uncomfortable territory in which one voice begins to speak for everyone from this position, a dynamic that begins to silence and homogenize rather than diversify and deepen our understanding. So as students become more adept at naming how their own identities shape their readings, I also begin to note the complexity of an individual's perspective. I read a text not just as a female-identified cisgendered person but also as a Christian, as an academic, as a New Yorker. Not all of our identities will feel relevant to a single text at any given time but the "I" that I bring to a text is never contained by any single identity. Therefore, one person cannot claim to name a singular African or male or deaf position on any issue. This all may feel quite obvious for those of us cultivated in the cradle of academia and particularly the social sciences but for students, this often is revelation.

Seeking a Vocation vs. Finding a Job

The first week of *Humanitarianism and International Aid*, I introduce the idea of vocation. We approach the question from several angles, considering the difference between a job and a career, between work that pays the rent and work that gives meaning. When they are surveyed at the end of the first class about what they want out of the course as a whole, about a third of them tend to mention finding their vocation.

Pace University was originally founded as a business school. Much of our focus, even in the liberal arts college, tends to be on how our graduates will find work when they leave us. As an institution, the university is proud to be on the list of colleges that make you rich. Many of our students are the first person in their family to attend university and they carry the hopes of the family with them through the doors. Their families imagine them leaving Pace to embark on careers that will enrich the whole family – accountants, lawyers, managers. Most of their families do not imagine a career in humanitarian aid for their children.

And yet the students pour into the *Humanitarianism* class each spring, bright with the notion of traveling overseas and helping people. A few of them have traveled abroad, all of them want to. We begin with the idea of vocation because I want to be clear about motivations. To engage in aid work because one wants to travel is very different than because one has the gifts and talents to do so. I tell the students that I left the world of humanitarian aid for the world of academia because I wanted to reshape the way humanitarian aid is currently conceived in North America. I realized that the biggest contribution I could make was not something I could teach in South Africa or Palestine but that I could contribute to changing the way that North Americans thought about aid and who they thought should be doing it. My goal in *Humanitarianism and International Aid* is not to train 25 new aid workers each spring. My goal is to give 25 students a rigorous introduction to humanitarianism and working abroad and to help them discover whether this field is something they feel drawn to – beyond their conceptions of aid work as glamorous or adventurous and their conceptions of themselves as heroic.

Every few years a new exposé of aid work hits bookstores – the characters shift but the basic message remains the same – many aid workers go into the work because they are running away from disenchanting careers or marriages and hope to recreate themselves abroad. These workers are unpleasantly surprised by the degree of paperwork and hopelessness that aid work often entails. They get burned out and cynical. I know these people; in my 20s, I was one of them. By the last week of class, students tend to be far more articulate about exactly what they want to do in the future. Some of them still want to be humanitarian aid workers. Most of them don't. This is certainly not a typical way of framing "success" from a pedagogical perspective but I am pleased with these results – not only because I want to prevent people from ending up in aid work if they would be unhappy and unhelpful there. But at the end of the course, students seem to have maintained most of their idealism, energy and passion but now have a clearer idea of what they might do that could productively engage their desire to help.

I first encountered Frederick Buechner's (1993) definition of vocation while I was in high school: "Vocation is the place where our deep gladness meets the world's deep need" (118). In the field of Peace and Justice Studies, we are doing our best work with our students when we enable them to discover how their own passions can be used to address and abate suffering in the world. When I have a student who is a brilliant musician but they believe that they have to become a diplomat in order to contribute to peace in the world, the task is not retraining but redirecting. Most of my humanitarian aid students certainly have the capacity to become tenacious, efficient, compassionate aid workers. However, most of them will go on to become wonderful nursing home attendants, compassionate elementary teachers or benevolent police officers.

I never suggest to students that aid work might not be for them. Nor do I promise to give them a set of skills that will immediately translate into overseas deployment. What I can pledge to them is that I will empower them to understand the most important themes and theories and help them ask all of the right questions to determine if this is a good field for them. This path together has two parts: one entails encountering and understanding trends, theories and practices in relief, development and peacebuilding work; the other entails knowing themselves and being able to identify their own gifts and challenges.

Weekly Adventures in Reflexivity

Humanitarianism and International Aid, as an upper level class, demands a significant amount of writing each week as well as considerable amounts of reading. Each week, students produce two very different written assignments. The first is a précis of the reading assignments for the week. These must identify the main argument, case studies and central points of each article or chapter. I ask students to imagine that they are briefing a senior manager at an aid organization about what they have read in a way that might be relevant to daily work. For the first few weeks, students seem to find this engaging but this framing of it wears thin eventually. However, I point out that as students they are asked to consume massive quantities of reading – this assignment asks them to succinctly summarize what they want to remember about this piece in five years. We talk briefly about mortality, about the fact that we almost never get to read everything we want to read in our lives and will likely never reread what we read in college. Suddenly a short way to remember the hours they put into digesting the week's assignments seems relevant again when considered in the span of lives that extend beyond the moments we are together in the classroom.

The second writing assignment each week is entirely personal as I ask students to consider a "Big Picture" question related to vocation. The first week the students write about their strengths, the next week they address their weaknesses. They are initially wary of this assignment: what is my agenda as the grader of this paper? How will their weaknesses be assessed? Intellectually they recognize these questions as standard job interview questions and they are torn between producing an honest answer or an instrumental one (that gets them the grade or the job). The early weeks are an ongoing trust-building exercise during which they begin to trust that I am on their side, that I am capable of simultaneously holding the role of professor/assessor as well as advocate/guide. To be honest, this is not always easy. The agreement that I have with students is that these assignments will be assessed primarily in terms of completion rather than quality. This is counter to my expectations for outstanding writing in all of the other classes that I teach and can be a confusing shift for students that have had me as an instructor in other classes.

As the class progresses, these weekly personal reflections go beyond what one might expect in a job interview. One week I ask students to go for one hour without using their cell phones, laptops, iPads, televisions or other electronic equipment. The initial explanation I offer them – that it is not uncommon when working abroad to have periods of time without the electronic connectivity that they expect at home – is an incomplete one. Yes, it is true that one is more likely to encounter unpredictable wireless networks abroad but this is not the primary purpose of the experiment. (And I sometimes worry that the initial explanation deepens the sense of Othering that students have of other parts of the globe …) My real intention in this assignment is that I want students to encounter themselves when they do not have the option of distracting themselves with music, images or demands from the rest of the world. I also ask them not to interact with friends – they can speak to strangers but not friends. This specification doesn't mirror any part of the world or of aid work *per se*. I believe that my students are able to encounter themselves, to think more clearly – even if just for an hour – if they know that this is an assignment. Many of them really struggle with this assignment and I have had anxious emails from students about how much they dread and even fear the idea of being alone for an hour. One student told me that she felt that I was endangering students by asking them to go without communication from their parents for an hour. I assured her that she could prepare her parents for this digitally-free hour in advance and that if she felt she was in danger, she could certainly pull out her cell phone and call for help. After the hour is over, the students write a short reflection on what they did with their hour, why they chose to do this and what it says about them. For the most part, they are amazed by how calm they felt, how different this time/space was from the rest of their lives and how much they long to do this more often. A few admit that the hour was extremely difficult – even harrowing for them – but introspectively ponder what this might indicate about the rest of their lives.

Critical reflexivity demands the ability to identify the Self – to have a sense of one's own preferences, fears, experiences, and aspirations. In order to name and analyze why we believe what we believe or do what we do, we have to be able to know something about who we are. While the millennial generation is also criticized as being selfish, I am far more worried that they are self-less, that they are so accustomed to swimming in a sea of the thoughts and experiences of others, that their own experience is indistinguishable from the lives they follow on Twitter, Instagram and Facebook. The ability to connect across geographical divides has presented the peril of losing the ability to sense what is happening in this moment.

I also ask the students to go to a new part of the city that they haven't seen before and to spend an hour observing this undiscovered place. Who do you see here? What do you think the people here value? What is important in this space? And always the reference back to standpoint theory: what is it about you that causes you to see this place the way that you do?

The final week of class, I offer what appears to be an easier assignment but often proves difficult. I ask them to spend one hour doing something that makes them happy and to write a reflection explaining what they did and why. On one hand, this is about helping them develop the ability to resource themselves, a skill which proves useful in many settings but can be extremely useful in stressful situations overseas. But the exercise also requires thought and intentionality – it demands that the students think about a subject (themselves), consider the desired outcome (happiness – no small thing for anyone) and identify emotional states (how am I feeling now? How could that be changed?)

The Affective Fallacy and "Good" Work

Even as I am encouraging and training students to be able to identify what makes them happy, I am also trying to help them see that this impulse alone cannot be trusted as a rubric for peacebuilding and development work. It is difficult to manage the tension between helping students articulate what brings them happiness while simultaneously asking them not to assume that this will result in work that benefits other people. In an effort to broaden the interdisciplinarity of the Peace and Justice Studies program, I began using the book *Draw it with your eyes closed: the art of the art assignment* as a source of inspiration for designing assignments and classroom activities that integrate aesthetics and creativity. I was particularly interested in the assignment that Harry Roseman (2012) provides for his students:

> Bring in four reproductions of artworks: 1) A work that you like and think is good. 2) A work that you don't like and don't think is good. 3) A work that you like, but suspect might not be good. 4) A work that you don't like but have to admit is good.
>
> (21)

I am intrigued by this assignment because it helps students to differentiate between their own opinions/feelings/intuitions about the world and received technical feedback. I modify the assignment for my own classroom by asking students to simply name things (music, TV shows, movies) that fit into each of these categories. We talk (and often laugh) about how to be honest and intellectually rigorous about what we like vs. what we know to be good/deep/reliable/valid/effective/ethical/wise.

The teachable point here is that not everything that makes us feel happy is necessarily good – a notion expressed in literary criticism by the term "affective fallacy". In the *Humanitarian Aid* class, we address this in the context of the Kony 2012 phenomenon – a widely shared video which played upon the emotions of millions of people but ultimately suggested a deeply simplistic and flawed approach to the complexity of the post-conflict Ugandan society. The slickly produced video used music and images in a powerful way that left people feeling righteous urgency about "helping" Uganda but proposed solutions that neither Ugandans nor the majority of the aid community could endorse.

I believe that training my students to identify the affective fallacy within their own thinking is an important contribution towards strengthening the field of Peace and Justice Studies theoretically. One of my fears for our developing field is that it is too easily side-tracked by what makes us feel good rather than engagement with data (be it qualitative or quantitative). As I hope I have made clear, I believe that feelings are important and that it is impossible to remove the human person with all of their individual longings, desires and feelings from our epistemology. Certainly, feelings affect how we do the work as both practitioners and as academics.

At the same time, I am annoyed by the feel-good nature of much of what is identified as "peace" (somehow justice seems to have a more serious undertone to it). I am discouraged by the way that many peace-related listservs to which I subscribe often engage in discussion of serious issues only to be sidetracked by the sharing of a video that claims "love is the answer" or "just be kind". If we are to be taken seriously as a field of study and answer the skepticism of many about our work then we need to teach our students to distinguish between that which makes them feel good and constructive, sustainable approaches to conflict transformation and peacemaking.

Chris Argyris and Reflexive Thinking

While it often appears to be *en vogue* among radical academics to eschew business theory in an effort to protect our disciplines from monetization, I have found the insights of organizational theorist Chris Argyris at Harvard Business School very useful in thinking about reflexive teaching and learning. Argyris and Donald Schon (1974) wrote about the tensions between espoused theories and theories-in-use, that is, between what we say our motivations are and what our actual reasons are. As professors many of us have likely all chosen a book for a syllabus at some point because we are familiar with it and find it teachable or because we would relish the opportunity to read something new with an engaged group of students. If we tell them that we are asking them to read this book because it is critical to the subject matter, there may be a gap between our espoused theory and our theory-in-action. Argyris argued that the role of reflection was to help people close the gulf between these two which could result in more honest, principled and satisfying outcomes.

When an organization attempts to address problems it may engage in one of two types of thinking – single or double loop learning:

> When the error detected and corrected permits the organization to carry on its present policies or achieve its presents objectives, then that error-and-correction process is *single-loop* learning. Single-loop learning is like a thermostat that learns when it is too hot or too cold and turns the heat on or off. The thermostat can perform this task because it can receive information (the temperature of the room) and take corrective action. *Double-loop* learning occurs when error is detected and corrected in ways that involve the modification of an organization's underlying norms, policies and objectives.
>
> (Argyris and Schön 1978: 2–3)

In the field of Peace and Justice Studies, this is mirrored in our professed desire to address the roots of violence rather than just incidents as they occur. As practitioners and academics we argue that society must engage in double loop learning to name and rectify the roots of structural violence – sexism, racism, classism, homophobia, etc. – rather than simply deploy force to quell each wave of unrest that occurs. Our efforts to advocate for this societal switch must be mirrored in our classrooms. Rather than ask students to simply learn facts or theories to answer the problems we pose to them, we need them to acquire the skill of double-loop learning, to name what it is that they don't know and why.

Beyond Reflexivity?

In spring 2018, I taught *Humanitarianism and International Aid* again after having taken a year's break from it. The world had changed, seemingly dramatically, from the last time I had taught it in 2016. There was a different president of the United States. Students came into the room feeling less hopeful about the world they lived in and more fearful. While students often expressed anxiety about finding employment after graduation, now many of them were opening expressing more existential fears – were they safe? Were they at risk of losing some of their basic human rights? Would there be a nuclear war? What was the value of focusing on the idea of suffering elsewhere when the suffering felt imminent "here"?

This presented an opportunity to continue to deconstruct the connections and fractures between our notions of "here" and "there" as well as to name the ways that the United States had not suddenly become a site of suffering and threat, indeed for many indigenous students, students of color, students whose bodies had already been sites of violence, very little had changed. Reflexivity helped us to unpack some of this without assuming that we could evaluate how fearful or safe anyone felt. What we could do was to dwell critically in the space together, to ask how to show up for one another in a space of solidarity and to not become so focused on "here" that we decided that "there" didn't matter.

Another discursive turn had also emerged on campus among many of the Peace and Justice Students. The year before, several of them had taken a powerful class on philanthro-capitalism and had come away with the strong feeling that all humanitarianism was flawed beyond repair and must be ended immediately. Oddly, they had decided to enroll in the Humanitarianism class the next year despite their reservations or judgment that this was a worthless, imperialist, colonial endeavor. Thus about half of the class consisted of idealists who needed to move towards a more critical understanding of humanitarianism and the half were cynics who believed that the only reason to better understand humanitarianism was to be empowered to shut it down. This presented a pedagogical problem. The syllabus had been designed largely to ask students to become more aware of how their own identity, in the ways explored above, might impede their conception of "helping". For the idealist group, this was the right material paced in the right way. But for the cynics, this was all just further confirmation of what had become a badge of pride – that they knew better and could assume a superior position to the naïve idealists. For this group, my challenge as the educator was, surprisingly, to suggest that reflexivity was not enough.

The central tension with the rigorous critique of humanitarianism based on its often colonial/racist/imperialist tendencies (a valid and important critique for the field) was that its endpoint for this group of students positioned them in a nativist, isolationist landscape that they would have found repugnant in other terms. By deciding that as white, American women they were thoroughly implicated in the violence of humanitarianism, they had concluded that they should therefore do nothing about suffering that occurred anywhere else. Imagining a non-colonial, non-imperial, non-racist form of helping felt like an impossibility for them. When I asked whom they felt obligated/able to help, who they felt they could trust themselves to help, they concluded that they could really understand those with a similar subject-position. We had arrived together in a moment in which reflexive self-understanding did not result in better, more careful accompaniment of suffering people; reflexivity resulted in a withdrawal from the world. They allowed that they might be able to research aid or be ready to offer aid if their own community was affected.

Conclusion

This year I taught Louise Erdrich's poem "Advice to Myself #2: Resistance" as part of a class on poetry and art as a means of peacebuilding and resistance. The poem contains the line, "Resist turning your back on the knife of the world's sorrow, resist turning that knife upon yourself." As a class, we ruminated together on the tension between hope and despair, between believing in the possibility of the world and describing the world as it is and asking what the part that we might play is. To resist turning one's back on the sorrow of the world and resist turning entirely inward is at the heart of teaching Peace and Justice Studies. So much of my experience teaching in this field has been guided by going beyond the binary thinking that dices the world into good/bad, peace/violence, men/women, Self/Other and perhaps most often, hope/despair. As the facilitator of the classroom space, I have to nurture a place that can support both rage and serenity, both commitment to change the world and nurturing of the self.

References

Argyris, C. and Schön, D. 1974. *Theory in practice: Increasing professional effectiveness*, San Francisco: Jossey-Bass.

Argyris, C., and Schön, D. 1978. *Organizational learning: A theory of action perspective*, Reading, MA: Addison Wesley.

Buechner, F. 1993. *Wishful thinking: A seeker's ABC*, New York: Harper.

Cunliffe, A. 2004. "On Becoming a Critically Reflexive Practitioner" *Journal of Management Education*, 407–426.

Gilbert, J. 2005. "Self-knowledge is the pre-requisite of humanity: personal development and self awareness for aid workers" *Development in Practice*, Volume 15, Number 1, 64–69

Jensen, D. 2005. *Walking on water*. White River Junction, VT: Chelsea Green Publishing.

Paper Monument, editors. 2012. *Draw it with your eyes closed: The art of the art assignment*. Brooklyn, NY: Paper Monument.

3 Queer Possibilities in Peace and Justice Studies

Geoffrey W. Bateman

A little over twenty years ago, Lauren Berlant and Michael Warner (1995) published an editorial commentary in *Proceedings of the Modern Language Association*, asking the provocative question, "What Does Queer Theory Teach Us about X?" Their response helped open up an evolving understanding of the possibilities of queer scholarship as a critical tool for social justice, not only within the discourse of critical theory and literary studies, but also across a range of other disciplines and fields. They argued that "queer commentary has tried to challenge some major conditions of privacy" with regard to the regimes of sexual shame that we live within, as well as "driv[ing] into visibility both the cultural production of sexuality and the social context of feeling" (347). Within this then nascent intellectual movement, they saw great potential to "challenge the comforts of privilege and unself-consciousness" and to resist (sexual) systemization, embracing instead a theoretical orientation of "unsettlement" (348). Ultimately, Berlant and Warner write, "As difficult as it would be to spell out programmatic content for an answer, this simple question still has the power to wrench frames" (348).

It is this productive wrenching of frames that this chapter takes up in relation to teaching, learning, and pedagogy within peace and justice studies. What does or could queer theory—and its accumulation of insights, knowledge, and critical practices—teach us about peace and justice studies? What would it mean to *queer* our field and more fully apply the frameworks and insights of queer theory to work that we do specifically in our curriculum and classrooms? On the one hand, it challenges hidden or lingering heteronormative assumptions about privacy, sexual shame, and respectability within the work that we do. It also renders visible the social constructions of sexuality and gender embedded in our discourse and practices and unsettles what we think we know about these categories, especially in relation to non-normative or non-binary identities, desires, and their expressions. Despite what has emerged as a robust and evolving set of theories, knowledge, methods, and practices that has come to signify queerness, the impact of queer theory or queer studies remains limited on peace and justice studies in terms of both research and teaching. How might such queering open up new understandings and practices within our curriculum and pedagogies, fostering meaningful transformations of what we teach and how we teach it?

From major journals to textbooks within peace and justice studies, we lack a robust critical engagement with LGBT issues, much less with queer theory or queer approaches to sexuality and gender, if we take queer to signify not an umbrella term for sexual and gender minorities but a fuller embrace of fluidity, resistance, and non-normativity. Even less clear is a dedicated exploration of the connection between these issues and the central concepts and pedagogical practices of peace and justice studies as a field. Why is this? This lack of critical engagement has much to do with the fundamental assumptions—historical, theoretical, and methodological—of these two interdisciplinary fields, as sometimes diffuse and hard to pin down as they both might be. In the broadest brush strokes, we might even say that there's a deep tension between the normative foundations and empirical basis of peace and justice studies and the non- or even anti-normative impulses of queer theory and its origins in critical theory. Historically, there is a tension between the historical roots of peace and justice studies and its attachment, at times, to a politics of respectability, given its roots in religious traditions and, unspoken or not, middle-class norms of reform, propriety, and the family. To wrench the frames of peace and justice studies, then, is to question and possibly trouble what we teach in ways both deeply challenging and profoundly promising.

To return to the opening question of what queer theory might teach us about pedagogy in peace and justice studies leads to four tentative answers, and further questions, that provide us with powerful new directions for what we teach in our field and how we might teach it. First, the urgent need for greater queer visibility within our classrooms: how visible are LGBT and queer desires, identities, expressions, communities, and social movements in our research and teaching? Second, normativity and the role and meaning of identity, especially non-normative genders and sexualities: how normal and normative are these understandings within what we teach and how we integrate LGBT issues, and sexuality and gender more broadly into our curriculum? Third, respectability and sex, desire, and sexuality in knowledge production and methodologies in our field: how do norms of respectability shape what counts as legitimate knowledge and forms of political organizing and resistance in our educational practices? Fourth, intersectionality: how do our understandings of queerness intersect with, shape, and get shaped by other differences and structures of oppression and violence? Raising these questions opens up spaces of queer possibility within our research and teaching. Ultimately, engaging the frameworks and insights of queer theory and studies allows us and our students to position ourselves more creatively and justly in relation to the regimes of sexuality and gender that we inhabit, especially as those regimes inform and shape the work we do, students and faculty alike, in our classrooms and communities. There is much work to be done, especially in relation to engaging meaningfully with intersectionality and LGBT and queer sexualities and gender identities and expressions.

Engaging Queerness in Peace and Justice Studies

Before we can reflect on how we might transform our pedagogies and teach more queerly within peace and justice studies, we must confront the relative thinness of queer content in the field, for we cannot teach what we do not know. A review of scholarship within peace and justice studies journals reveals some focus on LGBT and queer issues, but not a robust integration of them. Since 1997, *Peace and Change* has published nearly ten reviews on book-length studies related in some way to LGBT issues, but only three actual academic articles that focus substantially on them. Two of these studies—"'The War on Terror' and Same-Sex Marriage" and "Joyfulness as a Community Organizing Strategy"—appeared in the 2005 special issue, "Queer Studies Meets Peace Studies," which announced the promising intent to bring these two fields into better dialogue (Shepard 2005; Bloodsworth-Lugo and Lugo-Lugo, 2005). It also included interviews with two lesbian activists, one Palestinian and the other Israeli, as well as a substantial review essay on the Cold War and sexuality and gender (Krahulik 2005a; Krahulik 2005b; Baxter 2005). As the editor, Kathleen Kennedy (2005), writes:

> It is my hope … that this issue will begin to introduce the field of queer studies to peace studies and vice versa in a manner that goes beyond the now infamous paradigm of adding a different method or group of people to a dominant paradigm and stirring.
>
> (434)

Despite her hope that the "methods pioneered by both peace scholars and queer scholars can positively inform one another" (434), such reciprocity remains elusive, given the lack of consistent engagement with such issues since this publication.

Scholarship outside of this special issue points to a similar interest in LGBTQ issues, but also confirms a lack of integration. Ian Lekus's (2004) interview with Amber Hollibaugh opens up a clear sense of queerness's role in liberation movements of the late 1960s and early 1970s. As she says, "You were queer and the fact that you were queer and the way you were queer made you radical" (303), highlighting the connections between queerness and social transformation. Additional articles have explored feminist anti-nuclear activism, gender and violence, and masculinity in Norway in WWI, all in ways that resonate with queer interests and commentary, but not explicitly. Scott Bennett's (2013) analysis of pacifists David McReynolds and Vern Davidson's resistance to the draft during the Korean War illustrates this critical stance. Even though both were radical gay men, the essay fails to address the relation between their sexuality and their anti-war activism, even though in a footnote he expresses his intent to do so in his forthcoming book about them (109). Such deferral illustrates a larger tendency in our field, representing an acknowledgement that LGBT issues deserve attention but may not be as important as other critical issues, even as gay historians have explored the significance of McReynolds' sexuality much more fully (Duberman 2011). More promising, Jacob Juntunen (2015) argues that *The Normal Heart*, a play by ACT-UP founder, Larry Kramer, "mak[es] the radical palatable," constituting "one of the first major actions that helped combat apathy, homophobia, and ignorance" in the early years of the AIDS epidemic (64, 78). In promising ways, such work has set in motion a greater appreciation and understanding of LGBTQ activism within one of the main journals in our field. Still, for those of us who turn to this publication for guidance on the content of what we teach, this engagement has yet to construct a sufficient foundation to help re-imagine our pedagogies as sufficiently queer.

In other journals, there has been some, but limited, attention to LGBT issues, which suggests promising directions to move in. In the past few years, *Peace and Conflict: Journal of Peace Psychology* has featured two studies that have focused on homosexuality or gay and lesbian identity in relation to political attitudes. The first demonstrates that despite valuing universal equality for all people, adults in the United Kingdom extended this value inconsistently to homosexual people (Abrams, Houston, Van de Vyver, and Vasiljevic 2015). Examining the activist motivation of LGBT Australians, a different team of researchers found that positive contact between gay men and lesbians and their heterosexual friends impacted their intent to engage in collective action differently depending on their specific social position: for gay men these kinds of positive interactions tended to increase their intent to participate in collective action, but for lesbians it undermined it (Techakesari, Droogendyk, Wright, Louis, and Barlow 2017). *Peace and Conflict Studies* has not devoted much attention to LGBT or queer issues, although in their reimagining of Gandhi's constructive noncooperation through behavioral systems science, Mark Mattani and Kristen Atkinson (2011) focus on queer culture as an important illustration of constructive noncooperation.

The *Journal of Peace Education* has been somewhat more inclusive of LGBT issues, insofar as a handful of studies address homophobia as a part of the many social injustices that peace education addresses. For example, in interviews with peace educators, Pamela Bolotin Joseph and Leslie Smith Duss (2009) report that those working with high school students included homophobia in their teaching about peace and human rights, and one teacher, in particular, acknowledged her activist background as having had roots "in organizations against violence to women and for gay rights" (196). Still, subsequent research has recognized that peace educators have more work to do to foster education that is responsive to the needs of LGBTQ people and the injustices they face, "since so much of the violence that occurs, especially against women, minorities, gay students, and others identified as that classic 'other,'" is "normalized almost to the point of invisibility" (Duckworth, Allen, and Williams 2012, 95). Robert Mizzi (2010) concurs, acknowledging that the "lives of sexual/gender minorities ... generally have been mute in peace education" (139). His interviews with community activists and peace educators who either identified as a sexual/gender minority or who worked actively on these issues fills this silence. Their experiences revealed their constant negotiation of the tensions between their identities and heterosexist and homophobic oppression that structured both the larger communities in which they worked and the peace education and community activism that struggled against these forms of injustice. This tension became pronounced when participants "received notable support and respect for being sexually/gendered differently and effectively started to build 'peace' in their workplaces or communities, but, at the same time experienced hate based on their identity-difference" (153). As they negotiated such attacks on their identities, these LGBTQ individuals felt their larger peace work threatened, even as challenging homo/transphobia was and should be integrated into the vision of what peace represents. In this way, Robert C. Mizzi and Sean Byrne (2015) argue that queer theory "can be helpful in deconstructing heteronormative understandings of peace and nonviolence, determining what kinds of 'performative' discourses exist" in the field of peace and conflict studies, "conceptualizing how violence acts as a form of (homo)sexual regulation" (367). In order for everyone, including LGBTQ people, to participate in peace and justice education, our field must take up these important lessons from queer theory and LGBT studies and generate both inclusive and transformative content and pedagogical practices.

Textbooks also provide an important window into what students in peace and justice studies experience in our classrooms. The most visible of these in peace studies also reflect little focus on sexuality, especially LGBTQ sexualities and gender identities and expressions. David P. Barash's *Approaches to Peace: A Reader in Peace Studies* (2018) does not mention sexuality, and only gives a brief nod to gender with selections from work by bell hooks and Betty Reardon (206–209, 262–269). *Nonviolence in Theory and Practice* includes a distinct section on "Women and Nonviolence," including an excerpt from Barbara Deming's "On Revolution and Equilibrium," but without situating her as an important *lesbian-feminist* nonviolent peace activist (Holmes and Gan 2012, 117–172). Houston Wood's (2016) more recent *Invitation to Peace Studies* devotes an entire chapter to "Building Gender Security," within which he addresses gender- and sex-based violence. This chapter includes a brief section that focuses on violence against LGBT people and their growing participation along with women more generally in the global peace network (78–80), and then a brief nod to the LGBT rights movement in the 20th century, in "Expanding Human Rights" (128–129). Wood's (2018) accompanying reader also includes an entire section devoted to gender and gender- and sex-based violence. One of the readings—George Lakey's "Lessons from the LGBT Equality Movement" from Waging Nonviolence—specifically explores the dynamics of this social and political movement (90–92).

Ultimately, the emerging queer content in our research publications and the LGBT additions to our textbooks are promising, for they move us toward greater inclusion and demonstrate both the power and relevance of sexuality within our teaching of peace studies, nonviolence, human rights, and social movements. But they don't reflect a deep engagement with LGBT issues, much less a queer orientation to them, nor do they complicate the field's orientation toward seeing sexuality and gender as central conceptually or in its teaching practice. That is, they appear as illustrative examples, rather than saying something to ourselves and our students about the ways in which entire social, political, and economic systems are deeply impacted by and implicated in how we order desire, sexuality, and all the ways we humans identify with and express these terms. Perhaps more importantly, they don't take up *queerness* and its destabilizing drives to unsettle what we think we know about any of these connections. What would it mean to complicate our foundational understanding of state power, terrorism, and nationalism by including texts like Jasbir K. Puar's (2007) *Terrorist Assemblages: Homonationalism in Queer Times* into our curriculum, which seeks to trouble our knowledge about the relationship between sexuality, international relations, and domestic policies on surveillance and marriage?

Resisting Norms, the Normal, and Identity

To queer a field like peace and justice studies and transform our teaching of these issues within it so that we more fully address the central questions of queer theory requires much more than making a gesture of inclusion to add minority or non-normative sexualities and genders to an expanding list of others who now deserve attention. It requires us to question the norms of identity, community, and perhaps even sociality itself, that continue to structure much of our world. As a field, peace and justice studies is a normative one, at least in its historical evolution and in certain foundational parts of the field. On the most basic level, "peace research has demonstrated a preference for empirical investigation" into conflict (Wallensteen 2010, 16), a methodological orientation with its own norms and epistemological structures. It does so, though, with a particular end in mind. As Kristine Höglund and Magnus Öberg (2011) write, peace research is "strongly normatively driven by concern to understand how violent conflict can be prevented and how peace can be made durable" (4), reflecting a particular "awareness of social values in research" (Wallensteen 2010,17). "Peace researchers," Wallensteen (2010) writes, "are not simply interested in empirically understanding the extent of violence in the world. They also hope to contribute to the *improvement* of the human condition," ultimately comparing peace research to medicine and its interest in "developing methods to cure and eliminate 'unhealth'" (17).

Even though many might not think twice about the goodness of such improvement, to queer ears, associating the purpose of a field or a discipline's introductory course with eliminating "unhealth" is disturbing, even if the disease is violence, if only because of the fraught history between medicine and LGBTQ people and the deep connections between non-normative sexualities and genders and illness, depravity, and deviance. As Michael Warner (1999) explains, modern medicine and its attendant notions about health developed in conjunction with the rise of the statistical norm. The effect of this development was that "normal came to mean right, proper, healthy. What most people are, the new wisdom went, is what people should be" (57). But "[h]ealth requires variation," Warner warns, "not a pregiven norm" (58). But queer scholars and activists are admittedly skeptical of anyone's confidence in their ability to know what might be good, healthy, or in the context of peacebuilding or social justice, appropriate for others. As Warner writes, "The history of the [LGBTQ] movement should have taught us to ask: whose norm?" (59).

It's not so much that the normative values espoused by teachers and researchers in peace and justice studies aren't potentially useful or good, for some of us, at least; it's that the power of such norms tend to re-establish moral hierarchies that marginalize and pathologize what's not normal. For many queer scholars, teachers, and activists, it can be difficult to separate our field's normative ways of understanding, studying, and responding to violence and the much larger cultural legacy of normalization that has pathologized sexual and gender difference more broadly. According to Warner (1993), "The preference for 'queer' represents" a direct challenge to these logics, as well as to "an aggressive impulse of generalization": this preference "rejects a minoritizing logic of toleration or simple political interest-representation in favor of a more thorough resistance to regimes of the normal" (xxvi). In this regard, queer functions not to hold space for LGBT people as sexual minorities who are seeking to enlarge the liberal state and its institutions like the academy in its distribution of rights and resources, but rather to interrogate and transform the very norms that frame such structures in the first place. In this way, Warner embraces a notion of queerness that "gets a critical edge by defining itself against the normal rather than the heterosexual, and normal includes normal business in the academy," ultimately suggesting that "we might even say that queer politics opposes society itself" (xxvi, xxvii).

These are powerful challenges to any field that privileges empirical and systematic methodologies in its production of knowledge, as well as investing in nonviolent resistance and collective action. Warner (1993) and other queer theorists, scholars, and teachers are deeply invested in "protesting not just normal behavior of the social but the very idea of normal behavior," which translates into a deep skepticism of "normalizing methodologies of modern social knowledge" (xxvii). Such skepticism challenges any peace and justice scholars and teachers who are compelled by queer theory to embrace a paradox, for we have to balance and resist certain values and ways of knowing that establish a normative discourse that shapes what is knowable and actionable. As one who strives to promote many of these values, I am equally troubled, though, by how these norms might also interfere at times with principled dissent and autonomy, and the possibility of what might emerge from the margins, specifically those that have been historically oppressed for being unnatural, depraved, perverted, or just not normal, especially when those being oppressed are queer students. Queer theory, in part, seeks to amplify the particularities of non-normative sexualities and genders, reflecting ways of knowing more amenable in the humanities and qualitative social sciences. For these reasons, even as the impulses of peace and justice studies, especially those that reject violence, are themselves countercultural and resistant to deeply held norms around conflict, they remain in tension with queer theory. These tensions help explain the challenge peace and justice studies faces in integrating queer theory or LGBTQ voices into the work we do, especially in our classrooms.

In its challenge of social norms and normativity, queer theory has also sought to unsettle the norms of identity, an impulse that my students—queer and non-queer—seem increasingly eager to embrace. In their early writing, both Eve Kosofsky Sedgwick (1993) and Judith Butler (1990) not only critiqued the categories of identity we use in relation to sexuality and gender, but also the notion of coherent, stable identity. In peace and justice studies, we often seem to take for granted such categories, seeing them as stable markers of social meaning, naturalized and transparent, even as the deconstructive and post-structuralist impulses of queer theory have opened up alternative ways to understand sexual and gender identity as a much more fluid, porous, and performative phenomenon, much less anchored in absolute and stable binaries. "That's one of the things that 'queer' can refer to," Eve Kososky Sedgwick (1993) writes: "the open mesh of possibilities, gaps, overlaps, dissonances and resonances, lapses and excesses of meaning when the constituent elements of anyone's gender, of anyone's sexuality aren't made (or can't be made) to signify monolithically" (8). For Annamarie Jagose (1996), "queer describes those gestures or analytical models which dramatize incoherencies in the allegedly stable relations between chromosomal sex, gender and sexual desire ... queer focuses on the mismatches between sex, gender, and desire" (3). To view identity, especially sexual and gender identity and their expressions, as dynamic in this kind of way poses serious challenges to any field that views identity as essentially stable rather than embrace the contractions, the mismatches, or the messiness of it, especially in relation to sexuality and gender. In this way, Judith Butler's (1990) argument that we can't ground feminism in a universalized, essentialist, commonsensical notion of "woman" or that people's sexual identities are not nearly as stable, nor binary, as we might want to believe remain provocative in a field whose norms are unquestioned when we take up issues related to these identities.

Such critiques can seem overly abstract, but such norms have consequences, especially when we study and respond to gender-based violence.

If we do not consider non-normative, or anti-normative identities, both as subjects of study and as present in our classrooms, or the bodies that we and our students inhabit that may not conform to binary structures, we risk missing very important experiences and insights into violence and the various ways we might respond to it in a transformative way. Especially for transgender individuals, or anyone whose sexuality or gender defies or is not reflected in our binary system, the gender binary itself enforces violence and is at the root of the oppression that many LGBTQ people face in the wider community and on our campuses (Confortini 2006, 355).

Even as this discussion reveals the challenges of integrating queer theory into peace and justice studies, there are promising connections to be made to the work of central scholars in our field, like that of John Paul Lederach (2005), that can animate our pedagogical approaches. In his definition of the moral imagination, and the capacities we must cultivate if we are to transcend violence, he argues we must develop the "ability to sustain a paradoxical curiosity that embraces complexity without reliance on dualistic polarity" (5). Because, in his estimation, violence results from reducing "complex history into dualistic polarities," Lederach urges us to refuse to "fall prey to the pressures of forced dualistic categories of truth" and embrace an "inquisitiveness about what may hold together seemingly contradictory social energies in a greater whole" (35, 36). Ultimately, to do this work well, we "require a capacity to develop and live with a high degree of ambiguity" (37). Living with such ambiguity isn't exactly the same thing as embracing a queer resistance to heteronormativity, but this line of thinking reflects a similar disposition to rigid moral hierarchies that resonates with queer theory's insights and imperative, provides a powerful entry point into queering what we teach in peace and justice studies.

Teaching Queerly in Peace and Justice Studies

What might it look like, then, to embrace queerness, not solely in terms of curriculum, but also approach? What kind of queer content should we teach and ask our students to engage? How best to teach it? What could queer pedagogy look like in our field? For the past six years, I've worked within this tension between peace and justice studies and queer theory and LGBT studies, and have sought ways to include LGBTQ voices and issues within our peace and justice studies curriculum in my department at Regis University and within our larger conversations at Peace and Justice Studies Association, working to unsettle our assumptions so as to re-orient ourselves so that queerness can be legible and be regarded as an important kind of epistemology and way of understanding nonviolence, social transformation, and justice. To teach queerly in peace and justice studies requires us to embrace the following dynamics: we might start by insisting that our notions of peace and justice are deeply tied to desire, our gendered bodies, and expressions of identity and deliberately engage with the politics of shame that often prevents us from seeing these connections. In our classrooms, we need to create space for authentic explorations of student identity, embodiment, and desire, even as we balance this with a more deconstructive move that unsettles any easy or simple way of understandings these facets of human experience. Fostering both identification and a kind of irreverence allows us to challenge the norms of our field, even as we hold them dear, in our larger promotion of radical inclusion and justice. We must do all of this while remaining committed to an intersectional approach, tying our teaching to other forms of marginalization and identity. That is, queer pedagogy must consider multiple identities and structures of oppression as they inform gender and sexuality.

For example, in an introduction to peace and justice studies course that I teach, I integrate readings that foreground issues of sexuality and gender in relation to violence and structure of oppression. A text like Dorothy Allison's (1993) *Two or Three Things I Know for Sure*, which describes her experience surviving sexual violence and abuse as a child, growing up in poverty, and her own coming out process as a lesbian, provides a powerful narrative that illustrates the deep connections between direct and structural violence, and the interpersonal dimensions that grow out of larger structures of oppression. It does so in a way that creates space for conversations and awareness about queerness and its relationship to peace and justice studies. As she asks in her own interrogation of how her step-father's abuse had shaped her sexuality and identity, "How does it come together, the sweaty power of violence, the sweet taste of desire held close?" (46). Allison's answers might make many of us uncomfortable, for in her embrace of her identity as a "lesbian, a dyke, stubborn, competitive and perversely lustful" (45), she confronts the unsettling interconnections that defy easy, normative notions of reclaimable identities. Her complex understanding of her own perversity acknowledges and integrates the traumas of her past, even as it seeks healing and resolution.

It's one thing to add this text to a course, to use it after one has established other conceptual terrain, like David Cortright's (2008) chapter on "What is Peace?" from his book *Peace: A History of Movements and Ideas*, but an important shift occurs when you start the course by centering a marginalized voice like Allison's and consider it foundational to the study of peace and justice. That is, queerness—and all it might represent, including sexuality, desire, and gender identity and expression—is not something we think about later after we come to understand peace; queerness is what we start with and use it as a lens through which to generate conceptual insights into peace and justice. In the next course our majors take, *Foundations of Peace and Justice Studies*, I take a step further and anchor the course in an intersectional analysis of the root causes of oppression and various forms of structural violence, often focusing on racism, sexism, and homophobia. Texts like Ta-Nehisi Coates' *Between the World and Me*, bell hooks' *Killing Rage: Ending Racism*, and *The Laramie Project* introduces students to forms of violence in our society in an intersectional way and requires their developing knowledge in anti-violence work, conflict transformation, nonviolent resistance, and various other methodologies and approaches that we might say characterize peace and justice studies. My larger point here is that if we don't center our core courses on issues like queerness, we will continue to re-inscribe our field as somehow not really concerned with issues like sexuality and gender identity and expression, and scholars, students, and activists who identify strongly with these issues might not feel welcome in our spaces, intellectually, pedagogically, or physically, or might not see peace and justice studies as relevant to their work.

Within the traditional scope of peace and justice studies, two queer figures feature prominently in the historical evolution of nonviolence as both a philosophy and a strategic response to oppression and violence: Bayard Rustin and Barbara Deming. Both activists provide powerful intersectional illustrations of the salience of race, gender, and sexuality in the context of the history of pacifism and movements for social justice. I often teach writings from both figures, and use the documentary about Bayard Rustin, *Brother Outsider*, to show both the punishing logic of mid-century homophobia in our national political context and the discomfort that leaders like A.J. Muste and Martin Luther King, Jr., felt about Rustin's homosexuality, especially its more public and scandalous moments. Further examples from Rustin's own writing also reveals how queerness functioned for him as a way to understand his own militancy and the extreme, nonviolent actions he took as an activist, especially in relation to pacifism and racial justice. "[W]e must," Rustin (2012) writes, "be prepared to be looked upon as queer" if we are to be effective in bringing about social change (120). Rustin's struggles to reconcile the public implications of his homosexuality with his more private sense of confidence and wholeness provides important insights to the relationship between pacifism, social movement, and queer desires, helping students see the importance and relevance of queerness to peace and justice studies.

Perhaps best known for her essay, "Revolution and Equilibrium," Barbara Deming provides another important example that illustrates the queer connections between nonviolence, anti-war activism, sexuality, and feminism. Long regarded as an important voice in the history, philosophy, and practice of nonviolence, Deming's lesbianism has not been seen as relevant in this regard (Cherus 2004). Yet Deming's (1984) commitment to and understanding of nonviolence is deeply rooted in her experiences, perspectives, and identity as a lesbian feminist, and to the recognition that we are "all one flesh," not separate male and female flesh. She integrates these deconstructed gender differences into a more androgynous whole and argues:

> nonviolence actions are by their nature androgynous. In them the two impulses that have long been treated as distinct, 'masculine' and 'feminine,' the impulses of self-assertion and the impulse of sympathy, are

> clearly joined; the very genius of nonviolence, in fact, is that it demonstrates them to be indivisible, and so restores human community.
>
> (230)

Building on her nonviolent embrace of gender fluidity, she argues that our sexual desires play an equally important role in bridging divides. As she writes:

> our sexuality is given to us so that we can commune with one another—and with our universe. It 'cracks our single selves' .... Without sexuality we would be impossibly isolated within our individualities. We could not experience community, could not experience in our flesh the truth that we are, all of us, 'members one of another', and of all that is.
>
> (244)

In focusing on figures like Rustin and Deming, we take steps in realizing what Robert Mizzi (2010) describes as "an anti-oppression program" that "include[s] a greater diversity of individuals, histories, contexts, and cultures during the peace-building process," respecting his call that a "general awareness of sexual/gender identity-differences be integrated into peace-building continua [sic] as an inclusive attempt to ending sexualized/gendered violence endured by sexual/gender minorities" (154). In addition to integrating this awareness into introductory and foundational courses required for our majors, we can also offer elective courses that explore these issues in greater depth, like I have in an upper-division special topics course called *Justice, Gender, Sexuality*. First and foremost, this course helps students develop a robust and critical vocabulary about queer sexualities, desires, and identities that is intersectional and allows and challenges them to see and experience and acknowledge the connections between the many facets of themselves and the structures that form them. For a pedagogy that aspires to be queer, we must help them situate themselves sexually and articulate these intimate aspects of themselves within the context of their studies, and that begins with narrating their own stories. A powerful assignment I've used in this course asks students to write a coming out narrative about some aspect of their identity. Even though this assignment works best with sexual and gender identity, it works well for other invisible, marginalized identities. It can also illustrate powerful truths about our normative regimes of sexuality and gender for students who identify as heterosexual or cisgender, for they can narrate and reflect on the moments when their more normative desires and identities became visible and salient to them.

In this course, students gain an introductory understanding of queer theory and activism with an overview of the history of LGBTQ activism in the 20th and 21st centuries, including the homophile movement, gay liberation, lesbian feminism, ACT-UP, and the struggle for marriage equality. Using texts like Anamarie Jagose's *Queer Theory: An Introduction* or

Donald E. Hall's *Queer Theories*, students grapple with the indeterminacies that anchor queer theory and gain a historical understanding of the evolution of the term queer and its significance for both activists and scholars. To provide students with a greater understanding of the importance of the AIDS epidemic and the activist response to it in shaping our sense of queer movements, nonviolence, and justice, they read Tony Kushner's play *Angels in America* alongside writings about AIDS activism and the documentary about ACT-UP, *How To Survive a Plague*. The third unit of the course takes up Michael Warner's *The Trouble with Normal* and focuses in large part on his critique of marriage equality and the larger normative impulses of our more recent LGBTQ activism. We follow up his more theoretical discussion with a more intersectional approach to LGBTQ politics, reading *Queer (In)Justice: The Criminalization of LGBT People in the United States*, gaining insight to the harassment and hostility queer people, especially transgender women of color, face. The course concludes by reading queer Chicano oral histories and Urvashi Vaid's writing about queer politics, looking towards possible futures for queer intersectional activism.

Conclusion

This course and the content integrated into other courses constitute a few ways that we might begin to imagine a queerer peace and justice studies, in both our classrooms and our larger research. It's certainly not the only way we might approach the queering of our field, but it is a start. As with any queer endeavor, though, it's the unexpected disruptions that we cannot predict that will likely make for the most promising paths forward. For our students, and for ourselves as well, it's essential that we grapple much more fully with the legacy of queerness that already exists, largely invisible and unrecognized, just under the surface, in the history of our field and those scholars, activists, and movements that have preceded us. As with many disciplines, queerness is right there, just waiting for us to ask the right questions to render it visible. Doing so has the potential to transform the knowledge and practices we hold dear. Foregrounding queerness within peace and justice studies provides an opportunity to better understand the central role that sexuality and gender has played in structuring knowledge, politics, and activism. Ultimately, it helps teachers and students position themselves more creatively and justly in relation to the regimes of sexuality and gender that we/they inhabit.

References

Abrams, Dominic, Diane M. Houston, Julie Van de Vyver, and Milica Vasiljevic. 2015. "Equality Hypocrisy, Inconsistency, and Prejudice: The Unequal Application of the Universal Human Right to Equality," *Peace and Conflict: Journal of Peace Psychology* 21(1): 28–46. DOI: doi:10.1037/pac0000084

Allison, Dorothy. 1995. *Two or Three Things I Know for Sure*. New York: Plume.
Barash, David P., ed. 2018. *Approaches to Peace: A Reader in Peace Studies*, 4th ed. New York: Oxford University Press.
Baxter, Randolph W. 2005. "Butch vs. Femme During the Early Cold War: Deconstructing Hyper-Masculine Ideologies," *Peace & Change*30(4): 540–547.
Bennett, Scott H. 2013. "Conscience, Comrades, and the Cold War: The Korean War Draft Resistance Case of Socialist Pacifists David McReynolds and Vern Davidson." *Peace & Change* 38(1): 83–120.
Berlant, Lauren, and Michael Warner. 1995. "What Does Queer Theory Teach Us about X?" *PMLA: Publications of the Modern Language Association* 110(3): 343–349.
Butler, Judith. 1990. *Gender Trouble: Feminism and the Subversion of Identity*. New York: Routledge.
Cherus, Ira. 2004. *American Nonviolence: The History of an Idea*. Maryknoll, NY: Orbis Books.
Confortini, Catia C. 2006. "Galtung, Violence, and Gender: The Case for a Peace Studies/Feminism Alliance." *Peace & Change* 31(3): 333–367.
Cortright, David. 2008. *Peace: A History of Movements and Ideas*. New York: Oxford University Press.
Deming, Barbara. 1984. *We Are All Part of One Another: A Barbara Deming Reader*, edited by Jane Meyerding. Philadelphia, PA: New Society Publishers.
Duberman, Martin. 2011. *A Saving Remnant: The Radical Lives of Barbara Deming and David McReynolds*. New York: The New Press.
Duckworth, Cheryl Lynn, Barba Allen, and Teri Triguba Williams. 2012. "What Do Students Learn When We Teach Peace? A Qualitative Assessment of a Theater Peace Program." *Journal of Peace Education* 9(1): 81–99. DOI: doi:10.1080/174002012.664548
Höglund, Kristine, and Magnus Öberg. 2011. "Doing Empirical Peace Research." In
Understanding Peace Research: Methods and Challenges, edited by Kristine Höglund and Magnus Öberg, 3–13. New York: Routledge.
Holmes, Robert L., and Barry L. Gan, eds. 2012. *Nonviolence in Theory and Practice*, 3rd ed. Long Grove, IL: Waveland Press.
Jagose, Annamarie. 1996. *Queer Theory: An Introduction*. New York: Routledge.
Joseph, Pamela Bolotin, and Leslie Smith Duss. 2009. "Teaching a Pedagogy of Peace:
A Study of Peace Educators in United States School in the Aftermath of September 11." *Journal of Peace Education* 6(2): 189–207. DOI: doi:10/1080/17400200903086615
Juntunen, Jacob. 2015. "War During Peacetime: Mainstream Theater, Mass Media, and the 1985 Premier of The Normal Heart." *Peace & Change* 40(1): 63–82. DOI: doi:10.1111/pech.12113
Kennedy, Kathleen. 2005. "Forward: Queer Studies Meets Peace Studies," *Peace & Change* 30(4): 433–434. DOI: doi:0.1111/j.1468–0130.2005.00327.x
Krahulik, Karen C. 2005a. "Aswat (Voices): An Interview with Rauda Morcos," *Peace & Change* 30(4): 492–520.
Krahulik, Karen C. 2005b. "The Jerusalem Open House: An Interview with Daphna Strousma," *Peace & Change* 30(4): 521–539.
Lederach, John Paul. 2005. *The Moral Imagination: The Art and Soul of Building Peace*. New York: Oxford University Press.
Lekus, Ian. 2004. "Interview with Amber Hollibaugh." *Peace & Change* 29(2): 266–321. DOI: doi:10.1111/j.1468–0130.2004.00291.x

Mattani, Mark A., and Kristen Atkinson. 2011. "Constructive Noncooperation: Living in Truth," *Peace and Conflict Studies* 18(1): 3–43.

Mizzi, Robert. 2010. "Let's Get This Straightened Out: Finding a Place and Presence for Sexual/Gender Identity-Differences in Peace Education," *Journal of Peace Education* 7(2): 139–156. DOI: doi:10.1080/17400201.2010.498996

Mizzi, Robert C., and Sean Byrne. 2015. "Queer Theory and Peace and Conflict Studies." In *Gender and Peacebuilding: All Hands Required*, edited by Maureen P. Flaherty, Thomas Matyók, Sean Byrne, and Hamdesa Tuso, 359–374. Lanham, MD: Lexington Books.

Puar, Jasbir K. 2007. *Terrorist Assemblages: Homonationalism in Queer Times*. Durham, NC: Duke University Press.

Rustin, Bayard. 2012. *I Must Resist: Bayard Rustin's Life in Letters*, edited by Michael G. Long. San Francisco, CA: City Lights Books.

Sedgwick, Eve Kosofsky. 1993. *Tendencies*. Durham, NC: Duke University Press.

Techakesari, Pirathat, Lisa Droogendyk, Stephen C. Wright, Winnifred R. Louis, and Fiona Kate Barlow. 2017. "Supportive Contact and LGBT Collective Action: The Moderating Role of Membership in Specific Groups," *Peace and Conflict: Journal of Peace Psychology* 23(3): 307–316. DOI: http://dx.doi.org.dml.regis.edu/10.1037/pac0000240

Wallensteen, Peter. 2011. "The Origins of Contemporary Peace Research." In *Understanding Peace Research: Methods and Challenges*, edited by Kristine Höglund and Magnus Öberg, 14–32. New York: Routledge.

Warner, Michael, ed. 1993. *Fear of a Queer Planet: Queer Politics and Queer Theory*. Minneapolis, MN: University of Minnesota Press.

Warner, Michael. 1999. *The Trouble with Normal: Sex, Politics, and the Ethics of Queer Life*. New York: The Free Press.

Wood, Houston. 2016. *Invitation to Peace Studies*. New York: Oxford University Press.

Wood, Houston. 2018. *Current Debates in Peace and Conflict Studies*. New York: Oxford University Press.

Part II

Experiential Learning in Peace and Justice Studies

4 Teaching Peace – Experientially

Edmund Pries

Student transformation is widely heralded as the "Holy Grail" or pedagogical pinnacle of teaching. It is, however, only the final stage in a process that I have elsewhere described as a "Five Step Arc of Learning" (Pries 2014) – and follows the four prior learning stages of (1) cognitive disequilibrium, (2) acquisition of new information, (3) knowledge and understanding and (4) learning integration. When teaching peace, especially, student transformation is not characterized by the alignment or capitulation of a student's views to the perspectives of the teacher; rather, it represents the student's acquisition and, ultimately, the "ownership" of the student's own beliefs, viewpoints and conclusions based upon study, scholarship and … understood experience. It is the latter, frequently classified as *experiential learning*, which will be explored in this chapter.[1]

While classroom academic study, broadly defined, is an ancient learning format, it can be argued that experiential learning (EL) has an even older pedigree. Apprenticeship for the acquisition of knowledge predates classrooms and textbooks. It has, however, become redefined and reemphasized via other terminologies by many great educational theorists of the twentieth century, including John Dewey (1933), Jean Piaget (Duska and Whelan 1975; Kibler 2011), Paulo Freire (2000), David A. Kolb, (1984), Alice Y. Kolb (2008), Donald Schön (1983, 1987) and many others. Learning through reflected experience has experienced its own renaissance (Baud, Keogh and Walker 1985; Brockbank and McGill 1998; Moon 2006; Schön 1983, 1987).

Experiential learning as a specific pedagogical field of both study and practice has not received the same popular valuation in academe as scholastic study until more recently. Peter November was an early adopter and has described his journey to experiential teaching methodologies (1997). Experiential learning is now seen as so successful, that even some governments, with their perennial concerns about job readiness of graduating students and with the additional concern that university faculties are not picking up the EL torch quickly enough, have more recently joined the chorus and taken initiatives to promote this form of learning back to the university (Conway et al 2016).

Experiential learning is also frequently known by other names, including *active learning, integrated learning* or *engaged learning*. While all are important pedagogical concepts and represent creative initiatives to harness a student's learning potential, experiential learning can also be distinct, because it focuses on real life problems and issues. These might include doing research on neighbourhood divisions for a local community organization. As discussed below, global problems and conflict issues can also be brought into the classroom by forcing students to confront a problem in a direct way. At its essential core, experiential learning is focused on having students discover for themselves the information and concepts we, as teachers, wish for them to understand. This is why it is also, occasionally, referred to as "student-discovered learning." Pedagogical theory suggests that when students discover the information themselves, the journey from discovery to intellectual ownership – knowledge integration and, ultimately, student transformation, whereby a student's outlook and actions in life are transformed by their learning – is much faster. Moreover, it also endures. The learning is retained because it has been owned and integrated. Once thusly adopted, it can also result in transformed action and in a new and suitably critical relationship to society.

Integrated and experiential learning is not neutral, but seeks to assist the student's educational journey towards informed and active engagement. This is particularly true of peace education. Larry Fisk has emphasized the pedagogical distinction between educating *about* peace and educating *for* peace (Fisk 2000, 159–193). His explanation of "problem-posing education" hews towards experiential education – at least in some form. Fisk's emphasis on a dialogical approach descends from the pedagogical architecture developed by Paulo Freire (2000). All of this sets the table for a deeply-engaged experiential learning methodology. There are, however, two primary questions that need to be considered. First, experiential learning may be fine and good, but – to borrow Fisk's terminology – how does it educate for peace? Or more precisely stated: how does it educate *better* for peace? Second, how might it serve to unshackle students from socio-cultural and socio-political views that militate against peace? The second question, if it is accurate, partially answers the first: peace education can only happen if transformation takes place and transformation can only result after the unshackling from anti-peace belief systems can be and has been effected.

It is my contention that experiential learning is particularly useful when it comes to unshackling university students from prior prejudices and belief systems – and from views that are reflexively articulated but that are frequently not their own. Rather, these views have been absorbed from parents, schoolteachers and, especially, popular culture and the media – and have been parroted without scrutiny. Before new information and perspectives can be accessed by the student, the unshackling from preconceived notions must be undertaken – and for this to occur, an experience of cognitive disequilibrium is both instrumental and essential. The critical importance of cognitive disequilibrium as a necessary learning stage was articulated most effectively by Swiss educational psychologist, Jean Piaget

(Duska and Whelan 1975; Kibler 2011). Piaget's identification of cognitive disequilibrium is widely referenced, and although he developed this notion to address the issue of childhood development, it is, I believe, equally applicable to undergraduate university education. Cognitive disequilibrium can be generated in many ways – including by the use of a provocative textbook. Significantly more effective, however, is an engaged student experience through experiential learning.

Experiential learning has the ability to engage the student on multiple levels – intellectual, emotional, physical – while effectively harnessing the curriculum. It is this multi-level – and multi-sensory – engagement that gives experiential learning its effective power. Experiential learning is also the most effective method for learning creative problem solving: skills can be obtained through experience. Most importantly, however, experiential learning can propel the student through the stages of the *Arc of Learning* more effectively (and quickly) than other teaching and learning approaches. In other words, not only does experiential learning open up prior beliefs for revision more quickly, it also speeds up the integration and adoption of new ideas – and aids, ultimately, the transformation goal discussed above.

Experiential learning cases proliferate through the academy, but they can be roughly divided into group-based and individually-based experiential learning models. Both have value but, it can be argued, group experiential learning multiplies the learning and accelerates learning integration because, additionally, it facilitates peer learning. This is why group experiential learning should be chosen over the individual experience whenever possible.

This chapter examines two cases of experiential learning geared to peace and conflict studies. The first scrutinizes how an international conflict and protest dilemma can be effectively brought into the classroom to serve as an educational vehicle for peacebuilding. The second takes the learning outside the classroom for a brief exploration of the potential of a pilgrimage pedagogy.

Case Study A: Confronting the Boycott, Divestment, Sanctions (BDS) Movement: How Do we Determine Ethically Legitimate Actions?

In the fall of 2014, I taught a case-study course on *Contemporary Global Conflicts* (Global Studies 331) at Wilfrid Laurier University which was focused on Palestine and Israel. The class read both Israeli and Palestinian authors as they described the history of the conflict from the perspective of their respective communities. The class also received guest speakers from each side, including a visiting Israeli scholar (post-doctoral student) who hailed from Tel Aviv and a Palestinian (a recent student) who lives in Ramallah. It was also important for us to examine the communities of support and opposition in the diaspora of both communities. This focused on the debate about the "Boycott, Divestment, Sanctions" (BDS) movement – a movement begun by Palestinians to boycott Israeli goods and interpreted variously regarding the degree of application (No boycott? Only products from settlements in Occupied Territories? All Israeli products? Educational services also? E.g. conferences, etc.). It bears mentioning that some students in the class were closely connected to the region through family. This resulted in some initial skepticism and, possibly, fears about how fairly "their" community or their views would be treated – especially through the risky dimension of experiential learning where classmates articulate their response from their own learning. However, for maximum learning to take place, student ownership of the outcome is required. And for students to feel ownership of the outcome, they also need to feel that they own the process of discovery – the learning experience. Like all experiential learning processes, this requires the instructor to trust the students and to have a well-prepared learning exercise that is sufficiently rigorous and well-developed to lend integrity both to the educational process itself and to the student's learning experience.

The Israel-Palestine Conflict course itself took place in an "active learning classroom" – a special classroom designed to foster group work and consisting of round group tables with computers, with each table also having their own projector and screen. Images from the instructor or any group table can be projected on all screens – or each group can work on their own screen. This class was comprised of 46 students, who were seated around eight round tables in groups – the same groups remained intact for the duration of the semester. The question for this exercise was whether BDS was a legitimate ethical action and applicable to this particular situation. Was it an appropriate response to the much greater dispute around land ownership, territorial integrity and international law, which forbids the settlement of occupied lands by the occupier, as articulated in Article 49 of the Fourth Geneva Convention (Article 49 of Convention IV)? The goal of the exercise focused on how to make the ethical dilemma of BDS real for the students. Moreover, how could I get the students to truly engage and grapple with this issue and thereby with the real dynamics of the conflict itself? One preparatory piece consisted of having leaders in the community who had crossed traditional lines (e.g. a synagogue president who wrote in favour of BDS) write letters explaining their position to the students. Another was to review some articles in the news media taking opposing sides. The critical instructional challenge was to find a way for students to *experience* the ethical dilemma by grappling with the key issues surrounding the BDS debate and to arrive at a well-argued determination based on their own research case. My solution to the dilemma of distance was, therefore, to create an exercise where each of the eight class groups was forced to make a choice about the justice and applicability of BDS and to justify their choice by providing arguments in support of their position. In order to achieve this, our experiential learning exercise would be focused on wine.

In the province of Ontario, Canada, all wine and alcohol products (except for some beer products and winery-owned outlets) are sold through the stores of the Liquor Control Board of Ontario (LCBO). The LCBO is, as a result, the largest bulk alcohol buyer in the world. They also provide detailed descriptions of all their products via their websites (e.g. vintages.com). My on-line research determined that the LCBO carried 54 Israeli-identified and labelled products in total (inclusive of both Israel proper and the Occupied Territories). From this list, I chose and purchased eight different bottles of wine. These were chosen according to several criteria: (a) location of the winery, (b) location of the vineyards producing the grapes and (c) ownership (and also price – I did not wish to go too far over $150 total for the eight bottles). I gave the list of chosen wines and serial numbers to my local LCBO wine consultant who collected them for me from across the province, since products are distributed to LCBO outlets based on perceived popularity in a particular region. The last of the eight bottles arrived with only two days to spare before the designated three-hour class. The big questions for me were this: would this experiential learning exercise work or would it explode in failure? Would it help students understand the fundamental issues involved? Would they truly grapple with the dilemma and would this experience help them to understand the ethical complexity of BDS?

I *gave* each classroom table (each group) a bottle of wine. It was, I informed them, theirs to keep (a gift); they owned it. Each bottle, it was explained, while from somewhere in Israel, was from a unique location and thus different from the others – and thus might face different issues; the bottles had been researched and chosen for that purpose. Their assignment, which they were required to produce via a PowerPoint document (each group had its own instructor-provided USB stick for such purposes, and which would be submitted to the instructor at the end of a class), was as follows:

1 Describe the bottle of wine, based on the label.
2 Provide some background research on the winery:

   a Where is it located?

      i Choose a suitable map from the course materials or as found on-line and place the geographical location marker to identify the location.
      ii Determine where the winery is located relative to both the 1947 UN borders and relative to the 1967 borders – and determine if that matters (see no. 4 below).

   b When was the winery founded?
   c Who owns and operates the winery? What can you learn or do you know about the owners?

3 Describe other relevant details that may be of interest and importance for additional questions below:

  a Where are the grapes from? (Where are they grown?) Remember that this may be hard to determine; some wineries may be seeking to camouflage exactly where the grapes are from. You will have to use alternative web sites that track this (by using volunteers on the ground who follow the harvested grapes to the winery as well as other methods) to find out.
  b So: does this winery use grapes from the Occupied Territories? (Golan or West Bank? BTW: no grapes are grown and sold to wineries from Gaza.) Some wineries will be located in one region, but their grapes may come from another.
  c Does it matter where the grapes are from?
  d A sample site for additional information (there are more available on-line; you can find them): www.whoprofits.org/sites/default/files/WhoProfits-IsraeliWines.pdf

4 Should your group's bottle of wine be subject to BDS (i.e. should it be boycotted)? Why or why not? Provide a thorough BDS analysis. The analysis can be of all aspects of BDS, including the legitimacy of boycotting products and the BDS movement itself.
5 Undertake one of the following options based on your conclusions under No. 4 above (you have to arrive at a consensus as a group):

  a You find nothing wrong with purchasing or consuming this wine (as per any BDS concerns/non-concerns). You choose to enjoy it as a group over a group dinner in the future.
  b You return the bottle to the LCBO and ask for a refund based on your beliefs relative to your analysis and conclusions about BDS. *(NOTE: Ontario's single-vendor alcohol sales system permits any bottle of alcohol to be returned without issue to any LCBO store – even if opened.)*

  What to do with the money?

    i You might donate the proceeds of the refund to a relevant charity related to the theme of this course – your choice of a charity is also arrived at by group consensus.
    ii You split the proceeds …

  c You come up with another alternative and explain to the class… (NOTE: Some students did come up with an alternative that demonstrates classic student ingenuity: they returned the bottle and traded it in for two bottles of cheaper Canadian wine.)

6 Provide a report to the class where you:

  a Present your research on the winery, its location, its history and its ownership.
  b Present your BDS analysis as explained above and describe your conclusions.

c Describe your group consensus-reaching process.
d Explain what you, as a group, have chosen to do with your bottle of wine and why you chose that option.

In addition to the above instructions, some resources were provided to the students, including a map of Israeli wine growing regions, a map of the various territories, including the three occupied areas under dispute, Gaza, the West Bank and Golan Heights, as well as some on-line resources that provided additional detailed information.

Student response to the idea – other than their amazement that their professor would buy them a bottle of wine – was enthusiastic. They dug into the material and produced surprisingly detailed analyses and well-developed arguments with excellent PowerPoint group presentations. They also worked hard at developing group consensus – and in all cases were able to do so. The group conclusions (to drink or to return the bottle) were quite varied. The trust placed in the students and their ultimate ownership of this learning experience was generously rewarded. Students were not only pleased with the creative experience but by the *learning* experience, recognizing that they learned more than they might have, had the instructor merely lectured to them about BDS. Unsolicited responses (received via email) from students regarding the exercise included the following:

> "... I really enjoyed the last class, and I know my group did as well. The idea was very original and quite entertaining! So thank you!"
>
> "... I always love alternative ways of learning. I find that I learn better through practical application and hands on research rather than article readings, although both are important."

Even a few years later, students still reference this classroom experiential learning exercise as a highlight of their university education. This exercise reinforced the earlier hypothesis that if an instructor lectures students about a controversial policy like BDS, it remains an intellectual concept for them. However, if students are creatively engaged in the issue and are required to make a decision, they can *own* the issue as relevant to them. It can lead to transformed thinking – and, potentially, to student transformation (changed behaviours).

It is also important for the instructor to have undertaken the requisite research and preparation. Experiential or actively engaged learning is definitely not a shortcut to less work; the opposite is almost always the case. However, the benefit to student learning is very rewarding and worthwhile.

The additional larger question, especially for this study, is also a critical one. Does this promote an understanding of peace? Does it contribute to peacebuilding? Education is about understanding but as stated earlier, it is also about student integration of that understanding and the resulting, more peaceable, transformation. Based on my observations, there was substantial student learning and a more enlightened understanding of the complexity of BDS. It is also true that students saw beyond the intricacies of the exercise to the complexity of the situation "on the ground" and, more importantly, to the difficulties that entangled the relationships between the people caught in the struggle between territories, regions, peoples, land ownership and rights. They were confronted with a decision which required them to weigh justice and to assess the factors that defined the struggle for all those directly involved in it. In this way, the conflict was brought into the classroom. Students grappled and debated – and the wine bottle before them was the simple device that sought their judgement. Justice being a prerequisite to a just peace, this learning provided an essential ingredient to their understanding of issues requiring resolution for peace to prevail.

For broader justice issues to be understood, justice also needs to prevail in the classroom. This includes the fair and respectful treatment of all participants and their right to express their views and opinions. It also means that the right to express these views does not include engaging in classroom violence against others. While this can be a difficult tightrope to navigate, a peaceable and just classroom ultimately begins with the instructor's respect for the students and the expectation that all students will be valued and that well-argued and properly researched positions will be welcomed. I mentioned above that for a few individuals in class, some initial skepticism existed about how fairly "their community" or their views would be treated. In each case, these students worked well within their group and helped mould the group consensus. Initial fears turned out to be unfounded.

The above focus on the unshackling of students from their preconceptions potentially overlooks an additionally critical dimension in experiential learning: the necessary unshackling of the teacher. Experiential learning unshackles the teacher – from the need to project a particular perspective or point of view to which they feel committed. If teachers truly believe that their cause and their views, whatever they may be, are rooted in justice based on available evidence, this ethical truth will also become clear to students as they work through the experiential learning exercise provided. Furthermore, it also allows for an ethical space to be created where students are permitted to learn and make their own ethical determinations without having the particular views of the teacher imposed upon them, especially in a situation where the power imbalance between teacher and student is frequently overlooked. For justice to be taught, it also needs to prevail in the classroom. And, for just and peaceful relationships between student and teacher to be maintained, experiential learning is an indispensable pedagogical tool.

Case Study B: Pilgrimage Journeys as a Way to Peace?

Experiential learning need not be confined to the classroom. Field study courses, travel courses and other travel-based experiential learning ventures continue to grow in popularity and number. This case study explores the potential value of pilgrimages for teaching peace. Utilizing a pilgrimage experience as an experiential learning tool is confronted by the same primary questions: how does a pilgrimage experience promote peace education? How are they even related? Furthermore, how does a pilgrimage experience contribute to a cognitive disequilibrium?

The answer to these questions is found in another central feature of experiential learning: *reflective practice writing* (frequently but inadequately referred to as journaling). Simply put: while *reflective practice writing* is, in its most frequent format, a form of journaling (also referred to as reflective practice journaling), not all journaling can be considered reflective practice writing. Peter November focused on this point. In his self-described journey from dissatisfied traditional teacher to experiential educator he used journaling extensively, beginning with a smaller amount of journaling and expanding it to 40% and eventually 100% of the student assessment (November 1997, 289–294). He borrowed extensively from David Kolb who had likewise emphasized "reflective observation" (November 1997, 295). But, reflective practice writing (RPW) is more than journaling. It is deeply-engaged reflective analysis. It is also designed to provoke ever deeper levels of analysis. A specialized RPW tool can be effective for this and has been developed in a manner that uses the symbolic process of spokes on a bicycle wheel (Pries 2016/2017, 2019). The RPW process is also known as *reflection ON action*, a procedural label first bestowed by Donald Schön (1983). The goal, however, is for students to become sufficiently familiar and proficient with the process of reflection to engage in *reflection IN action* and thus respond in a more reflective and considered way while still embedded in the experience (Schön 1983). The point is this: through reflective practice writing, another value stage of experiential learning is achieved. It is the reflective practice writing that allows students to critically engage their own past beliefs with the new experiences (Baud 2001; Baud et al 1985; Bolton 2009/2010; Brockbank and McGill 1998; Galea 2012; Moon 2006; O'Connell and Dyment 2013). It is reflective practice writing that permits personal change to occur – and it is reflective practice writing that connects a pilgrimage experience with the potential change, ultimately arriving at Fisk's education *for* peace.

While on one level pilgrimages can be compared to other travel courses, there are some ways in which they are markedly different. Most travel courses require students to travel as a group, preserving the "tribal" cohesion that can (although it may not need to) create an opportunity for resistance to change. A pilgrimage can include travel as a group, but also requires times of substantial physical, mental and social isolation that provides opportunity for deeper reflective analysis. Physical separation can initiate greater psychological separation. Indeed, philosopher Frédéric Gros (2015, 53–57) emphasizes the importance of solitude – and the value of silence when walking (58–63). This is why a pilgrimage is a fine way to create an experience of cognitive disequilibrium. It separates the pilgrim from the comforts, the patterns, the noise and the hustle of normal life and transfers the pilgrim into a world with different priorities: there is simply the road ahead and the final destination of the journey. The pilgrim has primarily heart, mind and feet by which to traverse the road. Gros emphasizes the physical and spiritual exile of the pilgrim: "… the pilgrim is never at home where he walks; he's a stranger, a foreigner" (107). The spatial placement of the pilgrim is simple: "Walk, cut yourself off, depart, leave" (109). One "becomes poor among the poor" by taking on the mantle of "poverty and humility" (like Christ, Gros says) and of "being poor among the poor" (114). Gros explains further: "The only wealth of a poor man is his body. The walker is a son of the soil" (Gros 2015, 114). It is this detached environmental context, combined with the perpetual pace of walking daily, and of being without – "cut off" from the world's noise – that creates the necessary cognitive dissonance for the contemplation of peace.

For this study of pilgrimage as a peace pedagogy, I will discuss only one particular pilgrimage route: the Camino de Santiago de Compostela (the Way of St. James). It is, however, a medial exercise – already and not yet. What I mean is this: I am scheduled to walk the Camino de Santiago with students in the spring of 2019 (April to May) and have, therefore, not yet done so. However, I also walked the Camino in the spring of 2015, but not with my own students. Instead, I ended up walking most of the way with four young pilgrims whom I met on the way to Saint-Jean-Pied-de-Port (the main starting point for the Camino Frances route) or on the first morning and who were the age of many of my students – or just a little older. This gave me the opportunity to explore the potential of using the Camino as a learning pilgrimage with students. What, from my own experience and observation, are the key potential ingredients for student learning provided by a pilgrimage experience? I will describe six valuable dimensions that contribute to transformational learning about peace.

1 *The Camino's Conflict History (Context of Place)*

The Camino de Santiago is approximately a millennium old. The first full description of the story was the five-volume work published by a French priest, Aymeric Picaud in 1139/1140 and known as the *Codex Calixtinus* (after Pope Callixtus II). Despite its reputation as a way of peace for those who walk it, peace has not characterized its history. All along the route, pilgrims encounter visible signs of a past that was steeped in conflict. One walks on ancient Roman-built roads and across Roman-built bridges from the imperial Roman occupation. On the first day, if one takes the Camino Frances (the French Way), one must choose between two military routes through the Pyrenees: the upper route taken by Napoleon and his army or the lower one taken by Charlemagne and his troops. One becomes cognizant of Spanish history that was dominated for several centuries by Muslim caliphs and emirs and their rich architectural culture. Santiago (St. James) was also nicknamed the "Moor Slayer" because it was his holy patronage that was employed by those driving out the "Moors" from northern Spain during the "Reconquista." Even Santiago's symbol is a sword. Likewise, there are visible signs of other wars and monuments to commemorate both victory and loss – especially during the Spanish Civil War. The opportunities for teaching about peace and conflict present themselves daily on this pilgrim road. In other words, a rich teaching environment is provided simply by noting the history of the people, their preserved architecture and their generations of conflict (Gitlitz and Davidson 2000; Brierley 2014).

2 *Global Character of the Pilgrimage Experience (Global)*

While the value of walking in solitude was noted above, the pilgrimage experience is also a richly communal one – and it is both culturally and globally diverse. In 2015, I met pilgrims from approximately 40 countries and encountered almost as many languages. However, the diversity of the Camino de Santiago is not only marked by the wide national representation of the pilgrims but by religious diversity (Mooney 1996). Although the Camino has its origin as one of the three main pilgrimage routes in the Catholic tradition that can grant indulgences (the others being Jerusalem and Rome), and while Catholic history and organizational support continues to be a defining feature of the Camino, there is also participation from members of many other global religions, including Judaism, Islam, Buddhism, Hinduism and, perhaps most popularly, the self-declaration of "non-religious but spiritual." David Gitlitz and the late Linda Davidson, who co-authored the popular cultural handbook of the Camino (2000), have explained how the religious diversity that flourishes on the Camino was a welcome experience for them, since they hailed from non-Catholic traditions. The diversity of the pilgrimage community, while enriching for pilgrims, is matched by its communal cohesion and unity, and which functions as a spiritual code for those on the Camino: all pilgrims are members of the same wandering community.

3 *The Spirit of Unity and Community (Social)*

A most-striking characteristic of the Camino is the instant community that is formed by the pilgrims. People who do not know each other reach out and support one another in a way that is not frequently replicated elsewhere. I was witness to people giving their shoes (an extra pair) to another pilgrim and many other signs of generosity and kindness – where those struggling are carried by others (figuratively speaking). For students who experience an alternate community of people, this can break open and challenge previously held prejudices about human relations and about the nature of people. It opens the possibility that perhaps people "out there" are all very much part of the same human community. People from all walks of life are able to bond as members of the same community. For a short journey, at least, a small human community experiences the inclusive uniqueness of their identity as part of a common humanity.

4 *Walking as Pedagogy (Physical)*

The rhythm, the strain, the stress and the repetition of walking for many hours each day and for many weeks leaves a physical, mental and spiritual imprint. The way pilgrims understand themselves in relationship to others changes in the midst of the stress and strain. This is particularly true when someone is injured – and most pilgrims, if not all, will battle some injuries. It is almost too obvious to state: a body in rhythmic motion sees and feels differently than one seated at a desk in the study, in the library or in the classroom or lecture theatre.

5 *The Unique and Transcendent Spiritual Dimension (Spiritual)*

Undertaking a pilgrimage is more than a complex physical and mental experience. It requires the yielding of self to context – of becoming a pilgrim. When walkers submit to an identity as a pilgrim – albeit for only a five or six week interlude in life – they also declare a readiness to become learners and open themselves to the richness of experience. This openness includes a willingness by student pilgrims to explore the spiritual side of their identity – however the "spiritual" dimension in life is defined.

6 *Finding Peace*

For people to be contributors to and promoters of peace, a biased personal disposition in favour of peace is required. A pilgrimage experience can facilitate this. While we first focused on the personal and then briefly explored the communal aspect above, we return to the personal – because the Camino is at its heart an intensely personal experience. Every pilgrim has a reason for walking; all pilgrims have questions they take on their journey. And every pilgrim seeks answers in solitude, often through intense physical and psychological or deeply emotional personal pain. This too binds people together. The most common question pilgrims pose to each other is this: why are you walking? (Why are you here?) The common goal is always to find peace. Peace between people is closely tied to each person's personal peace. Providing students with the opportunity to find peace with themselves in a context of larger learning of peace and conflict between people is certainly a multi-dimensional and well-rounded peace.

If we return to our initial statement that learning transformation begins with the teacher, providing an experience that creates cognitive disequilibrium, we can conclude that a pilgrimage provides this experience. It unhitches a student from the comfort of the known and injects sufficient uncertainty to provide cognitive disequilibrium. At the same time, the exposure to others and a physical, mental and spiritual context that is different permits the sought-after unshackling from previous tribal allegiances and from the prejudices that go along with them. This provides the necessary opportunity for new information and new perspectives to be considered. It is no surprise, then, that every person I have met who has been a pilgrim on the Camino de Santiago has described it as the greatest transformational learning experience of their life. Of further significance is that these persons have described themselves as passionate supporters of peace – something they credit to the Camino.

Conclusion

The two case studies of experiential learning, one within the university classroom and the other on an ancient and primitive multi-week-long pilgrimage trail, detached from the comforts of home, both provide ways in which students can be incited to examine and question easily held certainties and open their minds to better informed or new perspectives. Most importantly, they will have adopted these views through personal experience and examination and will have integrated and come to "own" them. But it is only a beginning. Experiential learning is cyclical pedagogy and the wheel of learning keeps turning as the process is repeated. The cycle moves from:

Action→Reflection→Theoretical Analysis→Integration→Revised Action (Pries 2016/2017, 2019). Ultimately, and with the right experiences, the goal is to move students in the transformational direction of peace.

Note

1 An early version of this chapter was presented at the International Studies Conference in Baltimore on February 23, 2017. With thanks to respondent Wendy Kroeker for her feedback.

References

Article 49 of Convention (IV) relative to the Protection of Civilian Persons in Time of War. Geneva, 12 August 1949: https://ihl-databases.icrc.org/applic/ihl/ihl.nsf/WebART/380-600056.

BaudDavid. 2001. "Using Journal Writing to Enhance Reflective Practice." *New Directions for Adult and Continuing Education* 90: 9–17.

Baud, David, Rosemary Keogh and David Walker. 1985. "Promoting Reflection in Learning: A Model." In *Reflection: Turning Experience Into Learning*, edited by David Baud, Rosemary Keogh and David Walker, 18–40. London: Kogan Page.

Bolton, Gillie. 2009. "Write To Learn: Reflective Practice Writing." *InnovAIT* 2: 752–754

Bolton, Gillie. 2010. *Reflective Practice: Writing and Professional Development*. London: Sage.

Brierley, John. 2014. *A Pilgrim's Guide to the Camino de Santiago: A Practical and Mystical Manual for the Modern Day Pilgrim*. Forres, Scotland: Camino Guides.

Brockbank, Anne and Ian McGill. 1998. *Facilitating Reflective Learning in Higher Education*. Buckingham: Society for Research into Higher Education and Open University Press.

Conway, Sean, Chair, et al. 2016. "The Premier's Highly Skilled Workforce Expert Panel: Building the Workforce of Tomorrow – A Shared Responsibility" Report submitted to the Honourable Kathleen Wynne, Premier of Ontario. https://files.ontario.ca/hsw_rev_engaoda_webfinal_july6.pdf.

Dewey, John. 1933. *How We Think: A Restatement of the Relation of Reflective Thinking to the Educative Process*. Boston, MA: D.C. Heath and Company.

Duska, Ronald F. and Mariellen Whelan. 1975. *Moral Development: A Guide to Piaget and Kohlberg*. New York: Paulist Press.

Fisk, Larry J. 2000. "Shaping Visionaries: Nurturing Peace Through Education," In *Patterns of Conflict; Paths to Peace*, edited by Larry J. Fisk and John L. Schellenberg, 159–193. Peterborough: Broadview Press.

Freire, Paulo. 2000. *Pedagogy of the Oppressed. Thirtieth Anniversary Edition*. New York: Bloomsbury Academic.

Galea, Simone. 2012. "Reflecting Reflective Practice." *Educational Philosophy and Theory* 44: 245–258.

Gitlitz, David M. and Linda K. Davidson. 2000. *The Pilgrimage Road to Santiago: The Complete Cultural Handbook*. New York: St. Martin's Griffin.

Gros, Frédéric. 2015. *A Philosophy of Walking*. Translated by John Howe. London: Verso.

Kibler, Jackie. 2011. "Cognitive Disequilibrium." In *Encyclopedia of Child Behaviour and Development*, edited by Sam Goldstein and Jack A. Naglieri. Boston: Springer. https://doi.org/10.1007/978-0-387-79061-9_598

Kolb, Alice Y. and David A. Kolb. 2008. "Experiential Learning Theory: A Dynamic, Holistic Approach to Management Learning, Education and Development." In *Handbook of Management Learning, Education and Development*, edited by Steven J. Armstrong and Cynthia V. Fukami. London: Sage Publications.

Kolb, David A. 1984. *Experiential Learning: Experience as the Source of Learning and Development*. Englewood Cliffs, NJ: Prentice-Hall.

Moon, Jennifer A. 2006. *Learning Journals: A Handbook for Reflective Practice and Professional Development*. New York: Routledge.

Mooney, Carolyn. 1996. "Battling Blisters and Finding Saints on the Road to Santiago." In *The Chronicle of Higher Education*. July 19.

November, Peter. 1997. "Learning to Teach Experientially: A Pilgrim's Progress." *Studies in Higher Education* 22, no. 3: 289–299.

O'Connell, Timothy S. and Janet E. Dyment. 2013. *Theory Into Practice: Unlocking the Power and the Potential of Reflective Journals*. Charlotte, NC: Information Age Publishing.

Pries, Edmund. 2014. "Leveraging Diversity: Teaching Peace in the Public University." *The Conrad Grebel Review* 32, no. 2 (Spring): 132–151.

Pries, Edmund. 2016/2017. *The Reflective Practice Writing Bicycle: The Integration of Experience and Learning*. Revised Edition. Available from the Author.

Pries, Edmund. 2019. "'The Reflective Practice Writing Bicycle': A Reflective Analysis Tool for Engaged Learning" *Religious Studies and Theology* 38 (forthcoming).

Schön, Donald A. 1983. *The Reflective Practitioner: How Professionals Think in Action*. New York: Basic Books.

Schön, Donald A. 1987. *Educating the Reflective Practitioner*. San Francisco: Jossey-Bass.

5 Simulating Reality

A Necessary Path to Critical Thinking and Perspectives Among Students

Amal I. Khoury

It is a challenging time to be teaching Peace and Justice Studies, especially with increasing structural and direct violence fueled by xenophobia, racism, sectarianism, sexism, and an array of other prejudices locally and globally. Teachers are not only responsible for facilitating student learning, but also for providing them with the analytical tools to understand, evaluate, and respond to the problems and issues around them. To get students to be enthusiastic about learning, and ultimately motivated to make positive change, I use several collaborative learning exercises in the classroom. I incorporate experiential learning activities in the form of simulations and role-play exercises that provide hands-on experience to students allowing them to be actively involved in and engaged with the issues we study. Such activities are effective tools to critically synthesize the material we cover in class and promote a critical perspective among my students.

My classes are student-centered and discussion-based. They are designed in a way that encourages open discussions on sensitive and difficult issues throughout the semester. Student participation is an important aspect of all my classes and I provide a safe and interactive space in which students can get involved and share their opinions on readings and issues openly and in a respectful way. To get students to think critically and become responsible members of society, it is important to offer different viewpoints and use examples of injustices from the United States and around the world. Being equipped with different perspectives and approaches allows each student to develop their own understanding of the systems in which they live and function. I always strive to include many perspectives on any given topic by assigning readings that present different viewpoints. I believe that, for students to be able to develop their analytical and critical thinking, they need to be aware of the various arguments and perspectives. At the same time, if students want to take a specific stand on a certain issue, they need to be able to build their arguments in a critical manner. My goal is to help students become more mature in their thinking regardless of their belief systems. It is not my aim or intention to steer students into thinking in one way or to adopt a certain perspective; but I always push them to expand their thinking and encourage them to understand and accept differences. Students in my classes have to learn how to articulate their arguments, evaluate various perspectives, and become motivated for further learning.

To complement such open discussions, the simulations and role play exercises I use in class help students navigate those issues, understand realities that they may not have experienced, and empathize (even sympathize) with others. Throughout the semester, I use smaller mini-simulations or role-play exercises when I need to highlight or explain a certain concept, such as the tragedy of the commons, relative deprivation, or police brutality. Those activities usually take place in one class session and in small group format, with an open, large group discussion or debriefing at the end. However, the main activity I do in all my classes is a 2–3-day simulation I schedule at the end of the semester. I believe that such collaborative, integrative, and experiential techniques and approaches are of utmost necessity for providing a hands-on and critical understanding of the material. These elaborate scenarios are my focus in this chapter.

What are Simulations?

Simulations are fun and engaging activities. They are scenarios designed to allow students to understand conflicts, practice negotiation and mediation skills, strengthen research and debate skills, experience emotions, embrace complexity, and bridge the theory/practice divide. They are effective tools to critically synthesize the material we cover in class, promote a critical perspective among students, and help them understand their role in the society and the world.

Such scenarios are usually elaborate and require intensive thought and planning from the instructor. The first step in the process is to decide which simulation to use in a particular class. Many factors come into play when choosing the right exercise: class size, subject matter, current events, and learning outcomes. In my *War and Peace in the Middle East* class, for example, I used a simulation on the Israeli-Palestinian Conflict that brought together ordinary Israelis and Palestinians to talk about their needs and interests from the perspectives of those directly impacted by the conflict. After deciding on the proper simulation, the second step in the process is to develop the scenario or modify an existing one to fit the class. This entails a detailed background and individual role cards. The third step in the process is to have all the materials that are needed, such as copies of the material, name cards and scratch paper, ready. When in class, desks have to be rearranged in a circle to create a set-up that encourages and facilitates everyone's participation in the activity.

Why use Simulations?

I use simulations in all my classes regardless of size, subject matter, class makeup, and the sensitivity of the material covered.[1] Those activities stimulate critical thinking and analytical skills and nurture problem solving and practical abilities in students. One of the most important goals of simulations is to challenge the students and help them develop critical perspectives on the range of complex issues we discuss in class and push them to reflect on and recognize their positionality vis-à-vis the issues and systems of injustices both in the US and internationally.

In addition to the above-mentioned array of skills and abilities simulations help develop, they also provide an opportunity for shy and quiet students to participate actively in class discussions. I have seen many students open up and speak for the first time all semester when they are engaged in the exercise. From my experience with simulations, I found that they provide students who are usually shy and hesitant an opportunity to engage and participate in open class discussions. In order for this to happen, however, the instructor needs to be conscious about the class dynamic and allocate roles accordingly (something I will discuss in more length below).

Simulations are also assessment tools for the instructor. An important result of simulations is that they contribute to a sense of understanding of how well the students are learning and grasping the material. I usually get a sense of how much the students learned by seeing them engaged in the activity and using concepts and techniques we covered throughout the semester. It is exciting, for example, to hear students use proper terminology when discussing the different approaches to transitional justice in the post-conflict, fictional country of Zamal. Even more importantly, simulations demonstrate how well they can synthesize the concepts and issues and navigate the complexities we address throughout the semester. I get a sense of joy when I hear some of my quietest students actively engaged in the exercise and able to identify concepts we had discussed earlier during the semester without me pointing it out to them.

Role-play exercises are also used to replicate real events. They directly and indirectly help students recognize the ways in which inequitable social relationships (through class domination, patriarchy, racism, etc.) are created as well as their roles in reproducing such social inequalities. For example, in the simulation I used for my *Introduction to Peace, Conflict, and Identity* class, students who played the role of the minority upper class that has control of all the resources in town reflected on how their unwillingness to consider change or hear the demands of the lower class for fear that reform may endanger their power, perpetuated the cycle of violence in town. Such hands-on activities also help students become aware of the extent of social injustices in the US as well as globally and provide them with the tools to address them. While results vary, one of the most important goals of the simulation is to promote critical thinkers that will work for positive change. During the exercise and in the debriefing, students were able to critically evaluate the root causes of structural and direct violence in their town; discuss possible short-term and long-term solutions to their problems; and connect the fictional scenario to real-world examples and problems. They also examined the role of each of the communities in the conflict and reflected on how change can happen.

The Role of the Instructor

Simulations require a lot of work from the instructor who has to prepare simulation materials carefully to make sure that the instructional scenario is realistic and meets the learning objectives. My simulations run over a period of two class sessions and are either based on real conflicts or fictional scenarios. The process of creating a detailed background and scenario for the role-play as well as individual or group role cards based on the goal I have for the class and the lessons I want the students to learn is lengthy and demanding. In my years of teaching, I have created several simulations from scratch and have used existing simulations I found online.[2]

Whether creating a new simulation or using an existing one, a lot of time and resources are needed to provide all the materials required for the exercise and build an assessment rubric to ensure a quality learning experience for the students. Contrary to what some may believe, "simulations are not a way for teachers to get out of the hard work of teaching. They take a long time to think through and prepare" (Brookfield, 1990, p. 122). It is important for instructors to prepare as much as possible in advance and ensure that the students understand the process before beginning the exercise. The instructor should explain the rules of the activity and give students time to read the material and ask for clarification. Even though there are many uncertainties in such an open-ended exercise, the instructor's role is to limit student frustration by having a clear set of guidelines and rules, by knowing what the instructional goals are, by having clear evaluation criteria, and by making students aware of the different possible outcomes from the exercise in advance. In a simulation I used in my *Reconciliation and Justice in Post-Conflict Societies* for example, the students were representatives of different political parties and NGOs in a fictional country of Zamal. In a session moderated by the UN Body for Transitional Justice, the parties came together to negotiate a way to address the past atrocities that were committed during the war. They were presented with different possible transitional justice measures: International Criminal Tribunal; National Criminal Tribunal; Truth Commission; Reparations; and Memorialization. The goal was for the parties to reach a consensus on how to proceed to address their country's violent past, even though they had conflicting interests and needs. I made it clear from the beginning that there are many possible outcomes: the groups can decide on one of the proposed measures; that they can as a group come up with a hybrid solution or a combination of measures; that they can be creative and think of additional measures rather than be limited with the options that were presented to them; or that none of these measures needs to pass and that they can decide, consensually, to take "no measure" and forget the past. Presenting those options clearly in advance helps release some of the stress. Students might find simulations stressful because they push them out of their comfort zone: they are taught to measure success by how fast they can reach a solution and agree on a favorable outcome. Understanding that in such scenarios, the process is more important than the result will lead to a more enjoyable experience.

While intensive and careful planning of the simulations is necessary, there is always an open-ended element to the ways they unfold that an instructor cannot predict. For simulations I have used repeatedly in a course, I have never had the same results from one semester to another: the way the exercise progressed depended on the students. For this reason, simulations should only be used if an instructor feels certain about and is familiar with the material that is the focus of the exercise. Furthermore, instructors should observe and learn from the simulation in order to continuously refine and improve it for better learning goals and results.

The instructor needs to know the students to determine whether a particular simulation is appropriate for the particular classroom. This becomes clear throughout the semester based on the group dynamic. For example, the dynamic of my *Introduction to Peace, Conflict and Identity* class in Fall 2017 led me to choose a fictional scenario instead of a real one to highlight the sensitive issues of identity conflict related to class and race. Even though the simulation dealt with sensitive issues we had discussed throughout the semester, having a fictional scenario with cartoon characters (Smurfs, Muppets, Power Puff Girls, Teenage Mutant Ninja Turtles, Care Bears, and Power Rangers) somehow lessened the tensions while allowing students to debate those sensitive issues. Class discussions throughout the semester were intense and despite my numerous attempts at engaging everyone in the conversations, some students were hesitant to actively participate. I wanted everyone to feel comfortable and safe discussing issues of racial discrimination, police brutality, power, and identity. Furthermore, reverberations from the fatal police shooting of Keith Lamont Scott close to campus and the resulting protests and state of emergency in Charlotte in 2016 made those issues more sensitive. Even though the characters were fictional, they still were realistic, had well-defined identities, interests, perspectives, and objectives (Gill, 2015, p.35). Rather than shy away from important and sensitive issues, I choose simulations that "involve students in re-creating within the classroom some of the dilemmas, crises, and problems they have experienced or are experiencing outside. Alternatively, they involve them in working through imagined, hypothetical situations that are recognizably close to those occurring in their lives" (Brookfield, 1990, 116). More realistic scenarios also help to develop the students' contextual awareness. In the fictional scenario of Hulapaloozaville, the shooting of a young Smurf girl by a police officer was a catalyst for the oppressed Smurfs to begin rioting in the streets and demand equal rights and justice. The objective of the exercise was for the different groups in society to negotiate for a final solution to the violence. It was exciting to see everyone engaged and excited during the simulation. According to the students who were assigned to the Smurf group, they felt weak, voiceless and discriminated against in the exercise. During the debriefing, they related their experience to racial minority groups and poor communities in the US. Furthermore, as the scenario attributed the rise of violence in the city to a little Smurf girl being shot in the back by a Teenage Mutant Ninja Turtle (law enforcement) as she was running away after stealing a loaf of bread and notes that all Michelangelo (the Turtle) "could see was her blue skin," the conversation in the debriefing turned to the issue of police brutality and racism in the US. In previous years, when I used this simulation, there was little to no mention of the issue of police brutality, but because of the current context, it became a central discussion issue in the debriefing. The instructor should have an open mind and expect students to make the connections they identify with and allow for an analytical and critical discussion of the issues that arise.

When creating the scenario, the instructor should provide a clear and detailed background of the conflict under study. The packet that the students receive should include the context or setting of the event, background or historical information, and scenario that they need to simulate (the same ones for all participants) and individualized role packets with biographical information of the characters, their goals, positions, interests, the obstacles they might face, the groups they might agree or disagree with, etc. While the instructor should provide as much information as clearly as possible, a lot of the information regarding the individuals or groups could be inferred from the scenario or from additional research that the students should perform to prepare and strategize for the exercise. After the material is distributed, the students should be given enough time to read through it and understand the context and their role. The simulation of current situations/conflicts or of conflicts that were closely covered in class (example: the Rwanda Genocide, etc.) can be helpful as students can easily relate to it. Simulations differ in terms of groups and roles: in certain exercises, students work individually to represent different members of a particular society; in others, students have to work with others in a group and agree on a strategy for the role-play. It is important to give students time to work in their small groups and strategize before convening in a large group negotiation. One thing I found helpful is to have a schedule or time table that details the time allotted to each of the sessions – for example, X minutes for small group meeting; X minutes for information consultations with other groups; X minutes for the large group discussion; etc. This provides structure and clarity to the students and a constructive learning process. Depending on the simulation and how it is progressing, I sometimes make more information available to students during the exercise to refocus the conversation.

One of the most important decisions that the instructor should make is how to assign roles in the simulation in a way that best challenges the students and assures productive group dynamics to maximize learning. Depending on the class, the instructor sometimes needs to assign the roles in order to make sure that each group is well balanced with vocal and shy students. Having some groups of strong and/or committed and other groups of weaker and/or less committed students does not provide for a good exercise or experience for the whole class. Having a balance allows for a better dynamic and for more active participation by everyone in the exercise – even those who are usually quieter and more reserved. Similarly, one should make sure that certain roles (such as mediators) that require strong and active participation, are assigned to vocal and committed students who will take the lead in facilitating the discussion/negotiation. Another consideration that the instructor should take into account is whether to "cast students in roles that are familiar to them or see a need to have the students play against type (role reversal) in order to encourage them to explore different perspectives" (Brookfield, 1990, p. 126), and broaden their horizon. This usually works when students are intolerant. Putting them in roles against type will challenge them and enrich their experience and help them appreciate the other side, despite the stress and discomfort that they might originally feel. In other classes, where the students are more balanced in terms of strengths and weaknesses, I randomly assign them to roles.

What makes a simulation succeed or fail is the creativity and commitment of the students. For that reason, it is important for the instructor to emphasize the fact that the exercise should be taken seriously and that each person has to stick to her/his role to the best of their ability – even when the characters are fictional. Role integrity is of utmost importance, even if it is against the student's personal perspectives. This is sometimes challenging, as students tend to fall back on their own personal thoughts and perspectives and try to "make things better." For example, in the above-mentioned Hulapaloozaville simulation, some students from the Muppets and Power Puff Girls found it difficult to ignore the Smurfs' plight as their role cards indicated and tried to compromise on certain issues to help the disenchanted group. Some students in the debriefing mentioned that "they found it very difficult to stick to their role specially when it was not how they would have acted if faced with the situation in real life." I repeatedly remind students that their classmates are aware that some of the perspectives and points they bring up in the simulation do not reflect who they really are as a person and that this is a role-play; that for the duration of the activity and for the sake of integrity, they are not Abby and John but a government of Sudan representative, a Muppet, or an international observer. At other times, I am really surprised by how well students stick to their roles and fight for their interests as dictated by the scenario: such attitudes makes the simulation more fun and reflect aspects of reality that draw students in and get them excited about the activity. Particularly for students who were assigned roles contrary to their personal beliefs, the exercise becomes more eye-opening and helps them build their arguments in a critical manner both in the scenario and back in the real world.

In a simulation I created on the Iranian Nuclear Crisis, for example, students were assigned different countries and they had to negotiate an agreement in the context of the United Nations. The Chinese delegation stuck closely to its role and left the negotiations table at one point, making any agreement impossible to reach. Another time I used the same simulation, students were more willing to compromise and were able to reach an agreement before the end of the first day. The group used the second day of the simulation to finalize the details of the agreement they reached. In other words, simulations are open-ended, they require critical and evaluative thinking, and encourage students to contemplate the implications of the scenario on their own role. When students take the exercise seriously, the situation starts to feel real and hence leads to more engaging interactions. Also, simulations help students understand the concepts covered in class in a more nuanced and practical way that goes beyond theoretical understanding.

After the original preparation and once the roles are assigned and the activity begins, the instructor should assume the role of the observer and not take active part in the exercise. I usually monitor the simulation process closely to ensure that students are benefiting from it and understanding the process. I only interfere to redirect the conversation if it begins to deviate drastically from the script/objective. I also will intervene to settle any issues that might emerge, control the situation if it becomes chaotic and non-conducive to learning, and answer any questions. I make it clear to students that I do not have expectations from the exercise in terms of specific strategies, approaches and outcomes: basically, they can do whatever they want if it is within the parameters and context of the simulation and is based on what we have been studying in class. It is interesting to see throughout the years how the same simulation has had totally different results from one class to another. When I first assigned the Zamal simulation in my *Post-Conflict Reconciliation and Justice* course, the parties were not able to reach a consensus on any transitional justice measure for the country. Intense discussions took place for the 2-day negotiation without an agreement. The second time I assigned that simulation for the same course, the parties were quick to run through the list of possible measures and agree on a hybrid approach to justice. They had reached a consensus before the end of the second day. It is sometimes challenging to convince the students that is it about the process, and not the end result: the success of such activities does not necessarily mean reaching an agreement, but that it is gaining knowledge and understanding of how the real world works and how challenging it is to address and solve conflicts in short periods of time.

At the end of the simulation, the instructor should facilitate the debriefing. In this session, students should be given the chance to talk about their feelings during the role-play. The students should also reflect on how realistic they thought the simulation was, what they thought were issues with the simulation, etc. This feedback is helpful for the instructor when updating and editing the simulation for future use. The debriefing session allows for everyone's voice to be heard and can provide an opportunity for students to reflect on the simulation both from their own perspective as well as from that of the role they played.

At the end, the instructor should assess the exercise and evaluate (and grade) the students based on how actively they participated in the simulation, how well they maintained the integrity of their role, how well they grasped and synthesized the concepts and techniques learned in class, etc. It is important to keep in mind that the simulation exercise itself is only part of the process of learning and not necessarily a comprehensive measure of the learning that took place. Depending on the scenario, the roles, and the group dynamic, not every student gets an equal chance of participating despite the instructor's efforts and intentions. Follow-up activities such as the de-briefing session and individual reflection papers give students the chance to voice their reactions to and thoughts about the simulation in general as well as their role in particular. Together, those requirements (participation in the exercise, de-briefing session, and reflection paper) give the instructor a clear idea of what the student learned and how they are processing the information they are learning.

Learning Outcomes for Students

The impact of such experiential learning on students cannot be understated. I have students who, years after participating in a simulation, still talk about how important and informative the exercise was and how much they have learned from it. One student noted:

> Simulations encourage students to examine nuances and understand complexity, which are great skills to have in life and they lead to personal growth. I still remember the simulation I participated in 5 years ago and how fun and eye-opening it was. It helped me look more critically at the world.

Other students mentioned how fun it was to discuss sensitive and challenging issues in a safe space and interactive context. Many students also talk about how emotional and stressful the exercise was, but highlight the benefits resulting from the experience – not only for the class, but also for their daily lives beyond the classroom.

In their class evaluations, students frequently commented on how "intriguing, stimulating, engaging, and creative" the simulations are. Many also talk about how much insight they gained about injustices and inequalities in society, what it means, and how it leads to conflict and violence. As one of my students noted, "When we were reading and talking about poverty, racism, and other social injustices, I still felt disconnected to those issues. I have not experienced any of this in my life and have not really thought about the impact such injustice has on others around me. Participating in the simulation exercise really opened my mind and motivated me to learn more, empathize with others, and work on making a difference."

Simulations are a reflection of what the students have learned and are able to synthesize and how they are able to process the information that was covered during the semester. These assignments motivate the students by increasing student involvement and by challenging them. Such collaborative learning also helps to promote discussion, improves relationships among students, and fosters students' ability to work with others. Through the use of small and large group exercises, students work together to maximize their own and each other's learning. One collaborative learning activity that I have designed and used is the "Transition Plan Commission to Propose a Peaceful, Successful and Acceptable Transitional Plan for Iraq". I created this simulation to incorporate several important themes in international relations and conflict resolution (e.g., anarchy, collective good, free rider problem, regimes, international organizations, and negotiations to name a few). It also allowed students to learn more about a complex world event dominating the news at that time (the Iraq War). The simulation allowed students to engage constructively in negotiations about how to address the Iraqi situation and to develop creative strategies and understand the different groups' perspectives, positions, and goals. It was a way in which we could address a controversial and divisive issue at the time in a positive and productive way. It encouraged students to learn about and humanize the different Iraqi groups and understand their different perspectives and needs. The use of instructional scenarios allows students to interact within a reality that is foreign to them. Such student centered constructive learning/teaching strategy, if presented properly, can transport students to a different world and reality that they experience and gather meaning from.

Simulations give students a sense of the importance and interconnectedness of some of the issues we discuss in class. The exercise aims at bringing together all the components and issues covered in class in a comprehensive interrelated way to help students critically and analytically apply and process the information from the semester and explore different perspectives of a situation. For example, the simulations I use in class are complex scenarios that highlight the multidimensional and multileveled nature of conflicts. Examples of such simulations are the Congo and Sudan role-plays I used in my *Peacebuilding in Divided Societies* course. Students had to discuss and agree on issues related to power sharing, economics, security, humanitarian issues, and reconciliation if they wanted to reach sustainable peace. Focusing on one particular issue or problem – rather than on the whole comprehensive picture – will not lead to an understanding of the conflict and hence to a long-term solution to the problem. In those simulations, students have to navigate the lines between direct and structural violence; between short term and long term approaches to peace; between reconciliation and justice, to name a few. Realizing the complexities of conflict and their role in perpetuating a system that lead to such conflicts and violence is central to positive change. My aim is for students to understand the complexities of social concepts and problems and encourage them to think critically about their lives, the world they live in, and their impact on that world. Some students welcomed the opportunity to walk in someone else's shoes for a few days. As one student noted, the experience was eye-opening and:

> had helped me understand the experiences and perspectives of those people: even those who commit atrocities during a war had reasons to do so. Even if we don't agree with them, we should understand their motives and address those concerns in any peace agreement for sustainable integrative peace to be possible.

Such activities also help engage students with different learning styles. Some students, who do not participate in class discussions actively throughout the semester, suddenly feel empowered to do so during those exercises. It might be that they find their voice through the characters they play or that the setup encourages them to step out of their comfort zone. I always feel a sense of pride to see those quieter students take control and argue their positions persuasively. Several students noted that the simulation made them feel confident about what they have learned in the class and welcomed the opportunity to actively engage in discussion with their peers without feeling intimidated or threatened. In general, it seems like simulations leave a good and strong impression on students and provide them with "unique opportunities to challenge participants personally and intellectually, bringing them outside their comfort zones and allowing them to make surprising discoveries about their strengths and weaknesses" (Gill, 2015 p. 33). Most students respond positively to active learning about events, concepts, and emotions related to the area of study and it is a good way to engage otherwise disengaged students.

Students experience simulations more deeply and remember them longer than they do readings. One student said that before participating in the exercise, he didn't "really have a deep understanding of the issues and that the exercise helped him have a better understanding of the things we read and talked about in class."

Can Simulations go Wrong?

Despite the advantages of simulations presented above, it is important to note that there are always risks involved with a poorly designed simulation and many ways in which the activity can go wrong. For this reason, the instructor should put a lot of hard work and thought in the choice, design and management of the simulations. It is important to be careful to avoid cultural appropriation or imitation in those scenarios. One way I try to do this is by avoiding stereotypes and promoting diversity: it is my role, as the instructor to step in and redress such problems if they occur. It is also important not to simplify the issues for the sake of the exercise: if the goal is to promote an understanding of the complexity of conflicts, then, the scenario has to be complex and there should be emphasis on the learning process instead of whether or not the students are able to reach an agreement or solution to the problem they are presented with.

Furthermore, the instructor has to make sure that the simulation continues to be interesting for the duration of the activity and that groups have equal opportunities to participate. When I see that students are starting to lose interest or too quickly try and reach an agreement, I might interject with new information that will ensure the integrity of the exercise. For example, in one instance, the Smurfs stopped fighting for justice for the murder of their little girl and for equal rights and were agreeing to the short-term fixes that discriminated against them. I decided that it was necessary at this point to step in with a "breaking news" story about the violent protests and rising death tolls occurring outside City Hall where they were meeting. This helped the Smurfs – and other groups – regroup and think about their goals and priorities and reenergized the class. Another drawback is the difficulty that some students might have to act in character, particularly when they do not agree with the values and perspectives of that person or group. The instructor should be proactive (as well as reactive) in addressing any risks that might emerge because I believe that the benefits from such simulations outweigh the disadvantages.

Conclusion

It is difficult to keep students motivated and aware of the injustices impacting them and others in the system. Simulation exercises help them make that connection in a safe space, a non-intimidating and non-threatening context. I have many students come up to me after the exercise to tell me how difficult, yet fulfilling, it was to participate in an activity that challenged their understanding and got them out of their comfort zone. Simulations generate enthusiasm and are a good technique that can help prepare students for crises they may face at some points in their lives (Brookfield, 1990, p.123).

I have always struggled with how to make students relate to the issues we cover in my Peace and Justice Studies classes and how to apply what they learn to contribute to positive change in the world. Getting students to appreciate and learn about experiences foreign to them is not an easy task, but I believe that the use of simulations – whether based on real life examples or fictional ones related to real life events – have helped with that goal. Students consider such activities to be useful, interesting, and engaging experiences with relevance to what is going on in the world around them. Many have commented throughout the years how the simulations felt real as they shed light on the complexities of conflicts.

I use different active learning, student centered activities in my classes and found that simulations engage students in ways that few other activities can.

They also allow for different aspects of learning – analytical and affective, theoretical and practical – to take place in one educational space (Gill, 2015, p. 49). Through simulations, students explore social injustices and begin thinking of ways in which a more just world can be pursued.

Critical thinking is a valuable skill to develop and many students, who are used to a "banking model of education" (Freire, 1990), are uncomfortable with such an approach. Simulations are ways in which to push both instructors and students out of their comfort zones and push them to critically assess their surroundings. Such activities also help promote life-long learning that is useful inside as well as outside the classroom.

Notes

1 I have been using simulations in classes ranging in size from 10 to 40 undergraduate students since I started teaching over a decade ago. Classes I taught include: *Human Rights and Conflict; Reconciliation and Justice in Post Conflict Societies; Peacebuilding in Divided Societies; Introduction to Peace, Conflict and Identity; Introduction to Peace and Conflict Studies; Gender and Conflict*; and *War and Peace in the Middle East.*

2 Some good sources for simulations are: The United States Institute of Peace Simulations database available at: www.usip.org/simulations and the Public International Law and Policy Group (PILPG) negotiation simulations available at: www.publicinternationallawandpolicygroup.org/knowledge-management-2014/negotiation-simulations/. Even though some of the simulations are dated, instructors can make changes and update them in ways they see fit for their class. This is not an exclusive list; there are many other sources for simulations and role-play exercises that instructors can access online for free.

References

Brookfield, Stephen D. 1990. *The Skillful Teacher: On Technique, Trust, and Responsiveness in the Classroom.* San Francisco: Jossey-Bass Publishers.

Freire, Pablo. 1990. *Pedagogy of the Oppressed.* New York: Continuum Publishing Company.

Gill, Natasha. 2015. *Inside the Box: Using Integrative Simulations to Teach Conflict, Negotiation, and Mediation.* Zurich: Center for Security Studies.

6 Learning Justice in the Streets

Community Organizing and Peace and Justice Studies

Margaret Groarke

Service learning, done well, is an important part of a Peace and Justice Studies curriculum. Through service in the community, students can develop the habits of mind and heart –critical thinking, an ethos of solidarity, optimism and activism –defined by the authors of this volume as central to peace studies. But if not carefully planned, service learning can reinforce existing stereotypes and encourage students to see themselves as "saviors" to dependent communities. Employing a critical service learning perspective avoids these pitfalls. In this chapter, I argue that community organizing is a particularly useful opportunity for Peace Studies students to engage in critical service-learning.

Many Peace Studies programs have made service-learning a central element of their curriculum (for examples, see Marullo, et al. 1999, Smith, et al 1999, Roschelle, et al 1999, Handley, 2017). Service-learning, also known as community-based learning, is

> ... a form of experiential education in which students engage in activities that address human and community needs together with structured opportunities intentionally designed to promote student learning and development. Reflection and reciprocity are key concepts of service-learning. (Jacoby, 1996, 6).

Since Peace Studies educators tend to focus much of their attention on global issues, it can be challenging to imagine a service-learning experience that immerses students in the issues we care about. One approach might be to look for local opportunities to engage in anti-war activism, or solidarity work for oppressed minorities in other countries. Another would be to use opportunities to engage with the local community to teach students concepts that are also relevant to international conflict. The students in Martha Merrill's introductory peace studies course volunteered in "a nursing home, a soup kitchen, [and] a battered women's shelter" (Merrill, 1999, 126), where they recognized that the people they met were more than, or different than, the stereotypes they expected them to fit into. She argues the experience helped students "understand the stereotyping and depersonalization that often precede conflict" (Merrill, 1999, 127), an important learning goal for her Peace Studies class.

As several authors in this volume have discussed, getting students to recognize their positionality is an important goal in the peace studies classroom. Students can find it challenging to recognize how poverty and inequality is shaped by structural forces beyond the control of individuals, and more profoundly, as Welty puts it, "their unique social location (including power and privilege – or lack thereof) affects what they know." (p. 29). Community service experiences can as easily reinforce stereotypes as they can counter them; students may focus on the personal faults of soup kitchen clients as the reason they are poor, and ignore the poor education system, inadequate jobs and wages, racism and other social factors that shape their life prospects. As Pompa (2002, 68) argues,

> Unless facilitated with great care and consciousness, "service" can unwittingly become an exercise in patronization. In a society replete with hierarchical structures and patriarchal philosophies, service-learning's potential danger is for it to become the very thing it seeks to eschew.

To address this problem, Tania Mitchell presents the case for a critical service-learning perspective, which requires a social change perspective, attention to structural causes in readings and classroom discussion, and, most importantly for my argument, careful selection of service activities:

> This requires rethinking the types of service activities in which students are engaged, as well as organizing projects and assignments that challenge students to investigate and understand the root causes of social problems and the courses of action necessary to challenge and change the structures that perpetuate those problems.
>
> (Mitchell, 2008, p. 53)

Peace Studies students stand to benefit greatly from critical service-learning as Mitchell defines it, and I argue that community organizing is a particularly fruitful arena for engaging in critical service-learning.

Community organizing is:

> the process of building power through involving a constituency in identifying problems they share and the solutions to those problems that they desire; identifying the people and structures that can make those solutions possible; enlisting those targets in the effort through negotiation and using confrontation and pressure when needed.
>
> (Beckwith and Lopez, n.d.)

Community organizing focuses students on the root causes of social problems, and engaging them in efforts to change them. Students work with community members not as clients or victims but as people with the ability to be change agents in their own lives. Each service-learning experience falls somewhere on a spectrum between prioritizing the needs of the community or the educational experience of the students; critical service-learning prioritizes the articulated needs of the community, aiming for a mutually beneficial relationship. As Brown says, "service learning activities and programs must be shaped to address *both* student learning goals *and* genuine community needs" (Brown, 2001, 16). Community organizing, with its central focus on bringing together groups of people to determine what they need and how to achieve it, is well-suited to do this.

Through community organizing, students are very likely to have the kinds of experiences that leads them to develop the habits of mind and heart we seek to cultivate in this field. As Cummings writes:

> Neighborhood-level [organizing] work would engage students across boundaries of culture, class, and race in activities that respond directly to pressing local issues. As organizers, students would interact as equals with capable, organized adults, thus avoiding the pitfalls of 'charity' … or of the 'social worker perspective.'
>
> (2000, p. 98)

Through organizing, and structured reflection on their experiences, students develop their ability to critically examine a situation, their empathy for and solidarity with people unlike themselves, an understanding of their own agency and that of other people, and the ability to invent and implement strategies for challenging power structures.

The Particular Benefits of Community Organizing as a Service Learning Experience

As Kim Cummings notes, despite the explosion of community service and service-learning in US colleges and universities, students are "rarely to be found doing direct organizing in neighborhoods" (p. 98). Cummings presents as a case study his own course, *Neighborhood Organizing Practicum*, and an organization he founded, Building Blocks, to show how neighborhood organizing can both rebuild community and revitalize education. In his initial conversations with local organizations in Kalamazoo, Michigan, Cummings learned that one problem that limited the reach and the growth of local civic organizations was the lack of time and person-power to reach out to non-members and invite them to join the organization. Cummings and the local organizations created "Building Blocks." Through Building Blocks, volunteer student organizers (working with a local supervisor) go door to door, inviting people to form a block association and plan a block improvement project. The small, highly structured, self-contained nature of the project works well with the semester-long commitment of the student organizers. Despite its small scale and narrow focus, it brings the benefits of community organizing to Kalamazoo. Through the project, neighbors – often strangers to each other – meet and communicate. They work together on a common goal they chose together through a democratic process. They overcome social divisions among themselves. They develop the social networks that would allow them to join larger associations in the community, and tackle larger common goals. The outreach by the students builds a base for larger neighborhood campaigns to demand public investment in their community, to lobby for changes in the law, or to hold private institutions accountable for their impact in the community.

My Organizing Class

I've offered a class in community organizing – originally called *Practicing Empowerment*, now titled *Community Organizing for Social Change*, three times. Twice I offered it during the summer session, to six students each time (about the average size for a summer class at Manhattan College). I offered it during the spring 2017 semester, and had 12 students. Some, but not all, of my students were Peace Studies majors. The summer course was an 8-week course; we met for two classroom hours and approximately three service hours a week. In the spring semester course, we averaged three classroom hours a week, and the students did 20 hours of community work over the course of the semester.

Each time I've taught the class, the students have worked with the Northwest Bronx Community and Clergy Coalition (NWBCCC), a local grassroots organization active since 1974. The NWBCCC works for racial and economic justice in what has long been the poorest urban county in the United States. Its membership mirrors the population of the borough – majority Latino, but also Black, White, Asian, and South Asian. Many Bronx residents are foreign born, and many are recent immigrants from across the world. Its mission is: "The Northwest Bronx Community and Clergy Coalition unites diverse people and institutions to work for racial and economic justice through intergenerational community organizing that transforms the Bronx and beyond."

The organization's small organizing staff works with hundreds of members to identify community problems, and to help members exercise their collective power to resolve those problems. They hold government agencies accountable, pressure elected officials to change the law, pressure private corporations or other institutions to act more responsibly, and imagine and create new community-controlled institutions.

Through community organizing, the NWBCCC has achieved many community victories. They defeated an unwelcome development proposal for the Kingsbridge Armory, an immense vacant property in the middle of the community, and later negotiated a ground-breaking community benefits agreement with an alternative developer. They successfully pushed for the redevelopment of numerous vacant buildings, creating thousands of units of affordable apartments for a mix of income levels, including homeless families. They've successfully pushed for legislation on the federal, state and city level. And they've rescued untold numbers of apartment buildings from decay.

My students have worked primarily on tenant organizing, a central focus of the NWBCCC. The vast majority of the residents of the Northwest Bronx are tenants in multiple-story apartment buildings, owned and managed by people and corporations outside of the neighborhood. The living conditions and the affordability of the rent are central concerns for many people. Like Cummings, we chose a small-scale project on which we could expect to make some progress during the class. In each class, NWBCCC assigned us buildings that the organization wanted to reach out to, but lacked personnel to do so. The buildings we contacted were part of the organization's larger strategy; for example, one semester, all the buildings belonged to the same landlord as several other buildings the organization was actively organizing, another semester they were all within walking distance of a tenant's rights workshop the NWBCCC was planning.

Pairs of students engaged in door-to-door recruiting in particular apartment buildings. The goals were to find out about conditions in the building, and to identify tenants who seemed interested in doing something to improve those conditions. The students either tried to organize a tenant meeting in the lobby, or invited tenants to tenant rights workshops or other larger meetings. Through these outreach efforts, students see the conditions that low-income Bronx renters often endure, and try to mobilize people into action. Sometimes they find that people don't want to talk to them at all; sometimes they find that people are resigned to their situation, or fearful that there may be retaliation if they stand up for themselves; sometimes they meet people who are cautiously or enthusiastically willing to talk about working with others to improve their situation. With the students, I reflect both on the reactions of tenants they reach out to, and also on their own approach – what statements or questions were the best conversational openers? Which pitches seemed most likely to get people involved?

The leadership model of the NWBCCC provides a particularly fruitful opportunity for student learning about democracy and empowerment. The organization works with individuals and institutions (mostly churches and smaller community organizations) to identify the issues community residents want to address. The NWBCCC does not primarily work with established community leaders, but helps develop the leadership potential of every member. Members are given opportunities to speak at meetings, to chair meetings, to recruit other people, and in other ways claim ownership of and develop the ability to lead the organization.

Students see this most clearly when they attended meetings of the NWBCCC, and observe the leadership and organizing staff in action. At a planning meeting, students observe neighborhood residents of different ethnic backgrounds, age, education and income, work democratically together to plan joint action toward a common goal. Translation and child care are provided to make it possible for parents and non-English speakers to participate in the conversation. At the end of the meeting, the chair usually asks for a volunteer to chair the next meeting, in a transparent effort to revolve the responsibility and open up leadership opportunities. My students who attended the NWBCCC's 2016 annual meeting were amazed to see rank-and-file members of the NWBCCC make demands of their elected officials in front of a supportive audience of three hundred local residents.

Participation in community organizing is more likely than other types of service learning experiences to offer students the opportunity to see less-privileged persons as persons with skills and abilities. When the students work with a group of neighborhood residents who are poor, people of color, and who take leadership roles in an organizing effort to solve their own problems, they are challenged to view these people not simply as clients or victims, but as people with agency over their own lives. One student reported about a tenant meeting he attended:

> They had people volunteer to go door to door with the Coalition to help get neighbors involved in the process to fix the building. This was one of the more interesting things I have seen because for the first time I had really seen progress from the tenants who took initiative to create their own change in their community.

This I have found as important for the Latino students who recognize their own parents in the tenants they work with, as it is for the suburban students for whom the largely immigrant, largely people of color population of the Bronx is not like the communities in which they grew up. The students in my organizing classes have generally been roughly half white suburbanites, and half urban Latinos. For the white suburban students, door knocking in Bronx apartment buildings was usually a step into an unfamiliar environment. The literature on service-learning is rife with examples of middle-class college students learning, through their community service, that poor people have knowledge to share, that they work hard, that they have dreams of a better life, and certainly my students shared those reflections on their experience.

The Latino students generally come from New York City neighborhoods and families similar to the tenants they were trying to organize. I was less conscious of the negative stereotypes these students would bring to their outreach and organizing work. Many of my Latino students express negative views about their own neighborhoods, and appear to believe that many of their own neighbors are not trustworthy, hardworking, or otherwise honorable people. As Cummings' students found, many people didn't know their immediate neighbors; this isolation leads people to distrust one another and, too often, to think the worst of their neighbors. In neighborhood organizing, I often hear people say that their neighborhood would be better if the other people who lived there cared; some of my students seem to hold this view of their own neighborhood. As they do outreach, and observe neighborhood leaders in meetings, they see Latino and Black residents work hard together to stand up for their rights, and demand justice for their communities. They begin to recognize how much of what makes a neighborhood "bad" is beyond the control of the people who live there, that in most neighborhoods there are many isolated individuals who feel that no one else cares, and how much of what may seem like apathy is fear or defeat. As one student said:

> I try to motivate the tenants by encouraging them not to be discouraged and not lose hope because if they don't fight this battle, no one can do it for them. I felt like there was a specific set of people that were willing to do what it takes and might show up to tenants rights night. I believe this building has a lot of potential it just takes the right people to encourage the rest.

By working with people willing to work for change, the student's own defeated perspective is transformed into a more hopeful one.

Opportunities for Reflection

As with all forms of service learning, it is important to incorporate opportunities for reflection on the experience into the course; it is in the reflection that real learning occurs (Bringle and Hatcher, 1999). No matter how much you structure the project, you don't know what students will experience, and you don't know how they will interpret that experience. In my first attempt at community-based learning, my students helped a local homeless organization survey welfare applicants and recipients as they left the welfare office. In preparing for the experience, we practiced approaching people, reviewed the survey questions, and discussed the different reactions people might have. We didn't plan on the security officers telling us we had no right to be on the sidewalk, which led to some great conversations about our rights to occupy public space, and the resistance of the welfare agency – why did they object to our presence there? We happened to have a lawyer with us the morning that we were first challenged, and that led to some interesting discussion of the importance of understanding one's rights. Whatever material the community service experience gives us to reflect on, we want to encourage our students to critically consider a variety of interpretations of, or explanations for, what they observe.

Good service learning, whether the service is serving food in a soup kitchen or organizing for the revolution, involves study and reflection that delves deeper, to think about why the need exists for that service. In good service learning, students help the homeless *and* consider *why* people are homeless and *how* that situation might be changed. The Georgetown Justice and Peace Studies Program encourages students to consider their service experience as part of a four-step cyclical social analysis model – "study, act, reflect, analyze" (Marullo et al 1999, p. 48).

When students engage in community organizing, reflection on these questions takes place not only in structured class reflection, but as a regular part of the organizing experience itself. In doing outreach, organizers discuss with people at their front doors *why* their apartments are cold and their rent is high, and *who* has the power to change that. In planning meetings, discussions of strategy often turn on who is responsible for creating the situation, or who has the power to change it. While all effective service learning gets students to reflect on understanding the structural reasons for the situations they observe, community organizing is particularly well-suited to raise their awareness of these issues.

When the community-based learning experience that students engage in is community organizing, students have the opportunity to reflect on some significant issues central to peace and justice studies, and to the activism for a better world that many of our students will engage in. One significant area for reflection is why and when and how people choose to participate. Because my students spend much of their organizing time doing outreach to involve people in the work of the organization, they reflected a lot on people's reactions to their mobilizing attempts. Why are some people willing to organize, while others are fearful, or insist that nothing can be done? In whatever way they are and will be involved in working for change, they will need to mobilize others to join them. Reflecting on their own initial efforts to do so is an important opportunity for learning.

Another significant area for reflection is questions of power and strategy. What decision-makers are responsible for the situation community residents want to change? What power does the community have to influence them? What strategies are most likely to achieve the group's goals? Students engaged in organizing see community members grappling with these questions, and can further think about them in their reflective writings and discussions. Community organizing tactics are always improvisational; people try tactics that have worked before, invent new tactics, and repeat the ones that work. Students learn a great deal about the critical analysis of power relations, and the development of effective strategies for action, by observing and participating in this process.

Challenges and Practical Considerations

Community organizing as a service learning experience also presents some challenges. The availability of a community partner, an organization which is engaged in real grassroots community organizing, may be the first challenge. While every community could benefit from having an organization building community power and leadership, not every community currently has a group that is doing this work. Another approach might be to work with community residents to create an organizing project; an example of this would be Paul Wellstone, who as an assistant professor at Carleton College in the 1970s, worked with two students and two local mothers to organize what would become the Organization for a Better Rice County (Wellstone, 1978).

In either case, it's important to think about the commitment you are making to the community. If your class will only be working on the project for a single semester, you must ensure that your participation doesn't raise expectations you can't fulfill. Will you be teaching a class the following semester that can carry on the work begun by the first group? Can another professor's class, or a student volunteer group, carry on the work? If not, through clear communication with your community partner, you can define a project for your students that will contribute to the organization without being unnecessarily disruptive when you and your students leave.

The variability of organizing can be a challenge for planning a college class. As a professor, you need to plan the class in advance, and be able to tell the students what will happen during the semester. The day-to-day work of many social service agencies is more predictable than community organizing, which makes it easy to slot in student volunteers – tutoring happens every weekday from 3–6 pm, for example. The organizing efforts of your community partner might shift as the leaders choose a new issue to work on, or confront an unexpected crisis. It can be frustrating if you planned a syllabus with readings about health care disparities, only to learn in the second week that the organization is shifting its priorities to a living wage campaign. Students might be asked to make phone calls, do street outreach, or help prepare for a public meeting or demonstration. But if you and your students approach your organizing efforts with flexibility, that shift can also be a learning experience. Many organizations have their bread and butter issues, ongoing organizing efforts that often are the way new members come into the organization. For Kim Cummings' class, it was the building of new block associations. For the Northwest Bronx Coalition, it is tenant organizing. Building a class project around the organization's core organizing campaigns increases the predictability of student assignments and experience, while exposing them to the excitement of the unexpected organizing campaigns.

Some might argue that doing a community organizing project as a class is only workable if the instructor has community organizing experience. I do have community organizing experience, and thus have done some skill development and role-playing in class. While I think my experience adds greatly to the course, having a strong partner organization makes this less crucial. You might arrange either for the community organization to plan to train your students at their site, or for an organizer or leader to come to class to prepare students for their organizing work, or even to have an organizer co-teach the class with you. I don't mean, however, to scare you away if you do not already have experience. The basic skills one needs to assist in organizing are easy to develop and useful in so many ways; you can learn along with your students.

Critical Service-learning and Democracy

Community organizing also, as distinct from most other service-learning experiences, trains students in a number of useful democratic skills. If one of the habits of mind we hope to engender in our students is activism, we need to teach them to be effective participants in local, national and international political communities. Exposure to and involvement in community organizing teaches students a number of important democratic skills, including:

- Organizing a group activity
- Identifying and resolving problems
- Speaking up for oneself
- Resolving disagreements among allies
- Resolving conflicts with persons in authority

It is a fundamental principle of community organizing that these are skills that everyone can develop. Through participation in community organizing, students often learn these skills along with people in the community, avoiding the dangers of students seeing themselves as swooping in to save the helpless neighborhood residents. And they are contributing in a way that responds to the articulated needs of community residents.

Conclusion

The perspectives and skills students gain through participation in community organizing are those our Peace Studies students need to be critical scholars of the state of peace and justice, and effective activists in shaping a more peaceful and just world. Through their participation in organizing, my students saw Bronx residents struggle to be inclusive of one another, across language barriers, religious differences, and racial divides. They became aware of how their own social position influenced the way the world treated them and the way they understood the world. They saw themselves in solidarity with people that they met who were struggling to improve the conditions in which they lived. They learned basic democratic skills, and watched as neighborhood residents and organizers evaluated their power and created strategies. And, by developing an understanding of the power organized people can wield, they became more optimistic about the possibility of change. Those skills and perspectives, once developed, are transferable to spaces well beyond the local community.

References

Beckwith, David, and Cristina Lopez, n.d. "Community Organizing: People Power from the Grassroots," COMM-ORG: The Community Organizing Website. https://comm-org.wisc.edu/papers97/beckwith.htm

Bringle, Robert G., and Julie A. Hatcher. 1999. "Reflection in service learning: Making meaning of experience." *Educational Horizons*, 77(4), 179–185.

Brown, Danika. 2001. "*Pulling It Together: A Method for Developing Service-Learning and Community Partnerships Based in Critical Pedagogy*" Washington DC: Corporation for National Service.

Cummings, Kim C. 2000. "John Dewey and the Rebuilding of Urban Community: Engaging Undergraduates as Community Organizers." *Michigan Journal of Community Service Learning*. Fall. 97–108.

Handley, James. 2017. "Pathways to Praxis: Moving from Peace Studies to Peace Activism" Peace and Justice Studies Association Conference, Birmingham, AL.

Jacoby, Barbara. 1996. *Service-learning in Higher Education: Concepts and Practices. San Francisco*: Jossey-Bass.

Marullo, Sam, Mark Lance, and Henry Schwarz. 1999. "Study, Act, Reflect, and Analyze: Service-Learning and the Program on Justice and Peace at Georgetown University" in *Teaching for Justice: Concepts and Models for Service-Learning in Peace Studies*, edited by Kathleen Maas Weigert and Robin J. Crews, 47–54. Washington, DC: American Association for Higher Education.

Merrill, Martha C. 1999. "Learning about Peace: Five Ways Service-Learning Can Strengthen the Curriculum" in *Teaching for Justice: Concepts and Models for Service-Learning in Peace Studies*, edited by Kathleen Maas Weigert and Robin J. Crews, 125–135. Washington, DC: American Association for Higher Education.

Mitchell, Tania. 2008. "Traditional vs. critical service-learning: Engaging the literature to differentiate two models." *Michigan Journal of Community Service-Learning*, 14(2): 50-65.

Pompa, Lori. 2002. "Service-learning as crucible: Reflections on immersion, context, power, and transformation." *Michigan Journal of Community Service Learning*, 9(1): 67–76.

Roschelle, Anne R., Jennifer Turpin, and Robert Elias. 1999. "Student Contributions to Public Life: Peace and Justice Studies at the University of San Francisco" in *Teaching for Justice: Concepts and Models for Service-Learning in Peace Studies*, edited by Kathleen Maas Weigert and Robin J. Crews, 65–72. Washington, DC: American Association for Higher Education.

Smith, David Whitten and Michael Haasl. 1999. "Justice and Peace Studies at the University of St. Thomas" in *Teaching for Justice: Concepts and Models for Service-Learning in Peace Studies*, edited by Kathleen Maas Weigert and Robin J. Crews, 55–64. Washington, DC: American Association for Higher Education.

Wellstone, Paul. 1978. *How the Rural Poor Got Power*. Amherst: University of Massachusetts Press.

Part III

The Power of Story in the Peace and Justice Studies Classroom

7 If These are Our Values, then What is Our Practice?

#BlackLivesMatter and an American Apocalypse

G. Michelle Collins-Sibley

> Trayvon Martin, Oscar Grant, Shereese Francis, Rekia Boyd, Kendrec McDade, Tamon Robinson, Shantel Davis, Jonathan Ferrell, Jordan Baker, McKenzie Cochran, Eric Garner, John Crawford, Michael Brown, Tanisha Anderson, Ezell Ford, Kajieme Powell, Akai Gurley, Tamir Rice, Dontre Hamilton, Bettie Jones, Roy Nelson, Tiara Thomas, Alonzo Smith, Anthony Ashford, Tyree Crawford, Samuel Dubose, Sandra Bland, Walter Scott, Natasha McKenna, Alton Sterling, Philando Castile ...

An incomplete listing of the dead: damning evidence of our American history of violence against black bodies just since 2012. Five years ago, on February 26, 2012 George Zimmerman shot and killed Trayvon Martin as the seventeen-year-old was walking home from a convenience store where he had bought a snack. A month later in an unscripted response to a reporter's question about the teenager's death, President Barack Obama responded, "If I had a son, he'd look like Trayvon" (Jonsson 2012); a year later, on the occasion of the Zimmerman verdict, he would elaborate, saying, "Trayvon Martin could have been me 35 years ago" (Obama 2013). That same summer of 2013, Alicia Garza, Patrisse Cullors, and Opal Tomei founded #BlackLivesMatter.

There is a larger and much, much longer history of violence against men and women of African descent in these United States of America dating from our colonial history and the late August 1619 arrival of some "20 and odd" Africans in Jamestown, through the "peculiar institution" of American slavery, the age of lynching culminating in the Red Summer of 1919, the Civil Rights movement bringing us to our present moment. Two years ago the nation marked the 50th anniversary of Selma, the march across the Edmund Pettus Bridge, and, the passage of the Voting Rights Act of 1965. Four years ago, one month before George Zimmerman was acquitted of all charges in the death of Trayvon Martin, the Supreme Court eviscerated the Voting Rights Act of 1965, declaring Section 4 of the act unconstitutional. Writing for the majority, Chief Justice John G. Roberts declared, "Our country has changed. While any racial discrimination in voting is too much, Congress must ensure that the legislation it passes to remedy that problem speaks to current conditions" (Liptak 2013). Hmmm …

So, let's think together about this for a moment. Black Lives Matter is the most recent iteration of black people standing up to assert the value of our existence, our experiences and our humanity. It's us rejecting the historical and cultural assumptions at the foundation of these United States of America that we are objects rather than subjects, means to an end rather than ends in and of ourselves. In Garza, Cullors, and Tomei's words it is "an ideological and political *intervention* (my emphasis) in a world where Black lives are systematically and intentionally targeted for demise … an affirmation of Black folks' humanity … contributions to this society, and … resilience in the face of deadly oppression" (Herstory). When people respond to #BlackLivesMatter with the counter assertion, "All lives matter," what does that mean? Of course, all lives matter except that in these United States of American that isn't true, it has never been true.

I could go on at length about the history of racism – institutionalized and overt – but however necessary such a history may be, this is not that history; nor is it a history of Black Lives Matter as a movement.[1] My intent is rather to engage with #BlackLivesMatter as a teachable moment located in the gap between our collective practice(s) – e.g. the three fifths compromise, the Naturalization Act of 1790 *et alia* – and our national principles articulated in the Declaration of Independence: "… we hold these truths to be self-evident, that all men are endowed by their creator with certain inalienable rights, among these the right to life, liberty, and the pursuit of happiness." My thinking begins with the oft repeated rejoinder, "All lives matter," what I hear is "Yes, but …": a denial, a reaction grounded in fear. What I see in my students in our small midwestern comprehensive university is the dismissal of the murders – and their video record – which give rise to this movement. Our collective challenge, my pedagogical challenge then becomes that of moving my students from fear to acceptance thereby creating space for responses located in a place of understanding rather than that of fear. In this context, I name the current moment "apocalyptic" not in the popular cultural sense of the end of days but rather in its Greek origin, *apokalypsis*: the disclosure of something that has been hidden, an uncovering, an unveiling. Rather than bemoan or condemn my students' lack of history or of empathy for black victims of police violence, my goal is to engage them actively in this critical disclosure: our values are *not* our practices. I proceed from the radical assumption that it is through the study of literature – poetry, fiction and memoir – that we may be able to reach that place of understanding, advancing a poetics or politics of humanity, by telling "stories about the lives of others, we learn how to imagine what another creature might feel in response to various events. At the same time, we identify with the other creature and learn something about ourselves" (Nussbaum 2014).

The study of literature, indeed of the Humanities generally, has gotten a bad rap of late. In these days of rising tuition costs practical, vocational education takes priority over the traditional liberal arts, sometimes called values, education. This is certainly the case for my students and their parents. Yet in our current apocalyptic moment the study of literature is eminently practical as it transmits both necessary historical context and our national values in ways that can move us to action. It is literature rather than philosophy, even political philosophy, that creates the social and cultural context in which action takes place; it, through language, shapes and creates our shared reality. Black literature, black art in general, has long been recognized as a pillar of black political expression; from the Harlem Renaissance through the Black Arts Movement to the present day artists have struggled to re-define American democracy through aesthetic expression. Charles Chesnutt understood himself to be preparing white readers for a world in which black people would be full and equal participants in democracy. Toni Morrison explains that she writes the stories she wanted to read, just as comedian and filmmaker Jordan Peele asserts that "Get Out" is the horror movie he wanted to see. Works of fiction, like film, function both as artifacts and as *performances* and audience emotional responses the reenactment of events in the text or on the screen. Perhaps most importantly, in the tradition of call-and-response, the storyteller not only recounts a story, she actually forges a connection between audience and story. Reading becomes initiation into the world as perceived by the author, and so:

> When the writer's aspirations are truly literary, his dedication to the art of fiction is tantamount to a social commitment to human well-being and self-realization. His sense of art is inseparable from his sense of what is beneficial and what is detrimental in human existence.
>
> (Murray 2016, 359)

"Human well-being and self-realization" for me involves a commitment to wholeness and unconditional acceptance of self, to self-compassion along with critical self-reflection. If we move back for just a moment to the idea of fear as undergirding the unspoken "yes, but" of all lives matter, the significance of critical self-compassion and self-reflection is all the more significant; it is part and parcel of the preparation for responsible citizenship promised in the University of Mount Union mission statement.

While this case for story as conducive to poetics of humanity, preparing students for empathy can be made through a variety of texts and authors I argue specifically for *Home*, a recent novel by Toni Morrison in which she engages with this question of healing through the development of self-compassion.

Set in the immediate aftermath of the Korean conflict, *Home* is the story of Frank Money, an African American veteran living in Seattle, who is called home to Lotus, Georgia to rescue his sister Cee from the hands of a eugenicist who has enlisted her unwitting cooperation in a series of experiments on black women. This period coincides with that period of American history now sentimentalized as the good old days when it wasn't so much a question of black vs. white as it was that of right vs. wrong. It was for which many now wax nostalgic in which our values and our practice seemed to accord with each other. But many of us, Morrison included, remember it rather differently; she tells us "I was trying to take the scab off the 50s, the general idea of it as very comfortable, happy, nostalgic. Mad Men. Oh, please. There was a horrible war you didn't call a war where 58,000 people died. There was McCarthy" (Brockes 2012). Frank suffers from PTSD, forced repeatedly to relive events and memories even though "remembering seemed unwise" (Brockes 2012). While the novel takes the shape of a first-person narrative, Frank regularly breaks the third wall to address directly the writer/reader to whom he seems to be telling his story; with each such interruption he challenges this "you" to tell/relate/write the "truth" of his experience, even as he contends that this simply isn't possible. With these abrupt shifts in perspective from first to second person, Morrison directly involves the reader in the narrative, making us witnesses to Frank's struggle and initiating us into his world. We come – literally and figuratively – to see the world through his eyes.

Just as Morrison frequently defies readerly expectations regarding the roles of storyteller, protagonist, and reader, here she takes that defiance a step further; this time to challenge readerly expectations about race and the racial identity of her characters. She had done this in an earlier novel *Paradise* (1997) with its cryptic opening lines, "They kill the white girl first. With the rest they can take their time." My students, not to mention a wide range of scholars, spend hours debating the identity of "the white girl," all for naught. By denying us easy evidence of the white girl's identity, Morrison not only pulls us into active engagement with the story, she also challenges us to consider why answering that question is so important to us. She further suggests the possibility of a world in which racial identity is a trivial question. In *Home*, she tells us she "tried again to create work in which color was erased but [this time] could easily be assumed if the reader paid close attention to the codes, the restrictions black people routinely suffered" (Morrison 2017, 50).

It works. With only minor prompting my students engage themselves in just such close attention to the smallest of details in their readings: Googling the "Green Book" to discover it's full title – *The Negro Motorist Green Book: an International Travel* Guide – and purpose; decoding the symbolic significance of place – Lotus, Georgia – and character names – Frank *Money*, the Reverend *John Locke*, along with other characteristics to determine racial identities. Frank and his sister are the only avowedly African-American characters in the early chapters of the novel, but Morrison is an African American writer famous for her treatment of black life and experience indeed most of her novels center exclusively on African American characters and communities, so they reason these unmarked characters *must be black*, mustn't they? In an earlier draft of the novel Frank himself was unmarked but her editors were so unnerved by her success in removing all markers of racial identity and fearful that her fans would be disappointed that she was persuaded to layer in details verifying his race. Through these two simple techniques Toni Morrison creates the space for truth telling conversations about race and our cultural assumptions about its significance; we are forced to engage with characters as human beings first, members of a specific racial category second. She initiates us as readers into Frank Money's world; he demands our attention and implicates us as witnesses to his journey out of fear and denial to acceptance, self-compassion, and, healing. In her own words, which I also share with my students,

> I was eager to manipulate, mutate and control imagistic, metaphoric language in order to produce something that could be called race-specific/race-free prose, language that deactivated the power of racially inflected strategies – transform them from the straitjacket a race conscious society can ... buckle us into – a refusal to "know" characters or people by the color of their skin.
>
> (Morrison 2017)

Neither Toni Morrison nor her protagonist Frank Money allow us to refuse to know him or his sister. In the process of engaging that recognition Morrison also unveils for her contemporary readers the ugly truths of nostalgic memory. In 1950's America, like 2018's America, there was a horrible war, returning veterans suffering post-traumatic shock, lynching, eugenic experiments on black women and men. As Frank travels south, back to his home, he is forced to remember not only his traumatic personal history in Georgia but also his repressed memories of Korea and we remember with him, we become his witness. It is this experience of *witnesses*, this forced change in readerly perspective that is essential to seizing upon #Black Lives Matter as a teachable moment.

It is one thing to consider the events #BlackLivesMatter protests – police shootings of unarmed black men and women – in the abstract, as just another story on the 6:30 pm news; just another YouTube video circulating across social media platforms or as a link on the New York Times website. To borrow Morrison's language, our "race-specific" prose and video constructs artificial walls between video and viewer enabling the viewer to refuse to know them. It is another thing to, as Morrison invites us to, to *bear witness* to these events rather than passively and superficially viewing them. When a storyteller's narrative strategies work, when the reader connects with and is drawn into the world of story, it is difficult to return to our old habits of passive and superficial engagement. Could it be that the contemporary video testimony with which we are inundated will become harder to ignore? Some may well argue we have become desensitized to this and other visual records of violence in movies, on television and social media in the digital age. If that is the case, can reading – dead letters on paper – succeed where the video record has failed? I believe that it can and not simply in the abstract context of theoretical discussions of orality and literacy, storytelling and literature. These are the lessons I have learned from my students over the course of decades in the literature classroom. Once the veil has been lifted it becomes very difficult to unsee what we have seen or to avoid witnessing its repetition.

In addition to more traditional literature courses, I regularly teach a course about forgiveness – *Why Forgive?* – in which we work through religious, philosophical, and literary texts raising and attempting to answer the question articulated in the class title. This fall marked an exceptional group of students who not only engaged with the range of challenging assigned texts but also were eager to draw analogies with and apply the readings to the contemporary moment in a seminar format. We read and discussed Toni Morrison's novel *Home* together in seminar. One morning's discussion began with the following question, raised by one of the seminar participants:

> Dr. Collins-Sibley, a friend and I were talking about race the other day and he said that if black and white people are going to talk about race productively then black people need to humble themselves. I'm wondering what you think?

In what I hope was in the best Socratic tradition, I turned the question back to the seminar – lively discussion ensued. Over the course of the semester, through their experience of closely reading a range of stories in the form of biblical tales, poetry, short stories, memoirs and this novel, my students had moved from passive readers to engaged witnesses who had begun to free themselves from the straightjackets of our race and class-conscious society. Why assume, they asked each other, that white and black people could only have productive conversations about race if black people humbled themselves? And what would a productive conversation be like?

These questions and our discussion brought us to the issue of the disconnect between our values and our practice with which I began this chapter. It is a truth pretty universally acknowledged – to paraphrase Jane Austen – that racism is a bad thing and racist behavior something to be avoided and condemned. Yet we continue to commit acts whose consequences can only be described as "racist." It's the paradox of systemic racism: a racism without racists. A disconnect grounded, I would argue, in fear and more than fear, in *shame*. This feeling of shame, the perception that any discussion of difference that does more than merely "celebrate diversity" is intended to make white students feel at best uncomfortable, at worst ashamed of being white; this in turn inevitably leads to defensiveness and the assertion that black people must humble themselves before engaging in such conversations with white people. These are the conclusions my students reached. How had their classroom become a space in which they had learned to tolerate discomfort and move past shame? To move beyond the need for an *appearance* of humility on the part of black participants[2] without which such conversations often result in defensiveness and ultimately frustration for all parties. Literature – the close and engaged reading of literature – bridged the gap; or more accurately, empowered us to bridge it. We were empowered to conduct conversations about race and systemic racism in the context of a course called *Why forgive?*

Remember for a moment the distinction Albert Murray is careful to make in the above cited passage about the writer's "dedication to the art of fiction" as "tantamount to a social commitment to human well-being and self-realization." By characterizing an author's aspiration as "truly literary," Murray draws an important distinction between "protest writing" and literature, similar to James Baldwin's excoriation of protest literature in "Everybody's Protest Novel." Baldwin would agree, I suggest, with Murray's assertion that

> American protest fiction … is predicated upon assumptions that have more to do with philanthropy than with the dynamics of antagonistic cooperation … with representing a world of collective victims whose survival and betterment depend not upon self-determination but upon a change of heart in their antagonists, who thereupon will cease being villains and become patrons of social welfare!
>
> (Murray 2016, 370)

Protest fiction evokes moral outrage, grounded in a commitment to hierarchical principles in which racial inequality is a problem of social value; shame, on the other hand, can be understood as a moral reaction demanding a shift in perspective. Toni Morrison, by Albert Murray's definition, is literary in her aspirations; she does not write protest fiction. As a storyteller, when she initiates us into her world – and by extension that of her protagonist – forging that connection between audience and story, making us witness to events in the novel, Morrison compels such a shift in perspective. The storyteller helps us to see the gap between what we value and what we practice. The concomitant practice of close reading as taught in the study of literature, can help us to appreciate such a shift in perspective in ways that make us our own audiences; critical close reading can help us to engage in the kinds of critical self-reflection that can emerge from truth telling conversations. Sympathy, or even empathy, resulting from the imaginative projection of readers into the experiences of protagonists is not enough. If we are to move from guilt or shame as merely the experience of personal shortcomings and/or moral failure – e.g. feeling guilty for being white – this kind of critical self-reflection can become a resource for action, and thereby, for positive change. At best protest fiction stops with outrage but literature may lead us through shame as the recognition of the rupture between our values and our attitudes or actions whenever confronted with social injustice. We move from being passive bystanders to becoming active witnesses.

Conclusion

If #BlackLivesMatter – as Garza, Cullors, Tomei define it – is an ideological and political intervention, an affirmation of Black folks' humanity, contributions to American society, and, resilience in the face of oppression, it is more than simply the demand that "you stop killing us!" It is a demand for equal opportunity – in the spirit of our founding document, The Declaration of Independence – to *flourish*. Life isn't a zero sum game; in the spirit of *ubuntu*, a person is a person *through* other people, and, a:

> flourishing life … is not an egotistic endeavor … to truly be virtuous, thus to flourish, we must attend to the circumstances necessary for others' flourishing … [and] the most immediate circumstances for which we can reasonably be held accountable are the ways in which we treat others.
>
> (Lebron 2013, 23)

I believe that the study and teaching of the Humanities, especially literature, is one way to profit from this teachable moment. But then, I have to believe. I have a son; he looks like Trayvon. Black lives matter.

Notes

1 See political philosopher Christopher J. Lebron's recent, excellent work *The Making of Black Lives Matter: A Brief History of an Idea* (Oxford University Press, 2017) for just such a discussion.
2 An important context, the participants in our seminar consisted of two African-Americans (one the professor herself), one Muslim man (and international student), three young white men, and, four white women; a pretty diverse group at the university.

References

Black Lives Matter. "Herstory." https://blacklivesmatter.com/about/herstory/

Brockes, Emma. 2012. "Toni Morrison: I Want to Feel What I Feel. Even If It's Not Happiness." *The Guardian* (April 13)

www.theguardian.com/books/2012/apr/13/toni-morrison-home-son-love

Jonsson, Patrick. 2012. "Obama on Trayvon Martin Death: A Time of 'Soul-Searching' for 'All of Us.'" *The Christian Science Monitor* (Mar 23). www.csmonitor.com/USA/2012/0323/Obama-on-Trayvon-Martin/death-a-time-of-soul-searching-for-all-of-us.

Lebron, Christopher J. 2013. *The Color of Our Shame: Race and Justice in Our Time*. New York: Oxford University Press.

Liptak, Adam. 2013. "Supreme Court Invalidates Key Part of Voting Rights Act." *The New York Times* (Jun 25). www.nytimes.com/2013/06/26/us/supreme-court-ruling.html.

Morrison, Toni. 2017. *The Origin of Others*. Cambridge: Harvard University Press.

MorrisonToni, . 2014. "How Can We Find Paradise on Earth?" *The Telegraph* (May 27). www.telegraph.co.uk/culture/hay-festival/10848569/Toni-Morrison-can-we-find-paradise-on-Earth.html

Murray, Albert. 2016. "The Hero and the Blues." In *Albert Murray: Collected Essays And Memoirs*, edited by Henry LouisGatesJr. and PaulDevlin. New York: The Library of America/Penguin Random House: 345–409.

Nussbaum, Martha J. 2014. "A Newly Rich Life within Yourself." *Awaken.org* (Sept 8). www.awaken.org/read/view.pphp?tid=1020.

Obama, Barack. 2013. "America is not a Post-Racial Society." *The Guardian* (July 19). www.theguardian.com/commentisfree/2013/jul/19/america-not-post-racial-society-barack-obama.

8 Storytelling as Peace Pedagogy in Higher Education

Amanda Smith Byron

Storytelling plays an important role in student learning, whether stories are taken from literature, shared from personal experience, or elicited directly from students. Existing scholarship on storytelling covers a wide swath of disciplines, audiences, applications, and purposes; and offers disparate ways to define storytelling. Senehi (2009) describes storytelling as "a universal way human beings deal with knowledge" (203), and has found the process of telling and receiving stories to continually form and reform our view of the world. Similarly, Michel de Certeau (1984) explains the function of storytelling as authorizing, founding, and settling in place the way people experience and understand the world.

The stories heard throughout our lives influence how we understand and interact with the world and, as such, inform the kind of solutions we are able to imagine to the conflicts we encounter. This is particularly significant in Peace and Justice Studies, because the stories circulating about war and violence dramatically outnumber stories about peace and justice. One of the most important tasks for Peace and Justice Studies educators is to unsettle the dominant narrative of adversarial engagement by offering counter stories of collaboration, shared power, and mutual engagement. Senehi (2009) explains, "Stories encode and transmit everyday understandings of conflict and what to do about it" (205). Storytelling is a key strategy for imparting the importance of Peace and Justice Studies as a discipline and as a pursuit, personalizing the significance of social injustice, and promoting the value of engagement in action to create social change.

This chapter examines the vital role that storytelling plays in the peace pedagogy of higher education. A robust understanding of peace pedagogy has yet to be formalized, and much of what is known about it is framed within the primary, secondary, and war-zone focused discourses of peace education. This chapter begins with background information on peace pedagogy and storytelling, exploring their vital role within Peace and Justice Studies, and examines storytelling as a tool of peace pedagogy in higher education, drawing from peace education and critical theory. This is followed by an exploration of the underlying issues, controversies, and problems that surround this inquiry. The neoliberal trend in higher education is examined as a challenge to both the critical thinking skills and democracy building skills that are foundational to Peace and Justice Studies. Storytelling is elaborated upon as a method of peace pedagogy, and as a means for effective praxis in Peace and Justice Studies in higher education.

Peace Pedagogy

Peace pedagogy refers to the method and practice of teaching peace, and is the means through which peace education occurs. The practices of peace education are based in the rich legacy of learner-centered approaches to learning (Jenkins, 2008), and include diverse applications that range from administrative protocols intended to create peaceful school culture, to curricula focused on cooperation, skill-building and personal transformation, to classroom resources designed to teach the history of peace. Harris (1990) describes the goals of peace education in terms of personal transformation, with an emphasis on orienting people "toward caring for others, using compassion, respecting diversity, seeking nonviolent alternative and mediating conflict" (255). In contrast, Jenkins (2008) focuses on the social action that transformation can facilitate, describing the goal of peace education as nurturing "the types of changes in thinking, attitudes and behaviors that will help learners to understand, confront, resist, transform, and ultimately eliminate violence in all of its multiple forms" (168). In both cases, there is a shared recognition that "how we come to know, what it is we know, largely influences how we will use or act upon that knowledge in the world" (Palmer, 1993, 21).

Though peace education was historically framed as war abatement, or as a negative form of peace recognized through the absence of violence, during the 1960s the women's movement drew attention to the positive nature of peace education's relational and transformative potential (Morrison, 2008). Feminists brought focus to the significance of the personal consequences that result from violence, and a recognition that peace cannot occur in the outer spheres without regard for the human impact of violence within the inner spheres. Boulding (2000) is one such feminist who, through her scholarship and activism, has fought tirelessly to bring attention to the social realm of peace, and the role of education in contributing to a culture of peace. Reardon (1988) describes peace education as facilitating transformation that registers change in human consciousness and society.

Critical peace education draws from the strength of critical theory, and the work of the Frankfurt School of Social Research, to challenge the dominant ideologies that contribute to systems of oppression, and to encourage strategic actions toward peace. Critical peace education embraces the goal of raising critical consciousness about systems of oppression, and mobilizing student action toward change. Bajaj (2008) distinguishes critical peace education from other categories of peace education by attending to the role of, "issues of structural inequality and research aimed towards local understandings of how participants can cultivate a sense of transformative agency" (135). Cultivating this agency, Bajaj argues, is central to the task of critical peace educators, because while learning about injustice and peace are vitally important, agency is what liberates oppression. Giroux describes this task as linking knowledge and learning to the performative and worldly space of action and engagement, energizing people not only to think critically about the world around them but also to use their capacities as social agents to intervene in the larger social order and confront the myriad forms of lives. (Giroux, 2009, 22)

Betty Reardon (1999) similarly articulates the importance of individual and collective agency as *global action*, which "refers to the skills and practices of active citizenship in global civil society, and actions taken to benefit the whole of human society, including unfamiliar and distant peoples" (16). The importance of encouraging concern for and righteous action toward social justice is central to critical peace education. Illustrating Maxine Greene's concept of *possibilizing*, Bajaj describes peace education as having a goal for learners to develop

> [a] sense of possibility that enables them to become agents of social change. Freirean ideas on the necessity for educators to inspire a critical optimism among students that is aimed at promoting solidarity and diminishing the distance between social groups—whether they are stratified by race, ethnicity, religion, class, or any other ascriptive characteristic. (Bajaj, 2008, 3)

Since the institution of education not only mimics prevailing ideologies, but co-constructs the ideas and values that are disseminated, critical peace education recognizes the importance of acknowledging the vital role of educational process in shaping the way democracy will work (or not) in the future. Central to this is the types of stories that are present (and absent) in the context of that educational process.

Storytelling and Social Change

There has been a trend for scholars hailing from diverse disciplines to recognize storytelling as an essential tool in higher education, especially for its capacity to garner "deeper insight into the lived realities of peoples and communities" (Carmona and Luschen, 2014, viii). Soling, Fox, and Irani (2008) claim the time of their writing as being the time where "narrative is more broadly recognized than ever as a significant, simple, crucial vehicle for reawakening, disseminating, and sustaining social justice impulses" (1). Increasingly, storytelling is recognized as having the capacity "to engage, transform and catalyze social action" (Carmona and Luschen, 2014, 1), and as having a central role in educating for social change:

> For many of us who would describe ourselves as teaching for social change, storytelling has been at the heart of our pedagogy. In the context of social change storytelling refers to an opposition to established knowledge, to Foucault's suppressed knowledge, to the experience of the world that is not admitted into dominant knowledge paradigms. Storytelling is central to strategies for social change.
>
> (Razack, 1998, 36)

Barone (1992) distinguishes between regular and critical stories, qualifying critical stories as those that situate experience in a sociopolitical context, and those where critical educational storytellers "prick the consciences of readers by inviting a reexamination of the values and interests undergirding certain discourses, practices and institutional arrangements..." (143). Lederach (1995) exemplifies this type of critical storytelling in his writing on peacebuilding, which situates both the conflict and the resolution within cultural contexts, steeped within the theory of conflict resolution. The point in sharing critical stories is to "recognize the gaps and silences in dominant ways of knowing, and seek to illuminate counternarratives" (Carmona and Luschen, 2014, 2).

Storytelling as a vital tool for social change is something that has been touted by critical theorists and critical pedagogues over many decades. McLaren (1989) charges critical theorists with the essential task of finding creative strategies "to empower the powerless and transform existing social inequalities and injustices" (160). The critical storytelling of counternarratives is a means for just that, offering a creative method to inspire action toward change.

Issues, Controversies, Problems

One of the greatest challenges to Peace and Justice Studies education in general, and to the use of storytelling for social change in particular, is the tremendous neoliberal influence in both educational policy and national climate. Current practice is to measure learning in terms of how well students are prepared for future employment, or how well they are prepared to fit into the dominant system. This focus on career preparation threatens the time and space required for adequate exploration of the humanities, and within that, the depth of critical reflection that storytelling can provide. At its core, Peace and Justice Studies encourages a critical unsettling of dominant narratives, sufficient analytical thinking skills to question dominant systems, and an activist orientation in support of a flourishing democracy. Giroux (2009) recalls that, "education became one of the first targets of neoliberals, neoconservatives, religious extremists, and fundamentalists advocating market interest over social needs and democratic values" (14).

This commercialization of learning in higher education has had far-reaching implications. Giroux (2009) explains that the "language of market fundamentalism and the emerging corporate university radically altered the vocabulary available for appraising the meaning of citizenship, agency, and civic virtue" (16). While there are compelling arguments for making higher education relevant to students and valuable to society, emphasizing individual employability over the goal of creating a citizenry capable of analyzing complex social issues and judging political decisions has impacted our ability to participate in democracy—and has, therefore, impacted the efficacy of our democracy itself.

Peace is dependent upon democracy, and an effective democracy is dependent upon an engaged citizenry. Without adequately developed critical reflection and thinking skills, civic participation declines; there are fewer people interested in or willing to commit to democratic processes, which results in a marginalized form of democracy. The literature shows a direct relationship between exposure to critical-thinking skills in higher education and long-term participation in public life, which is a key indicator of a functioning democracy (Abilock, 2005; Gates, 2006; Roosevelt, 2006). Higher education, where academic freedom exists to protect critical debate on even the most controversial topics, is perhaps the last bastion of hope that there will continue to be critical debate on controversial topics in an otherwise civically disengaged landscape (O'Neil, 2005).

Research Implications

While recent trends locate storytelling as an important element in facilitating social change, understanding its role in Peace and Justice Studies is a new field of inquiry. In my years as an educator in higher education, many of my students reported that my style of teaching had impacted their learning as much as the content of my instruction. While I consciously employ the practices of engaged pedagogy (hooks, 1994), experiential learning, and critical analysis, I was interested in knowing more about how my presence and choices as an educator impacted students, and specifically how it increased students' ability to reflect and act upon peace and justice issues. This piqued my interest in understanding more about my role as a post-secondary educator, and inspired a research project that overtly investigated how other post-secondary social justice educators inspire new and critical perspectives, and increase students' willingness to act on their convictions (Byron, 2011).

The specific question I posed in my research was how post-secondary educators use storytelling to address issues of social change, and to inspire action toward social justice (Byron, 2011). In collecting post-secondary educator narratives, I noticed how and when respondents used storytelling, and examined how those stories humanize the struggle of oppressed groups, how they engaged learner empathy, how they encouraged critical perspectives, and how they mobilized students to take action toward social change. This qualitative inquiry investigated the narratives of social justice educators to understand how storytelling in post-secondary transforms student perspective by positively complicating the context of conflict. When conflicts are oversimplified, it is easy to succumb to a dichotomous view of right and wrong, with one side to blame and one side to sympathize with. Encouraging and sharing counter-stories, which highlight the lived-experience of parties in conflict, deepens our understanding of conflict, and its corresponding context, and allows a humanization of the actors in conflict, which transcends the dichotomous view, and imagines new roads toward peaceful solutions. This process enables us to turn objects into subjects, which inspires increased compassion and empathy, and leads to the humanization of all sides. The #metoo movement provides a powerful example of how transformative counter-stories are in social movements, and in the journey toward greater social justice.

The study concluded that storytelling functions as a kind of ideological critique that can radically alter worldviews and transform perspectives about the practices and structures that hold systems of oppression in place. Ideology critique can be regarded as a formalized version of critical thinking, with the specific purpose of deconstructing ideologies in order to liberate people from unconscious influences. Mezirow (1991) refers to ideology critique as systemic critical thinking, and Brookfield (2005) further articulates ideology critique as a "critical distancing from, and then oppositional rearrangement with, the dominant culture" (13), and names this process as the central learning task of adulthood. According to my research, storytelling is regularly used as a method to engage students in a deeper critique of the world, and an expanded understanding of their own place within that world. The Storytelling Project Model (Bell, 2010), which maps storytelling as a means to transform racist narratives, was identified as a theoretical framework that explains the role of story in ideology critique, and offers a visual understanding of storytelling as a means to actualize social justice.

Conclusion

By investigating the relationship between storytelling and Peace and Justice Studies, we can recognize the profound impact that dominant narratives of war and violence have on society, and see how fostering and sharing counternarratives has the possibility to generate stories that can inspire peaceful action toward social change. Speaking about youth, but addressing a common need for students of all ages, Greene (2009) plaintively notes that, "If situations cannot be created that enable the young to deal with feelings of being manipulated by outside forces, there will be far too little sense of agency among them" (139). The awareness that allows us to recognize the limitations in the discourse of war and violence, is the first step toward creating social change. Hegemony remains in place until we realize that we need to take action toward change.

Greene (2009) notices that, "only when we envisage a better social order do we find the present one in many ways unendurable, and hence stir ourselves to repair it" (141). Imagining a better world may seem like an easy task, but it is one that takes critical and analytical thinking skills, a sense of hope about what the future holds, and a capacity for creative vision. Antonia Darder describes the task of critical pedagogy as being one that "cultivates imagination and seeks to create opportunities to insert students into new and unfamiliar contexts so they can grapple with the cognitive dissonance and ambiguity, which is intrinsic to a highly diverse society" (2009, 164). In gaining comfort with the unknown and unfamiliar, which happens through exposure to counternarratives and personal stories, students have the opportunity to expand their consciousness and, through that, cultivate their imagination.

Emily Dickinson (1960) wrote, "The Possible's slow fuse is lit by the Imagination" (689). In response to Dickinson's poem, Maxine Greene (1995) explains that the

> fuse may be slow because of the ways in which the imaginative capacity has been ignored. In the many education reports that have appeared in recent years, imagination plays no part. In plans for cooperative work among teachers and professors, the stress is on pragmatic issues: standards, disciplines, benchmarks, approaches to assessment.
>
> (Greene, 1995, para. 1)

The need for imagination is perhaps at the heart of the neoliberal crisis in education. And the solution is perhaps rooted in the humanity and compassion that results from storytelling. Greene (2009) writes that "[i]magination, moreover, is enriched and stimulated through live encounters with others, through exposure to diverse vantage points and unfamiliar ways of looking at the world" (142). Paolo Freire (1994) speaks to a similar need for poetic imagination to be pragmatically applied to social concerns, and directed to adult educators so that they can show students that, "the lovelier world to which they aspired was being announced, somehow anticipated in their imagination" (39). The sense of possibility that is generated from an enlivened imagination is possibly the force that John Dewey (1954) imagined would enable humanity to break through "the crust of conventionalized and routine consciousness" (183), to create the change needed to work toward greater social justice.

Storytelling is presented as a means to effectively engage in social change, as a core component of Peace and Justice Studies. But one of the most powerful effects storytelling offers is its ability to illustrate what is possible when voice and agency are engaged, and when people are willing and able to step up to the task of democracy. This sense of possibility is a refreshing dose of hope in a time when the prevailing messages of our culture speak of hopelessness, and is a welcome clue about how to cultivate the imagination needed to create a peaceful and just tomorrow.

References

Abilock, Debbie. 2005. "Six promising approaches to civic engagement." *CASA Journal*, 29(1), 8–11.

Bajaj, Monisha. (Ed.). 2008. *Encyclopedia of peace education*. Charlotte, NC: Information Age Publishing

Barone, Thomas. 1992. "Beyond theory and method: A case for critical storytelling." *Theory into Practice*, 31(2), 142–146.

Bell, Lee Anne. 2010. *Storytelling for social justice: Connecting narrative and the arts in antiracist teaching*. New York: Routledge.

Boulding, Elise. 2000. *Cultures of peace: The hidden side of history*. Syracuse, NY: Syracuse University Press.

Brookfield, Stephen. 2005. *The power of critical theory: Liberating adult learning and teaching*. San Francisco, CA: Jossey-Bass.

Byron, Amanda. 2011. *Storytelling as loving praxis in critical peace education: A grounded theory study of postsecondary social justice educators*. Portland, OR: Portland State University.

Carmona, Judith and Kirsten Luschen (Eds). 2014. *Crafting critical stories: Toward pedagogies and methodologies of collaboration, inclusion and voice*. New York: Peter Lang Publishing.

de Certeau, Michel. 1984. *The practice of everyday life*. Berkeley, CA: University of California Press.

Dewey, John. 1954. *The public and its problems*. Athens, OH: The Swallow Press.

Dickinson, Emily. 1960. "The Gleam of an heroic act." In T. Johnson (Ed.), *The complete poems*. Boston, MA: Little Brown, pp. 688–689.

Freire, Paolo 1994. *Pedagogy of hope*. New York, NY: Continuum.

Gates, Brian E. 2006. "Where is the moral in citizenship education?" *Journal of Moral Education*, 35(4). Retrieved from www.informaworld.com/smpp/content?content=10.1080/03057240601025636

Giroux, Henry. 2009. "The attack on higher education and the necessity of critical pedagogy." In S. Macrine (Ed.), *Critical pedagogy in uncertain times: Hope and possibilities*. New York: Palgrave MacMillan. pp. 11–26.

Greene, Maxine. 1995. "Metaphors and responsibility." *On Common Ground: Partnership and the Arts*, 5. Retrieved from http://www.yale.edu/ynhti/pubs/A18/greene.html

Greene, Maxine. 2009. "Teaching as possibility." In S. Macrine (Ed.), *Critical pedagogy in uncertain times: Hope and possibilities*. New York: Palgrave MacMillan. pp. 137–149.

Harris, Ian M. 1990. "Principles of peace pedagogy." *Peace & Change*, 15(3), 254–271.

hooks, bell. 1994. *Teaching to transgress: Education as the practice of freedom*. New York : Routledge.

Jenkins, Tony. 2008. "The International Institute on Peace Education: Twenty-six Years Modeling Critical, Participatory Peace Pedagogy ." *Journal of Peace Education and Social Justice*, 2(2), 166–174.

Lederach, John Paul. 1995. *Preparing for peace: Conflict transformation across cultures*. Syracuse, NY: Syracuse University Press.

McLaren, Peter. 1989. *Life in schools: An introduction to critical pedagogy in the foundations of education*. New York: Longman.

Mezirow, Jack. 1991. *Transformative dimensions of adult learning*. San Francisco, CA: Jossey-Bass.

Morrison, Mary Lee. 2008. "Elise Boulding and peace education." *Encyclopedia of Peace Education*. Retrieved from www.tc.edu/centers/epe/entries.html

O'Neil, Robert M. 2005. "Academic Freedom: Past, Present, and Future beyond September 11." In P. Altback, R. Berdahl, & P. Gumport (Eds.), *American higher education in the twenty-first century: Social, political, and economic challenges* (2nd ed.). Baltimore, MD: The Johns Hopkins Press. pp. 91–114.

Palmer, Parker. 1993. *To know as we are known: Education as a spiritual journey*. New York: Harper Collins.

Plummer, Ken. 1995. *Telling sexual stories: Power, change, and social worlds*. London: Routledge.

Razack, Sherene. 1998. *Looking White people in the eye: Gender, race, and culture in courtrooms and classrooms*. Toronto, Canada: University of Toronto Press.

Reardon, Betty. 1988. *Comprehensive peace education: Educating for global responsibility*. New York: Teachers College Press.

Reardon, Betty. 1999. *Educating the educators: The preparation of teachers for a culture of peace*. Peace Education Miniprints No. 99. Retrieved from ERIC database, ISSN 1101–6418.

Roosevelt, Grace. 2006. "The Triumph of the market and the decline of liberal education: Implications for civic life." *Teachers College Record*, 108(7), 1404–1423.

Rukeyser, Muriel. 1973. "Kathe Kollwitz." In J. Goulianos (Ed.), *By a woman writ: Literature from six centuries by and about Women*. New York: Bobbs Merrill, p. 363–379.

Senehi, Jessica. 2009. "Building peace: Storytelling to transform conflicts constructively." In D. Sandole, S.Byrne, I.Sandole-Staroste, & J. Senehi (Eds.), *Handbook of conflict analysis and resolution*. New York: Routledge, pp. 201–214.

Solinger, Rickie, Madeline Fox, and Kayhan Irani. 2010. *Telling stories to change the world: Global voices on the power of narrative to build community and make social justice claims*. New York: Routledge.

9 Toward a Pedagogy of Radical Love

Karen Lynn Ridd

In 1989, while working in El Salvador with Peace Brigades International (PBI), I was briefly detained and imprisoned.[1] PBI carries out nonviolent accompaniment work, providing unarmed bodyguards to teachers, unionists, students, indigenous leaders, church workers, and activists of all types in countries where repressive regimes target such people and their organizations for the humanitarian and social justice work they do. At the time I was arrested, I was in a church refugee center, trying to improve safety for the refugees and the valiant Salvadoran church workers running the center. Despite our efforts, the Salvadoran military invaded the building, scattered the refugees, arrested and detained all the staff, and took five PBI workers to the Treasury Police Jail. There I was blindfolded, handcuffed, interrogated, kept standing without food and water, and threatened with rape and mutilation.

There is a long version of this story, but here's the heart of it. I was in a torture center. I knew that's what it was; I had had Salvadoran friends tortured in that prison and I could hear torture around me. While in detention I tried to speak out against the torture but was unable to stop it. Under my blindfold I caught glimpses of people lying broken on the ground. However, when the officials were ready to release me, I refused to leave. I had been imprisoned with Marcela Rodriguez Diaz, a Colombian colleague, and in our unjust world my North American life was being valued more than hers. I refused to leave the jail without her, and was re-imprisoned, staying with her until we could both be released.

Before we were released, an astonishing thing happened. My refusal to leave had confused the guards, who challenged me: "Do you miss us? Do you want us?" with all the sexual innuendo this entailed. I was frightened and I didn't know how to answer. But I had been learning about nonviolence from the Central Americans I was accompanying, and an answer poured out from me. I said, "No, of course I don't want to be here, but you are soldiers, you know what solidarity is. You know that if a comrade is down or fallen in battle, you wouldn't leave them, and I can't leave my comrade, not now, not here. You understand."

I don't know what response I thought I would get. After all, I was speaking to torturers. Yet, intuitively—and influenced by the Latin

Americans whom I'd been supporting—I had placed the torturers in what George Lakey and Martin Luther King, Jr. before him have called a "dilemma demonstration," (Lakey 1987, 103; King, n.d.) a Catch-22 where there is no "good" way out. Do the torturers agree with me and implicitly acknowledge our joint humanity? Or do they disagree and show themselves to be, even to themselves, inhumane tyrants?[2] They became still, silent. Then, gently, and after a long while, one said, "Yes, we know why you are here." From then on, the most amazing thing kept happening. Guards kept coming, apparently from all around the jail, looking for the two women they had heard about, the "inseparable ones," and responding with respect for love, friendship, and connection.

In that Salvadoran jail, I faced and learned many things. I learned the importance of what I call the "futile gesture": my small, hopeless act of returning to the jail for my friend, combined with the phone calls and messages PBI supporters around the world sent to the Salvadoran government on our behalf, led to our release. I learned that we do get second chances, and that a mistake—allowing myself to get separated from my colleague—can be rectified. I learned, incarnate, King's dilemma demonstration whereby you put your opponent in a no-win situation, and Mahatma Gandhi's conviction that liberating the oppressed also liberates the oppressor. But most importantly, I learned, embodied, the possibility and the power of connection.

The importance of connection has profoundly influenced both my understanding of how to teach and my practices in the Conflict Resolution Studies program at Menno Simons College (MSC), where I have taught for the last 15 years. Connection is crucial to any form of teaching, I would argue, but especially in Peace Studies, which seeks to move students and the world towards greater connection and greater compassion. In this article, I will make some observations on the importance of connection—and love—for teaching both generally and specifically in reference to Peace Studies, and offer a few remarks on teaching within an Anabaptist institution.

Those Who Went Before

Who were the teachers who inspired us? What made them great? Of course there are disconnected, cynical teachers out there, too many of them. Sometimes I too am one of them. But there are also great ones. In my case, one was Mrs. Stern, my ninth grade Language Arts and Art teacher, who as a rookie in the classroom didn't know where to set the bar. She set it too high and had 14-year-olds reading and reciting Chaucer, Milton, and Shakespeare. She didn't know these things were beyond us; she believed we could do them. And we did! I learned from her that people will rise (or fall) to expectations. In high school there was Mr. Dickens, a South African refugee to Canada, who made me feel that education mattered and had something to do with making a difference in the world. At university there was Professor Arthur Walker-Jones, who trusted us to design our own assignments and gave us the freedom to set our own goals. Three different teachers and three different styles, but they shared one attribute: they loved what they were doing and put that love into action.

Love the Students

George Lakey (1990), the noted peace educator, activist, and author, offers a simple teaching mantra: "Love the students, love the material, love yourself." But what does "love" mean in the educational context? What does it mean to love the students? It takes an act of courage, trust, resilience, and vulnerability on the instructor's part. It can be heart-breaking, because to love is to risk. It can be exhausting; at the end of an academic year I sometimes feel utterly spent, like a marathoner just making it across the finish line, with nothing left to give. It can be challenging: if we give our hearts to our students, we will have theirs, not only this year, but next year and the year after, with the number of people wanting, needing, and deserving our time growing exponentially. And it can be very rewarding.

Students in Peace Studies programs are deeply aware that they are living in a world which is falling apart, where we remove mountain tops—literally blow them off—to get energy. This is a world where the addiction to oil leads to slate fracking and the devastation of the tar sands. All my generation had to worry about when growing up was nuclear war! Now, we have a world of melting polar ice caps, pending global economic and environmental collapse, and peak oil. The issues are overwhelming, and students drawn to Peace Studies realize to a large extent that the world is at risk. At the same time, they and other young people are not getting increased connection and support in our culture. Instead, they are becoming increasingly isolated, hooked into computers and videogames. The soldiers in the story with which I began this chapter were also lost in detachment, prisoners in their own jail, isolated in horror. In a smaller way, students get lost in the isolation of technology and consumerism, afraid of the horrors that surround us all. It makes them easy to teach, because they are longing to be attached, cared about, and loved. I too benefit from this dynamic, since fracking, global warming, and peak oil terrify me too. The students support, motivate, and inspire me, and I'm glad to be in this world with them.

It is becoming clear that to learn at their best, students must have their hearts engaged. Gordon Neufeld, the Canadian developmental psychologist, promotes an attachment-based development model. Children need to feel a strong connection to a mature caregiver in order to thrive and grow (Neufeld and Mate, 2006). At a lecture several years ago, Neufeld (2005) described a study that examined the impact of early reading on children. Brain scans showed that reading to the children caused a significant, measurable increase in activity in the brain's language centers. Researchers subsequently concluded that children's brain development could be stimulated by reading to them from an early age. However, to their consternation, subsequent studies failed to show the same surge in brain activity. Trying to explain this difference, they realized one variable had changed: in the first study, each child was sitting on the mother's lap, whereas in the later studies they were being read to by research assistants. Neufeld concludes it was not that the children were being read to at a young age that made the difference. It was that they were being read to by someone who loved them and whom they loved. It was their attachment to the beloved reader that opened them to learning.

I contend that our students will do best—as learners, as people—if their hearts are engaged. It is perhaps even more crucial, in that the world desperately needs them to have engaged hearts because only then can they act in the peacemaking ways that are required. School shootings, mass attacks, war—all these ultimate acts of alienation demand detachment, a separation of self from other. Increasingly, war itself is detachment: fighting unseen foes, firing high-tech missiles from rooms in North America on targets in another continent, and employing drone strikes and robots. If detachment enables one to kill, then attachment is surely the antidote. If acts of violence require detachment from the victim and ultimately from the self, then the way out of this conundrum is through connection. What we need is for students to engage their hearts. But they will not and cannot do so unless we engage ours with theirs. This is at the core of peace education. In our courses and in our pedagogy,[3] we must model attachment, connection, and love, and support students to be loving in their journeys into the world.

Love and Peace Education

What I am arguing is distinctly counter-cultural. Universities are bastions of intellect and rational thought. Teaching through the power of connection is probably slightly disconcerting to some administrators; it is unnerving to some students. But peace education instructors are accustomed to creating alternative cultures and upending oppressive ones. We, of all people, should know that unsettling the status quo opens opportunities, as my unsettling of the soldiers in the Salvadoran jail opened the opportunity for Marcela's freedom. We, of all people, should be able to move past a culture that tells us repeatedly *not* to love the students and warns us that getting "too close" means losing perspective and becoming biased.[4] Implicitly we are told—through big classes and institutional red tape—not to love. Explicitly we receive directives; even elementary teachers are told, "Don't hug."

Several years ago, the University of Winnipeg, where Menno Simons College is located, received an explicit threat that was taken very seriously. Among other things, professors were given instructions from Security on how to respond to an intruder. Many of these instructions made sense: lockdown procedures, emergency contacts, locating exits. But one stipulation rather horrified me. We were explicitly told "not to engage with an intruder." What else could one possibly do, if not engage? Pretend the intruder didn't exist? Surely, engagement is the only human way to respond and, at least for me, the only chance to affect a situation positively. Ultimately, I can't be certain how I would react in a campus crisis. I hope I would react like professor Liviu Librescu of Virginia Tech, who tried to protect his students during a shooting in 2007. Whatever I would do, I would be reacting through engagement.

Given our culture of disengagement, it is not so simple to love the students. What does it mean to try to do so? For one thing it means really knowing who the students are. According to Neufeld, attachment happens in various ways. At a surface level, it happens through "sameness." I work this angle consciously on the first day of class. From my colleague Rick McCutcheon, I have learned to greet and shake hands with every student as they enter the room or settle cautiously into their seat. With each one, I look for some point of connection, or sameness, and I say things like: "I love that shirt! That shade of blue is one of my favorite colors, too." Or, "Oh, you're reading a book by Kenneth Oppel. Have you read *Silverwing*?" Or, "Jets jersey, eh? What did you think about the draft picks this summer?" It's a great way to start, but only a superficial way of connecting, which is why it's easy.

Much more profound is attachment through being known. Bruce Tuckman's research on group development indicates that a group becomes a high functioning team only when it has moved past the stage of polite sameness ("Oh, look how alike we are!") to a stage where members allow their real selves to show (Tuckman and Jensen, 1977). At this point the profound question is "Will these people still like me if they know how I really am?" Teachers need to really know their students, and this means providing space—in classes, curricula, assignments, and offices—for students to be themselves. We must be ready and willing to learn, from them, who they are.

Truly knowing the students requires awareness of the complex structures of classism, racism, sexism, ableism, and heterosexism that color their lives and that privilege or de-privilege them. Consider this example. At the University of Winnipeg the number of aboriginal students is continually on the rise. Several years ago, for instance, I had nine aboriginal students in a class of 27. Thirty-three percent—what a gift! I intentionally structured the class towards this demographic. Obviously, it would have been ideal to have an aboriginal instructor (in the not-too-distant future we hope we will), but in the meantime I had a curriculum with aboriginal content, aboriginal authors of readings, a text by an aboriginal author, and aboriginal guest speakers. Still, seven of the nine students failed to pass the course.

It is not enough to have registration numbers. We must have classes, structures, and professors who can meet students' needs. Disturbed by losing so many students, I approached Neil Funk-Unrau, coordinator of my department. He found the same rate of failure existed in other department courses, so he contacted Julie Pelletier, chair of the Indigenous Studies program, who confirmed that the dropout rate in their department too was roughly the same as ours. Her analysis was that many students were arriving terrified, filled with the post-colonial legacy of residential schools and society's messages about their inadequacy. These students, she suggested, largely drop out when the first assignment is due, or the first exam is conducted. Force-fed self-limiting beliefs, they are afraid to hand a paper in lest it confirm what they already "know," namely that they aren't "good enough."

It is not enough to have aboriginal curricula, or even aboriginal instructors. One of Pelletier's solutions, which I've since implemented, is to have all the students on the first day write a short piece in class and hand it in, not for grades and not as an assignment. It is only for feedback, for starting to make a connection, and, most important, for getting past the fear and beginning a new pattern in handling assignments.

Instructors who want to know their students will profit by acquainting themselves with Howard Gardner's work on "multiple intelligences" (Gardner, 2011), and implementing it in the classroom. In particular, we must be aware that kinesthetic learners, those perhaps most marginalized in mainstream school systems, are entering universities and colleges in ever-increasing numbers. Again, it is not enough to have such learners gain access to the academy; we must also welcome them, and we can do that by accommodating their various learning styles.

Loving the students also means trusting them, an act that is counter-cultural in hierarchical institutions such as schools and universities. Several years ago, my department leaders asked me to teach a course in Conflict Theory and Analysis, an area that was not my bailiwick. They acknowledged it was a course that likely could not be taught in participatory ways, and that many students considered it unremittingly boring. I was discouraged, since I'm committed to a teaching philosophy that highly values engagement. I couldn't imagine teaching a whole course through lectures.[5] Nor could I see myself learning a wholly new course and finding ways to make all 12 weeks engaging in the short time frame I'd been given. In near desperation, I decided to trust the students. I set them the challenge of coming up with an activity each week that was participatory and would help them remember the theory. I would still teach the theory and make sure everyone understood it, but the students were responsible for helping each other engage with it. They succeeded magnificently, and this assignment is now a standard part of the curriculum.

Love as a Challenge to the Academy

Loving the students means loving the whole of them, and that takes us to controversial ground for the academy, namely the realm of spirituality. To love someone is to make space for the whole person, including the person's spirituality. This is anathema to many in academia, and often for good reasons. The legacy of colonialism and residential schools should make us deeply wary and puts us on dangerous ground. I teach at Menno Simons College, a college of Canadian Mennonite University (CMU), a "Christian University"—a term that many of my secular colleagues may see as an oxymoron like "dry wine," "jumbo shrimp," or "just war." I'm an outsider to this place in many ways; I was brought up in a firmly mainstream Protestant, but not Anabaptist, religious tradition. From my perspective, one benefit of teaching in an Anabaptist institution is the relative lack of attachment to hierarchy. Universities are, may I say, almost ridiculously hierarchical. Consider the theatrical display of robes and hats at convocations, or note the nuanced and rigid terms that speak volumes to the insider but are virtually ignored by everyone else (full professor, associate professor, adjunct professor, instructor).

Of course, there are power and rank differentials among Mennonites (perhaps most notably along gender lines), but there also seems to be a kind of disdain for the hierarchical ordering of humans, a disdain that in my experience creates a less hidebound institution. The President of CMU, the Deans of MSC, the Program Coordinators—all the people who fill these roles—interact with us with a sense of the equality of our humanity and a respect for the gifts each of us brings. In practical terms, I've experienced great respect for my style of teaching, and much openness and support for the quirky or unusual things that I try. This is fortunate, because one distinct problem with teaching from a place of love is that students tend to do "too well." It's a problem I find deeply ironic; if we were doing our jobs brilliantly, wouldn't our students do brilliantly too? Every year the computer discovers that my students' marks are too high, and I must justify their success. I wonder how I'd fare in a system with a stricter hierarchy or a less generous administration.

To be clear, while I don't see a role for mandatory religion in higher education, I also don't see higher education (at least in the arts) without a created space for potential expressions of spirituality. I've come to this perspective not because of the dictates of my Anabaptist institution, which, as noted, has been highly flexible, open, and supportive, but because of many indigenous students in my classes. They see the separating out of the spiritual world as a weird western and colonial phenomenon that has led to a dangerous detachment from the world and the environment. These students are not advocating for religious education per se, but they are declaring a need for space and support for spiritual reflection. They remind me of a southern Baptist pastor who once told me, "I try every year to become less religious and more spiritual." (People's Institute, 1987). For students to flourish as their whole selves without the forced self-dissection that results from—and leads to—detachment, we must find ways to accommodate their spiritual journeys even within secular universities.

What if we have large classes (although many peace educators fortunately have sensible class sizes)? How do we love the students then?

We love them in the moments of contact that we do have with them. We show them—their whole selves—respect, at all times. If the North Star of our teaching philosophy is love, then our practice will follow. Professor Harry Huebner, a long-time, well-loved CMU faculty member, told me one of his favorite methods. At the beginning of the year he tells students that not only is there no "stupid question" but if they don't have a question formulated they should just speak their thoughts, and he and they will formulate a question together. We need not be afraid of not having enough time for students. If we go forward in love, we will find methods, like this one.

Lastly, we can love students by enabling them to love each other, which they will do only through connecting with each other. It is imperative that we build community in our classrooms, not just on principle but because it enhances the ability to learn. We create attachment between students by using small groups, circles, and buddy systems; attending to learning styles; making introductions and learning names; undoing the academy's "argument culture"[6]; valuing students' thoughts; and trusting students, and helping them trust and learn from each other. Further, as peace educators we must not fail to use the classroom as a form of mini-laboratory, a place where conflict resolution principles are not just discussed but put into living form.

Love the Material

Loving the students is where I started, but it is perhaps easier to love the material. Craig Kielburger, the Canadian activist, observes that in the face of the immensity of global issues people can become bogged down and overwhelmed. There is a way forward, however. It is, he once said in a radio interview, to "find something that breaks your heart, and then put your heart into it."[7] When we love our material—which we surely do, or we would not have been drawn to it as we have—then we put our hearts into it. When that happens, students will feel also feel our passion and be drawn in. In short, we cannot be afraid to be in love with what we teach and to show students that love.

Daniel Chambliss and Christopher Takacs (2014) have recently completed research on the impact that good teaching has on enrollment, and conclude that the professor a student first encounters in any discipline acts as a gatekeeper for the discipline. If the professor is "good," students will likely be drawn into that field of study, whereas a poor experience with a professor will push them away, not just from a department but even from the discipline (Jaschik, 2013). My own experience as a university student bears this out. In my first year I took courses in various disciplines, unsure of where I wanted to head. That all changed in a heartbeat, partway through the year. My English professor, Walter Swayze, read this aloud to the class:

I wandered lonely as a cloud
That floats on high o'er vales and hills,
When all at once I saw a crowd,
A host of golden daffodils;
Beside the lake, beneath the trees,
Fluttering and dancing in the breeze.
I gazed—and gazed—but little thought
what wealth the show to me had brought:
For oft, when on my couch I lie
In vacant or in pensive mood,
They flash upon that inward eye
Which is the bliss of solitude;
And then my heart with pleasure fills,
And dances with the daffodils.

As Swayze read Wordsworth's "I Wandered Lonely as a Cloud," he wept unabashedly. It was in that moment that I decided to major in English Literature, not because of this great poem but because Swayze's passion inspired me. He showed me this was a study that has meaning and value, that matters. My colleague at MSC, John Derksen, is similarly loved by students. One reason they routinely give when I ask what makes him exceptional is that he is not afraid to show his emotions in class. We teach what we teach because it is or has been our passion, because it matters to us. Peace educators are in a discipline that also matters to the world. We need to find or remember that passion and be unafraid to let it show. How else can we expect students to love what we teach if we don't love it ourselves? If we do not show them, through our honest emotion and passion, that something matters, how can we expect it to matter to them? If we must love the students because *they* matter, we must love also the material because *it* matters.

Love Ourselves

So, we must love the students and the material. This brings us to what is perhaps the hardest requirement of all: we must love ourselves. In *The Courage to Teach*, Parker Palmer (2007) contends that "we teach who we are." Teaching is not so much about "what" we teach or even "how" we teach, but about the "who." And who are we, when we're tired or not looking after ourselves? How can I be violent to myself, or to the planet, and not bring some of that into the classroom? To be at my best as a teacher, which admittedly I not always am, means to live my beliefs as consistently as possible. It also means to take care of myself, to be grounded, and to be living in peace with others and, fundamentally, with myself. It also means that I be loved, spend time with those I love, and laugh—and bring laughter to a place from which it is often excluded, the university classroom. If I can laugh and enjoy myself, perhaps the students can. It's crucial that we laugh, especially in these difficult times, for it is not an easy job that we do, and peace activism is not an easy path to walk.

One of Palmer's most helpful chapters deals with how much fear instructors must confront in order to teach, especially the fear of being vulnerable, of "looking stupid" or foolish (2007). Courage is not, however, being fearless but continuing on in spite of fear. It is, as Ernest Hemingway said, "grace under pressure." Loving ourselves means taking self-care seriously. It means, as I needed to do many years ago, finding our own individual true voices as educators, our own styles, using love as our compass point. Loving ourselves means taking risks. This is no minor thing. If we ask students to take risks and to expand their horizons, surely it is only ethical for us to do so too. Also, it means being willing to bring into the classroom our whole self—failures and struggles as well as successes—and our vulnerability, for being vulnerable is a gift to both students and instructors.

Lastly, loving ourselves means being committed to our own growth and learning, and to finding mentors and inspirations. Shirley Sherrod, former head of the United States Department of Agriculture, has become one of those for me. "I learned a lot of lessons from my parents growing up, but one of the most important ones is what my mother taught her children after our father was killed," she has written. "She told us we mustn't try to live with hate in our hearts … Life is a grindstone. But whether it grinds us down or polishes us up depends on us. We can't yield, not now, not ever" (2010). Sherrod, by word and example, calls on us to live in love, even in the most difficult times. Her words are echoed by retired South African Archbishop Desmond Tutu when he defines the virtue of "Ubuntu":

> It is the essence of being human. It speaks of the fact that my humanity is caught up and is inextricably bound up in yours. I am human because I belong. It speaks about wholeness, it speaks about compassion. A person with Ubuntu is welcoming, hospitable, warm and generous, willing to share. Such people are open and available to others, willing to be vulnerable, affirming of others, do not feel threatened that others are able and good, for they have a proper self-assurance that comes from knowing that they belong in a greater whole. They know that they are diminished when others are humiliated, diminished when others are oppressed, diminished when others are treated as if they were less than who they are. The quality of

> Ubuntu gives people resilience, enabling them to survive and emerge still human despite all efforts to dehumanize them.[8]

What we need in this broken world is to be polished and not ground down. What we need for the world and for peace studies students is to *be* Ubuntu!

Conclusion

I began this chapter with a story about imprisonment, and I'll end it with one about liberation. The Right Rev. Stan McKay and Rev. Frances Combs both tell a story of blades of grass, which I will tell in my own way here:

There is a section of highway that I know well, a piece of the "Trans-Canada" that runs through Ontario from the border with Manitoba to the town of Kenora. Years ago there was a smaller highway there, the first Trans-Canada, concrete and tarmac snaking its way through bush, past swamps and around hills. Not straight enough for modern travel, it gave way to the new highway laid down 50-plus years ago. As a child, when we'd travel that new road, it was a game to follow the old highway with our eyes. Concrete, rock-solid, invincible. Certainly stronger than the plants or blades of grass which it had subdued. But a miracle has happened there. Over the years, the concrete has bulged and broken open, revealing the strength of the plants, pulsating with life, beneath the hard surface. Plants whose vitality and energy of life gives them the strength to break open, break apart the tarmac above.

In each student, I trust that there are hidden "blades of grass" waiting patiently for their time to break forth. In the material that I teach, there too are "blades of grass," insights, that will burst open. And I trust there are "blades of grass" in me as well, upsurging love for the students, the material, and myself.

Notes

1 This chapter originally appeared as an article in *The Conrad Grebel Review* 32, no. 2 (Spring 2014): 177–91. Reproduced with permission. The article can be found at https://uwaterloo.ca/grebel/publications/conrad-grebel-review/issues/spring-2014/towards-pedagogy-radical-love.

2 My two-thirds world, white skin privilege gave me space and options not available to all, and not available in the same way for Marcela.

3 Here, and throughout this article, I use "pedagogy" while a more accurate term would be "andragogy." Unfortunately, "andragogy" is so little known as to be problematic.

4 It's an interesting reflection on our culture that we are warned about getting "too close" but don't have similar language or directives for being "not close enough."

5 Let me be clear here. Some people learn best through lectures, some people teach best through lectures, and all the principles I am outlining can be used by lecture-based professors. There are wonderful lecture-based professors out there, but I'm not one of them! In my earliest teaching experiences, I tried to imitate the styles of

my own university professors, and failed. It was not until I returned to Canada after my experience in El Salvador that I found my own voice and style. Passionately concerned for the fate of my Salvadoran colleagues, some of whom were imprisoned and perhaps facing torture, I found myself speaking and teaching from my heart, and in the experiential ways that work best for me as a learner. I realize there are students in my classrooms who are disadvantaged by the lack of lectures, but I accept this as a limitation I have as an instructor. Fortunately, those who learn best through lectures have many fine options to choose from at the University.

6 In this I have been influenced by the work of Deborah Tannen, especially *The Argument Culture: Stopping America's War of Words* (New York: Ballantine Books, 1999), where she shows how communication in universities often does not serve us well. Debate does not necessarily lead to greater truth or depth but into entrenchment and close-mindedness.

7 Craig Kielburger, in a radio interview in the 1990s, confirmed by private correspondence with Tess Finlay, Coordinator of Public Relations and Publicity for Free the Children, September 2013. See Craig Kielburger, *Free the Children* (New York: Harper Collins, 1998).

8 Tutu's definition can be found at http://ubuntuchoirs.net/Ubuntu_spirit.php, accessed October 2012.

References

Daniel F. Chambliss and Christopher G. Takacs. 2014. *How College Works*. Cambridge, MA: Harvard Univ. Press.

Howard Gardner. 2011. *Frames of Mind: The Theory of Multiple Intelligences*, 3rd ed. New York: Basic Books.

Scott Jaschik. 2013. "Majoring in a Professor," *Inside Higher Ed*. (August 12). www.insidehighered.com/news/2013/08/12/study-finds-choice-major-most-influenced-quality-intro-professor.

Martin LutherKing, Jr., "Meet the Press" television interview, n.d., in "A Force More Powerful Part 1: Nashville—We Were Warriors" (www.aforcemorepowerful.org/films/afmp/).

George Lakey. 1987. *Powerful Peacemaking: A Strategy for a Living Revolution*. Philadelphia, PA: New Society Publishers.

George Lakey. 1990. "Training for Social Action Trainers" workshop, Philadelphia, December.

Gordon Neufeld. 2005. Public lecture, Winnipeg Art Gallery, Winnipeg, Manitoba.

Gordon Neufeld and Gabor Mate. 2006. *Hold on to Your Kids: Why Parents Need to Matter More Than Peers*. New York: Ballantine Books.

Parker J. Palmer 2007. *The Courage to Teach: Exploring the Inner Landscape of a Teacher's Life*. San Francisco, CA: Jossey-Bass.

People's Institute for Survival and Beyond. 1987. "Walk Together Children" workshop, People's Institute for Survival and Beyond, Gulfport, Mississippi, July.

Shirley Sherrod. 2010. "Open Letter: "You and I Can't Yield—Not Now, Not Ever" NAACP, available at www.naacp.org/news, accessed October 2012.

Bruce Tuckman and Mary Ann C. Jensen. 1977. "Stages of Small Group Development Revisited." www.freewebs.com/group-management/BruceTuckman%281%29.pdf, accessed October 2012.

Part IV

Pedagogies of Hope and Resistance

10 Hope and Critical Thinking

The Challenges and Opportunities of Peace Education

Randy Janzen

Hope and critical thinking should be considered complimentary and inseparable, but in some ways, they seem paradoxically to represent polarities. In conventional understanding, our goal of critical thinking is to produce learners who question, evaluate and challenge set assumptions and ideas (Mpofu and Maphalala, 2017), which would logically fit closely with the intended outcomes of Peace and Justice Studies curricula. My years of classroom experience, however, have left me with a persistent discomfort that our critical analysis of the current global realities may unintentionally result in student sentiments of hopelessness for the future. Is there a way for us as educators to instill a robust skill set for critical thinking without our students losing hope? Climate change, militarization, growing economic disparity are common (and essential) topics in introductory Peace and Justice Studies courses. Is there a risk that critical thinking tilts the balance towards understanding conflict and injustice rather than the hope-filled visions of peace with justice?

As someone who teaches introductory Peace and Justice Studies at the post-secondary level, I am aware of the multiple expectations of students who choose to enroll in these classes. Some students seek to build on idealistic notions and to nourish their hope for a better world while some students wish to focus on a deeper understanding of the complex interconnections of current meta-themes such as neoliberalism, climate change, and increasing global disparity of resources and power. Among the varied expectations, however, there appears to be one unifying desire among the students: to engage in critical thinking. This outcome, similarly endorsed by faculty and administrators as well, lacks a common definition, however, and in spite of its ubiquitous presence in course outlines, visionary statements and post-secondary discourse, our understanding remains elusive. Critical thinking is sometimes defined in terms of behavioral outcomes – a surrogate term for problem solving or high academic performance (Behar-Horenstein and Lian, 2011) although it is neither of these. There is disagreement in the literature as to whether undergraduate education even corresponds with increased ability to think critically among graduates (Behar-Horenstein and Lian, 2011). Robinson (2016) even suggests that our global education system consciously aims to impede critical thinking in order to produce graduates trained for specific tasks that require neither critical thinking nor an awareness of a global system that is sustained on grave inequalities and repressive social control.

In contrast, hope, as a pedagogical concept, is rarely manifested in concrete ways in Peace and Justice Studies, such as course outcomes or departmental planning day agendas. Hope is mostly absent even in educational mission and vision statements which raises the question of how we conceptualize hope and operationalize a pedagogy of hope in our post-secondary curricula. Bovens calls it scandalous that a philosophical theme so central to how we should live our lives has gone virtually unnoticed in our education system (1999, 667).

In this chapter, I explore my own journey of discovering the essential connection between the two concepts of critical thinking and hope, which, I argue, are both fundamentally and equally paramount in our expressed purpose of preparing informed and capable citizens to participate in positive social change. After a brief discussion on the complex relationship between the two concepts, I explore how critical thinking is connected to three conceptual views of hope (Patient Hope, Sound Hope and Absolute Hope) based on the works of Webb (2013) and Halpin (2003). Through my own reflections based on my classroom activities, I suggest that a conscious attention to the relationship between critical thinking and hope can provide opportunities to further the goals of peace education.

A logical idea would be to locate critical thinking on the opposite end of a polarity with ignorance or naivety, and to locate hope on a spectrum opposite to despair. However, in this chapter, I begin by placing the concepts of critical thinking and hope on opposing ends of a polarity. Edgoose (2009,107) argues that engaging in critical thinking can potentially displace a naïve understanding of hope, where hope is an unreasonable expectation that one's future will improve. Hope is often embedded in religious discourse such as Christian doctrine, where hope can be seen as the promise of a better existence in an afterlife, which may be seen a promise for the dispossessed to cope with conditions that are often unbearable. Hope may be viewed as a naïve perspective that shrouds our ability to think critically, while critical thinking may be viewed a catalyst to displace the unsophisticated essence of hope.

As a peace educator, I argue that although hope and critical thinking potentially represent polarities; they are simultaneously both equally important and ultimately necessary components of our pedagogy. In a paradoxical way, polarities often represent two seemingly opposing concepts where one must choose to embrace either one or the other. However, in reality, polarities are probably better described as two perspectives that cannot be considered independently – each is untenable by itself and needs to consider the other one to be sustainable (Dembour 2001, 57). Peace and justice education can be seen as a pendulum – swaying steadily and equally between mutually interdependent polarities of hope and critical analysis. Thus, I posit that at the same time, we are able to view critical thinking and hope as connected and interdependent. This brings us to the core question of this chapter: how do we teach hope while retaining a critical perspective? Or alternatively: how can we engage in critical thinking while remaining hopeful?

Peace Studies is a normative discipline – one that is values-based, not neutral, and therefore explicitly seeks to engage in dialogue, inquiry and research in order to make our world a better place. This is a lofty order, but it seems logical that both critical thinking and hope are both essential pedagogical concepts to this calling. Critical thinking in a values-based discipline is necessary but not sufficient to engender a sense of hope. Following class discussions or readings, my students have demonstrated critical thinking in comments such as "eye-opening" and "transformative". These same students often add other descriptive words such "depressing" and "hopeless". I recall many years ago at the end of a course, a student asked me how I could possibly maintain hope in light of all the material we covered in class. I recall giving a response that seemed unconvincing, and since that time I have consciously reflected on the theme of this chapter and have dedicated my energy to prioritizing both hope and critical thinking in the classroom, to engage in learning that meets multiple student interests – from the emancipatory understanding of hegemony including critical perspectives on gender, race, class and the imperative that peace requires justice, to encouraging the student who possesses a drive to enact a utopian vision of the future.

The Banality of Ignorance

For my first consideration on the balance between hope and critical thinking, I refer to the famous phrase coined by Hannah Arendt (1963): "The Banality of Evil." After observing the genocide trial of Nazi war criminal Adolf Eichmann in Jerusalem, Arendt concluded that people who commit the most heinous crimes are not necessarily evil and grotesque psychopaths. On the contrary, they often are ordinary people who in no profound way are different from regular humanity. In Eichmann's case, Arendt uses his below average intelligence and approval-seeking behaviour to explain possible causes for his engagement in heinous crimes. By dispelling the myth that perpetrators of extreme violence are essentially different from the rest of humanity, Arendt also opens a pathway to demystifying violence, thus making space for new approaches to understand violent behavior.

I believe one can apply Arendt's axiom to another banal theme: ignorance. Because many students of peace studies are passionate and strongly committed to the value of justice, sometimes their reaction to people who hold opposing views is one of harsh judgment and distancing. I recall recently being at a peace lecture, where the presenter shared a shocking story of a fundamentalist Muslim scholar who claimed that allowing women to drive cars would lead to the end of virginity! The story was shared by the lecturer to exemplify an extreme view on women's rights. Both the lecturer and the audience were aligned in a view that this perspective was, in a strong and simple term, ignorant. The response from the audience was predictable – gasps, disparaging and uncomfortable laughter and shaking of heads. Overall, the judgment of the audience was explicitly uniform (at least outwardly) – this man must be ignorant for professing such beliefs. In a sense, this cultural performance of locating a radical and ludicrous declaration with a socially distant identity (Islam) brought the lecturer and the audience closer together, united in their collective ideological distance from the radical Muslim scholar. While exposing and debunking extremist views is a necessary part of critical discourse, examining our follow-up and reactions also needs to be a component of our process of critical analysis. Ignorance, in a sense, is similar to the concept of evil, in that we may achieve personal and group benefit by distancing ourselves from the ignorant other, in order to somehow more convincingly locate ourselves and our allies in a position of "knowing." It may be appealing to delegitimize the values and actions of not only radical outliers (such as the scholar in the above story) but also those who authentically seek understanding but may lack the analysis or background to be grounded in the critical perspectives aligned with social justice. Frances Lee (2017), who identifies as a queer person of color and a social activist, describes her own fear of not feeling adequately radical enough, of being afraid that speaking publicly on any issue will be met with righteous scrutiny from those who deem to be wiser on social issues. Lee states:

> The amount of energy I spend demonstrating purity in order to stay in the good graces of the fast-moving activist community is enormous. Activists are some of the judgiest people I've ever met, myself included. There's so much wrongdoing in the world that we work to expose. And yet, grace and forgiveness are hard to come by in these circles.
>
> (2017)

I believe Lee's fear of saying the wrong thing strikes a chord with many of my students who ask questions as a means to learn and better understand issues on which they may be, for lack of a better word, ignorant. They may choose to remain silent if their novice understanding is problematized. The challenge we need to consider is how to reframe ignorance, often represented by the unchecked perspectives of students from privileged backgrounds. At the same time, if we stand in solidarity with victims of oppression, as educators, we do not want our classrooms to become battlefields where those with less power (in terms of gender, sexuality, class or race) stand to lose. Exposing all the wrongdoing in our world (and in our classrooms) requires more than just critical thinking. In reflecting on what more we need, I am drawn to Webb's concept of Patient Hope (2013, 6). Patient Hope is underpinned by the notion that we, as human beings, are on a journey and as such, acknowledges that regardless of where we may be, there is a basic trust in ourselves and others and an underlying hope in the goodness in all. While Patient Hope does not allow for passive acceptance of injustice, it is characterized by patience, humility and silence. Patience is a primary trait of this form of hope so that we are allowed to view one another without a sense of rushed urgency but rather trust that each of our journeys has the potential to bring goodness to our collective existence. It is not an uncritical acceptance of ignorance, but rather an instilled hesitance to dismiss another human being. I believe it echoes Lee's call for us all to be gentler with those who are situated within our circle of solidarity and also with those on the outside of it.

Rather than creating social distance with those lacking a critical analysis, is it possible instead to view the outsider as a potential ally or co-collaborator? To answer this question, I think of the work of Paul Born, a Canadian facilitator of community conversations, who shares poignant examples of groups who have chosen to collaborate on critical community social issues such as poverty and homelessness – groups who traditionally are distantly situated to each other in terms of social connection. Participants are encouraged to reframe their perceptions of persons they may have previously not trusted and may have thought did not have the willingness or ability to extricate themselves from their own ignorance. In Born's examples (2012), business leaders and people for whom homeless is a lived experience intentionally teach each other and also listen to stories in order to transform ignorance into what Born calls a state of "unknowing" – a genuine acknowledgement that one's professional expertise or community status can be a detriment to listening to and authentically understanding the narratives of others. This process is only possible with a critical analysis of power differences in the group, but the process infuses a philosophy of Patient Hope that participants say they did not think was possible before they engaged in dialog with the other.

The Banality of Ignorance is a call to reframe the way we view individual and cultural beliefs and values that are ill-informed. This is not to say that ignorance is not dangerous. While Eichmann's personality may have been banal, the collective actions of the Nazis were incomprehensibly violent. It is exactly because of its destructive and violent potential that ignorance must also be addressed. However, this call is to acknowledge that ignorance is more closely situated to "normal" than it is to "evil". Our critical analysis equips us with the ability to identify ignorance and to understand its danger, and by valuing it as banal, we can then demystify the perceived distance between those who hold adversarial viewpoints.

Critical thinking in peace education is necessary to understand the way in which our political leaders can construct nationalistic narratives to justify war against a common enemy and also to justify violent repression against those who rise to challenge them. Leaders can often consolidate their support from an ill-informed citizenry by constructing the ignorant (the "other" whose values clash with our own at a fundamental level) into a dangerous enemy. The legitimate economic and political grievances of a foreign opponent group can be dangerously typified by their violent acts of justice seeking. Terrorism is a politically loaded term that invariably describes groups who, at the core of their ideology, are ignorant. To construct ignorance as evil, we permit ourselves to engage in behavior that exacerbates our social distance rather than address it. Governments can use this to their advantage as a way to sell a war on terror. "People are more frightened of confronting the unpredictable and irrational randomness of the deranged mind than a tormentor who seems like someone who can be reasoned with. The epithet 'insane' carries an aura of invincibility" (Mahoney and Eguren 1997, 89).

By constructing a war on terror, we exacerbate our social distance from groups who engage in violence. This can lend support to further dehumanizing of radical groups and justify escalating violence through retaliation and revenge. Students have lamented that they feel hopeless. I believe it therefore necessary for peace educators to be aware that critical analysis can exacerbate feelings of hopelessness for students already overwhelmed with the burden of personal stressors, such as debt and pressure to get a good job in an overly competitive market. Peace education needs to consciously work to create connections between disparate values and narratives to which the populace appears ignorant

I contend that it is necessary to create a culture within our classrooms that promotes understanding of (but not agreement with) individuals and groups that we deem ill-informed – in essence, to practice Patient Hope. Our understanding may break down any "aura of invincibility" or even inevitability that may be associated with ignorance. As an example of an activity for promoting understanding, I think of a recent opportunity I had to teach conflict analysis and transformation to university students in Albania. After a number of classes, the group became more comfortable and open to a point where we explored contentious community issues such as their relationship with the Roma community in their city. Due to the entrenched power differences between the dominant Albanian culture and the Roma, it was not surprising that there were no Roma present in this university class. The homogeneous make-up of the class created an atmosphere where the students felt emboldened to discuss their fear and mistrust of the Roma. While the students were able to acknowledge their own level of power and privilege in relation to the Roma, it was nonetheless comfortable for them to slip into a narrative of having all the answers and considering the Roma community as collectively ignorant of viable solutions. To address this issue, we engaged in a simple exercise of perspective taking. Upon one student's suggestion, we used the recent high-profile situation of a young Roma man who was charged with burglary in a case that escalated tension between the two cultural groups. The class identified many possible perspectives of the community crisis and personified them in characters including the young man himself, a Roma community leader, an ethnic Albanian community leader and the victim of the crime, among others.

Through this simple simulation, it was evident in the debriefing that the students realized the solutions to this community crisis rested not only on dialog but also on accepting the idea that the Roma perspectives were an integral part of that dialog. It was also evident that a crisis can be a catalyst to addressing long-standing inequalities in new ways. The Roma were seen as people who shared similar values and opinions – not simply as ill-informed as previously believed. Critical thinking perhaps led them closer to Webb's concept of Patient Hope. Peace education, therefore, should equip students with the capacity to engage with those who have wildly opposing viewpoints, and with the tools to bring disparate groups together, whether the disparity is real or perceived. Shapiro (2016) contends that teaching our students how we as human beings can live and relate to one another is essential to infuse hope into education. Human connection across divides is nothing short of bold and daring, but necessary part of our obligations to the education of coming generations.

Another case study I utilize is from Israel, which describes two disparate communities (one Israeli Jewish, one Israeli Arab) who awkwardly come together to solve a land conflict (Babbitt, 2009). With skillful facilitation, these two groups managed to find hope, but did so without sacrificing a critical analysis of history and disparate access to power. They addressed ignorance and fear directly through compassion and problem solving. This story emphasizes small but concrete victories and also the length of time and patience required to effect change. Critical thinking is enacted by dispelling long-held and entrenched cultural narratives. Hope is manifested in the collective epiphany that all people are gifted with reason and understanding, regardless of their cultural identity.

In my class called *Introduction to Conflict Analysis and Transformation*, students are required to write a conflict analysis paper in which they need to demonstrate an authentic understanding of both perspectives of the conflict they research. For some students, this presents a great challenge, as some inadvertently or unconsciously take sides. They therefore end up writing what I call an "advocacy paper" – where a conflict is presented from one perspective. Often the student has some type of relationship with the conflict. While an advocacy paper is a worthwhile academic endeavor, it does not require the student to reflect on the perspective and views of a position with which they vehemently disagree, and which they likely view as ill-informed or ignorant. These students are often surprised when they realize their omission. Usually the result, however, is ultimately a positive one, where the students understands the difference between advocacy (albeit a legitimate and critical component of peace education) and an exploration of the narrative of a position with which they disagree. The student may gain a deep understanding of a perspective – even empathize, without having to agree with it.

Students of Peace and Justice Studies must also understand the social psychological dimensions of learning that may contribute to the inhibition of critical thinking. Our built-in biases in the ways we process information contribute to our tendencies to become ill-informed. Kelman (2007) argues that these factors negatively impact our bargaining and decision making process where critical thinking is superseded by strong sentiments on identity and the mobilization of group loyalties. Understanding these processes can also demystify our understanding of disparate interpretations not only by offering rational explanations for perceived ignorance of the other but also by making it easier for us to reflect on our own ill-informed analyses. For conflicts ranging from the interpersonal to the international, critical analysis of dangerous and ill-informed ideologies are afforded more hope when we view them as banal rather than evil.

In summary, critical thinking is necessary to identify potentially dangerous ideologies that threaten our goal to build cultures of peace. Hope, however, can come through our emancipation from viewing ignorance as impenetrable and somehow foreign to our own ideas. Peace education should assist students in demystifying ill-informed beliefs and values so that they can be better equipped to co-create just and peaceful futures.

Critical Analysis of the Present, Hope for the Future

In 1979, a populist and well-organized nonviolent campaign managed to oust the unpopular and brutal regime of Shah Reza Pahlavi of Iran. The Iranian Revolution is a story of contagious optimism, collective nonviolent action, and ultimately of dashed hopes. Well-organized nonviolent strategies such as protests, strikes, and noncooperation achieved the removal of a despot in less than one year, and succeeded where assassinations and guerrilla warfare failed (Chenoweth and Stephan 2011), making the Iranian Revolution a showpiece of the potential power of nonviolent action.

This story of Iranian nonviolent activists could easily be a mainstay of Peace and Justice Studies discourse – a story that offers hope to fledgling peace activists who want to learn the theory and practice of nonviolence. However, the story takes a turn for the worse very shortly after the triumphant nonviolent victory, disqualifying it from the annals of best practices for Peace and Justice Studies. The long-term aftermath of the 1979 nonviolent revolution is far more familiar to our students than the short-lived but memorable nonviolent movement that preceded it. By all accounts, Iran's nonviolent revolution did not bring longstanding peace, harmony and social justice to its people. Even after taking into account the unrelenting Western biased rhetoric against the current regime, it is impossible to ignore the human rights abuses committed by it. What went wrong? Needless to say, the history is complex, but Chenoweth and Stephan explain the failure to build a culture of peace with the following summary: while nonviolent opposition forces managed to consolidate a wide range of divergent groups around the need to depose the dictator, they failed to unify around a shared vision of what post-Shah Iran would look like. The collective perspective of what was wrong with the old system did not evolve into a common and shared vision or blueprint to guide the new one.

I use this historical case study to reflect on another relationship between hope and critical thinking, and how we can learn from it to better integrate these concepts in peace education. Webb (2013) describes a specific form of hope that focusses action towards a concrete and specific endpoint. Webb calls this Sound Hope – a future-oriented aspiration on which we can strategize and organize in order to attain it. Sound Hope, I believe, fits easily into the framework of Peace and Justice Studies by encouraging us to operationalize our visions of what peace with justice would look like in our families, our communities and in our world. An integral component of Peace and Justice Studies is examining the current and pervasive themes of injustice such as poverty, racism, militarization of foreign policy and growing economic disparity. It seems relatively easy to rally students around and develop plans of action on issues that unite us in our anger, frustration and fear. As Kelman (2007) states, it is easier to campaign against something than to implement a collective community vision. However, like the Iranian Revolution exemplifies, rallying around a narrative centred on what is wrong with our world brings us only halfway to our goal. What Peace and Justice Studies students need is to additionally learn skills to operationalize peace with justice and to consider a more explicit relationship with Sound Hope.

In order to engage students in discussions on Sound Hope, I believe we need to define cultures of peace in ways that students can understand and relate to. We need to transform a broad and nebulous concept into a meaningful and even measurable definition of what we mean when we think of hope. In our Peace and Justice Studies classes, we do this by breaking down the concrete components of the United Nations definition of a culture of peace (United Nations 1999) which include the goals of gender equality, universal access to education and healthcare and demilitarization, among others. By comparing these ideals with current realities, we are also able to describe what a culture of violence looks like. Using this as a starting point, we move through a range of themes to bridge both critical thinking and concrete goals and aspirations that are achievable. One example we focus on is international development or humanitarian aid – a topic that most students connect with and an activity many have already participated in through school-based short-term "voluntourism". We begin by deconstructing these familiar experiences of humanitarianism and link them to concepts of charity versus social justice. At midpoint, the students often feel a sense of despair and cynicism due to the longstanding harm created by many forms of foreign aid. At endpoint, they feel cautiously hopeful, no longer at the point of abandoning their aspirations to engage in humanitarian work; instead they are emboldened with new tools to critically evaluate potential opportunities and have a clear idea on what a socially just humanitarian opportunity would look like.

Similarly, we examine the media with the same process. The students arrive already with a healthy skepticism of conventional media but tend not to possess a Sound Hope of what might be. As a final assignment, students write a paper to discuss how a specific aspect of culture can be used for creating cultures of peace or conversely further entrenching cultures of violence. For example, some students have chosen to explore organized sport, art, popular music or the construction of gender roles. By taking a broad concept and applying it to an area of their own communities, the students can understand peace not only in a way they can measure or describe concretely, but also understand peace as a process or a set of actions in which they are able to participate (and probably already do). The elusive and abstract concepts of peace (and the opposing ideas of injustice and violence) can now be tangibly seen all around them.

Engagement in visioning for world peace is not a process that comes naturally. It is far easier to collectively rally against highly visible atrocities carried out by groups of others. Likewise, it is not intuitive to determine whether one should pick up a protest sign or engage in dialogue. That is why I find it important to teach students simple yet effective frameworks, utilizing variables such as power, level of awareness, and stage of conflict to choose the most effective strategy (Lederach 1995; Schirch, 2004). Activism, advocacy, mediation, nonviolent action, reconciliation – these are highly skilled practices that need to be timed and operationalized with due care. They all can work toward the common goal of creating a culture of peace. It is important for students to learn this, as they may be challenged to reconcile how strikes, sit-ins, protests and other forms of nonviolent action (that may escalate conflict in the short term) actually work towards the goal of peace and justice. Equally, such frameworks offer the novice or future activist the opportunity to see bold defiance and civil disobedience as part of a large framework of peacebuilding. In our class, we aspire to a model of nonviolent action that coordinates with a conflict transformation vision where one's hope is that the victory afforded through well-planned nonviolent campaigns can, in the longer term, include the shifting to relationship building and reconciliation.

The case study of the Iranian Revolution also raises the concept of prefigurative politics, where social justice campaigns implement anti-violent practices and strategies within the movement itself. Many nonviolent movements, such as Occupy and other alterglobalization movements have explicitly engendered anti-authoritarian and anti-hierarchical practices as an integral strategy in order to enact social change. Many movements have incorporated these processes in spite of diverse backgrounds and values of their adherents (Maeckelbergh 2011, 2), and thus offer a contrast to Chenoweth and Stephan's interpretation of the Iranian Revolution. Additionally, if we wish, we can push the concept of prefiguration even farther with a critical analysis of our own classroom environments. What would it look like if we practiced radical justice in our own classrooms as a strategy to achieve

Sound Hope? I believe we have a long way to go to challenge the hierarchical and authoritarian structures and punitive disciplinary policies that are present in our colleges and universities and thus, our peace education pedagogies must pay more attention to the challenges and opportunities for critical thinking and hope that are right in front of us.

In Peace and Justice Studies, we engage our students in a dialogue that includes an analysis of the main social issues of our time, but by moving beyond the discourse of what is wrong and developing a vision with strategy of culture of peace, we can avoid future outcomes similar to that of the Iranian Revolution, and actually see our anger, frustration and fear channeled through a vision to create cultures of peace.

Critical Thinking, Cognitive Dissonance and Hope

The motives for enrolling in an introductory Peace and Justice Studies course are undoubtedly varied, but as an educator, I am intrigued by the seemingly unified reasons given by the students during our Week One discussions. Pragmatic reasons (looking for a class with easy marking and one that fits into work schedules!) aside, the students agree on two broad reasons for studying peace and justice: to have a better analysis of regional and global current events, and to use that analysis to help build a better future. It strikes me how these two reasons correspond with the concepts of critical thinking (analysis of current events) and hope (building a better future). Students often add that they no longer trust conventional news sources and thus seek more appropriate tools to understand the global socio-political events though a critical lens. Students also often add that they want to be positive change agents, as the future of the world often seems overwhelmingly hopeless. I suggest that these students are motivated, in part, by an underlying sense that despite their concerns, hope still exists in their consciousness – a hope which I suggest broadly corresponds to what Halpin (2003) describes as Absolute Hope: an openness of spirit with respect for the future and an anticipation of something better that is not yet occurring.

Through my experience and a peace educator, I have come to realize that an effective teaching strategy to promote a pedagogy of hope is to present the class with an inspiring story (best narrated in the first person) of someone who overcomes overwhelming adversity (in the form of violence and injustice) through a powerful nonviolent campaign. A story I have come to use regularly is that of Leymah Gbowee, the Nobel Peace Prize Laureate and leader of the nonviolent women's movement to oust Liberian dictator Charles Taylor. The students are predictably profoundly impacted by Gbowee's story of hope. As a Peace and Justice Studies class, we might stop there and ride high on the crest of hope and inspiration, but we would run the risk of fulfilling only half of our mandate to infuse hope with critical thinking. Focussing only on the inspiring stories of frontline peacemakers also has the potential drawback of allowing students to cope with their existential pain with powerful narratives that are reduced to simplistic stories of heroism, and that reinforce the powerful cultural message that justice and righteousness will always prevail. Pushing this further, these films may afford students the opportunity to identify with oppression and struggle in a way that alleviates their guilt from growing awareness of their own privilege.

In my class, my goal is to not allow the students to remain in the safe but unscrutinised state of hopefulness for too long. Rather, my attempt is to connect this hope to the pragmatic and rational realm of empirical research on nonviolent action. By locating Gbowee's experience into the context of social research, we pose the question, what can we extrapolate from one single case study? The answer: not much. I remind them that one could still reasonably conclude that the women of Liberia somehow got lucky or that their techniques would not work in other circumstances. A sample size of one is not sufficient to conclude that nonviolence is strategically superior. We then review Chenoweth and Stephan's (2011) research comparing the outcomes of more than 300 campaigns (spanning approximately the past century) that sought to overthrow unjust political regimes. Their comprehensive study reveals that nonviolent campaigns are more than twice as likely to achieve success when compared to violent ones and are significantly more likely to lead to longer term gains, as measured by sustained democracy and absence of further outbreaks of civil war. The students can then see that the hope-filled story from Liberia corroborates with the empirical evidence, thus propelling their hope forward to include a critical analysis of the empirical evidence on the effectiveness of nonviolent action.

This, however, raises my concern that Peace and Justice Studies students comprise a rather homogeneous group of learners – one that has already embraced the ideals of nonviolence prior to even enrolling in the class. Thus my attempts to expose them to opposing viewpoints such as Ginsberg's (2013) treatise on the value of violence may be futile. Maybe their apparent acceptance that nonviolent action is supported by empirical evidence is not the outcome of rigorous critical thinking exercises in class, but rather an example of a noncritical reinforcement of pre-existing values. Or, perhaps just as likely, because they have been socialized to passively accept information provided by their teachers who are constructed as wise and knowledgeable. I add this because my experience with more seasoned activists is that many are reluctant to accept the empirical evidence of the effectiveness of nonviolent action, even in spite of being the practitioners of it. For example, in one instance I was a presenter at a workshop on nonviolent action, where I offered the participants (who already believed that nonviolent action was morally superior to violence) encouragement that their principled actions were also strategic and effective, as demonstrated by Chenoweth and Stephan's research. Overall, the evidence provided reassurance and hope, but among several attendees, including one of the co-facilitators, there was a refusal to accept that nonviolence was an effective strategy.

In my classroom, therefore, I further challenge my students through an exercise of cognitive dissonance. I present them with a series of questions, which they answer anonymously via electronic clickers that create an aggregate picture of the class's responses on a screen. The questions delve into the commonly held belief that the world is increasingly becoming more violent. We review their answers by comparing them to various trend data that challenge this thesis. I am aware that the argument that we are living in the most peaceful time in human history, popularized by Stephen Pinker (2011) but examined more rigorously by the Human Security Report from Simon Fraser University (2013), is a deeply contentious one among academics and researchers. But for this exercise, this controversy is beneficial because after I present the argument, I encourage the students throughout the course to formulate their own opinion, by conducting their own research. In summary, my purpose is to encourage critical thinking through cognitive dissonance and then invite them to question, evaluate and challenge their own set assumptions and ideas. In a complementary discussion, examining the thesis that the world is becoming more peaceful opens up a parallel conversation on hope, which brings us back to Halpin's concept of Absolute Hope and the impetus to acknowledge and celebrate the generations of peacemakers that have preceded us. Heroes like Martin Luther King, Jr., and Gandhi need to be commemorated along with the countless unknown human rights and justice defenders throughout time whose Absolute Hope inspired them in their tireless dedication to create "something that is not yet." Perhaps one can say that our generation is experiencing that "something" that our forbearers fought for. Celebrating past victories for peace and justice is not a call to be complacent in our privileged and peaceful bubbles, but rather an exhilarating call to follow the lead of those courageous activists who created our world, to continue to struggle for those who do not yet enjoy peace with justice.

Conclusion

In the midst of writing this chapter, I had the opportunity to travel to South Sudan, a country mired in a civil war resulting in millions of internally displaced persons and a nation on the brink of widespread famine. I was there to learn more about unarmed civilian peacekeeping and I interviewed a number of staff of an organization who were a mixture of locals (South Sudanese) and internationals (from all over the world). While listening to their stories of how they viewed their work, I was struck by the noticeable differences between the reflections of the South Sudanese and the internationals. In broad terms, local staff reflections were packed with steadfast hope whereas many international staff tended to be caught up in worries of self-doubt and existential despair, wondering whether any of the work they were doing would ever make any difference. For the internationals, hope seemed so elusive. I personally could relate to the sentiments of doubt expressed by the internationals, and at the same time, was mesmerized and inspired by the unflinching hope of the South Sudanese. When I asked several of South Sudanese staff how they could remain so hopeful in such a desperate situation, they replied that there was really no other alternative. The reality of their country left them no choice but to hope for something that "was not yet".

As I reflect on their responses, I think of the pendulum swinging between the two polarities constructed in this chapter: hope and critical thinking. I become more resolved in my thinking that both are important and in complex ways, inseparable and interdependent. In this chapter, I give pragmatic consideration to how to encourage my students to nurture both their sense of hope and their skill of critical thinking, and consider Webb's concepts of Patient Hope and Sound Hope and Halpin's concept of Absolute Hope.

I often reflect on the question from the former student who wondered how I could retain hope in the midst of such an uncertain future. The question set me on a reflective journey in which I am still engaged. I think I would be much better prepared now to convey to her that hope and critical thinking cannot be considered separately, and that our critical analysis of "what was" and "what is" draws us naturally to hope for "what is not yet".

References

Arendt, Hannah. 1963. *Eichmann in Jerusalem: A Report on the Banality of Evil*. New York: Viking Press.

Babbitt, Eileen. 2009. "Combining Empathy with Problem Solving: The Tamra Model of Facilitation in Israel." In *Building Peace*, edited by Craig Zelizer & Robert Rubinstein, 157–178. Sterling, VA: Kumarian Press.

Behar-Horenstein, Linda and Niu Lian. 2011. "Teaching Critical Thinking Skills in Higher Education: A Review of the Literature." *Journal of College Teaching and Learning* 8, no. 2: 25–42.

Born, Paul. 2012. *Community Conversations*. Toronto, Canada: BPS Books.

Bovens, Luc. 1999. "The Value of Hope." *Philosophy and Phenomenological Research*, 59, no. 3: 667–681.

Chenoweth, Erica and Maria Stephan. 2011. *Why Civil Resistance Works: The Strategic Logic of Nonviolence*. New York: Columbia University Press.

Dembour, Marie-Benedicte. 2001. "Following the Movement of a Pendulum: Between Universalism and Relativism." In *Culture and Rights: Anthropological Perspectives*, edited by Jane Cowan, Marie-Benedicte Dembour, & Richard Wilson, 56–69. Cambridge, UK: Cambridge University Press.

Edgoose, Julian. 2009. "Radical Hope and Teaching: Learning Political Agency from the Politically Disenfranchised." *Educational Theory*, 59, no. 1: 105–121.

Ginsberg, Benjamin. 2013. *The Value of Violence*. Amherst, NY: Prometheus Books.

Halpin, David. 2003. *Hope and Education: The Role of the Utopian Imagination*. London: Routledge.

Human Security Report. 2013. *The Decline in Global Violence: Evidence, Explanation and Contestation*. Vancouver, Canada: Simon Fraser University.

Kelman, Herbert. 2007. "Social Psychological Dimensions of International Conflict." In *Peacemaking in International Conflict: Methods and Techniques*, edited by William Zartman, 61–102. Washington, DC: United States Institute of Peace.

Lederach, John-Paul. 1995. *Preparing for Peace: Conflict Transformation across Cultures*. Syracuse, NY: Syracuse University Books.

Lee, Frances. 2017. Excommunicate me from the Church of Social Justice. Posted July 13, 2017. Retrieved from: www.autostraddle.com/kin-aesthetics-excommunicate-me-from-the-church-of-social-justice-386640/

Maeckelbergh, Marianne. 2011. "Doing is Believing: Prefiguration as Strategic Practice in the Alterglobalization Movement." *Social Movement Studies*, 10, no. 1: 1–20.

Mahoney, Liam and Luis Eguren. 1997. *Unarmed Bodyguards: International Accompaniment for the Protection of Human Rights*. West Hartford, CT: Kumerian Press.

Mpofu, Nhlanhla and Mncedisi Maphalala. 2017. "Fostering critical thinking in initial teacher education curriculums: a comprehensive literature review." *Gender and Behavior*: 9256–9266.

Pinker, Stephen. 2011. *The Better Angels of our Nature: Why Violence Has Declined*. New York: Penguin Group.

Robinson, William. 2016. "Global Capitalism and the Restructuring of Education: The Transnational Capitalist Class' Quest to Suppress Critical Thinking." *Social Justice*, 43, no. 3: 1–24.

Schirch, Lisa. 2004. *The Strategic Book of Peacebuilding*. Intercourse, PA: Good Books.

Shapiro, Svi. 2016. "Educating for Hope and Possibility in Troubled Times." *Tikkun Magazine*, 31, no. 4 (Fall): 37–45.

United Nations. 1999. Declaration of a Culture of Peace. Resolution 53/243/A.

Webb, Darren. 2013. "Pedagogies of Hope". *Studies in Philosophy and Education*, 32: 397–414.

11 The Peace Professor

Decolonial, Feminist, and Queer Futurities

Sara Shroff

> Coming to know the past has been part of the critical pedagogy of decolonization. To hold alternative histories is to hold alternative knowledges. The pedagogical implications of the access to alternative knowledges is that they can form the new basis of doing things.
>
> (Tuhiwai-Smith 1999, 34)

In August 2015, I walked into a US university classroom in downtown New York City, around the corner from Wall Street, to teach my first-ever college course. Here, I would spend the next several years teaching an undergraduate introductory course in Peace and Justice Studies (PJS), a discipline I have come to appreciate and hold accountable. As class commenced, students trickled in, stylized in an array of New York fashion, searching for a seat in a classroom organized in rows. Obama was the U.S. President. The United Nations and the U.S. was signing yet another climate and trade treaty - the Paris Accord and the Trans-Pacific Partnership; the European "refugee crisis" was splattered on the front pages of newspapers, recounting how 800 migrants from Mali, Gambia, Senegal, Sierra Leone, Eritrea, Somalia, Bangladesh and Ivory Coast were left to drown in their unsuccessful attempts to cross from Turkey to Greece. Elsewhere, several countries had legalized same-sex marriage while others passed transgender laws; Canadian Prime Minister Justin Trudeau had promised that his cabinet would embody gender equality (i.e. 50% would be women); Cuba and US opened their respective embassies signalling an end to socialism and communism and a triumph of capitalist democracies, and the #BlackLivesMatter movement gained prominence as the modern day civil rights movement voicing loud protests over police brutality, state-sanctioned violence, and the deathly impacts of racial capitalism. Against this crisscrossing and deeply uneven transnational backdrop, we gathered to learn peace.

We opened our class, as we would every semester thereafter, with some questions: What is peace? To whom does it belong? Who enforces it? Who enjoys it? What is our role as scholars and students of peace? My engagement with these questions, and thus the narrative I share today, is part biographical, part pedagogical, where both inform each other. As such, this reflection is both an account of our classroom experiences as well as a vision into the polemics and possibilities on how to (un)/learn/study/teach peace. In sharing my experience, I hope to offer a wayward, feminist, queer and decolonial way of teaching *an/other* peace. My point of departure is the field of PJS itself, especially how it defines and deploys notions and dimensions of peace. While, PJS does not "own" the concept of peace it has contributed to our dominant understanding and framing of peace today. I begin with my working definition of decolonial, feminist and queer pedagogies and move into a discussion of three aspects of this pedagogical praxis: (1) spheres of knowledges (2) situated subjectivities and (3) speculative practice.

A decolonial, feminist and queer pedagogical practice is an open invitation to collectively unlearn and relearn knowledges, not simply as a method of instruction and indoctrination, but rather to practice a kind of pedagogy that moves towards collective justice, laboriously and lovingly. I draw, here, from what Linda Tuhiwai-Smith calls *alternative knowledges,* which question the roots of our thinking and truths. To teach *alternative knowledges* of peace means to teach the ongoing histories, truths and formations of violence (read: white supremacy, racial capitalism, settler/colonialism, orientalism, heteropatriarchy, heteronormativity and ableism) that has shaped that which comes to be seen as peace. Alongside the naming of cruelties and crimes perpetuated in the name of peace, *alternative knowledges* underscores how we have come to accept violence as peace-making par excellence. Centering *alternative knowledges* in the PJS classroom implies a defiant and disobedient way of teaching that is about re/building the classroom into what bell hooks might call a *location of possibility* (hooks 1994), where we communally toil and tackle with/for and beyond peace, non/violence and justice to new futures and futurities.

Spheres of Knowledges

> So what does peace mean in this savage, corporatized, militarized world? What does peace mean to the poor who are being actively robbed of their resources and for whom everyday life is a grim battle for water, shelter, survival and, above all, some semblance of dignity? For them, peace is war.
>
> (Roy 2004)

Defining peace is a sobering exercise. The charge of selecting readings and assembling a syllabus meant I had to be critically conscious of my own politics of peace, non/violence and justice. It became clearer to me that my definition of peace and, more broadly, my practice of peace grounds my pedagogy. In this section, I lay out the contours of what I call *an/other peace.* My understanding of peace builds on the extraordinary archives of critical race, decolonial, intersectional feminist, postcolonial, queer and transgender studies scholarship. *An/other* peace is my articulation of the *subaltern* (Spivak 1988; 1999, Santos 2002, Salah 2014), the *"other"* (Said

1978, Bhabha 1994, Hall 1996), the *wretched* (Fanon 1963), the *mestiza/border figures* (Moraga and Anzaldúa 1981, Anzaldúa 1987), and the *undercommons* (Moten and Harney 2013). These are the diverse and dispossessed communities that continue to be marked by disposability, death and debt, in the pursuit of peace. Gayatri Spivak (1988) calls the systemic subjugating and silencing of their knowledges within dominant frames of what constitutes "real" knowledge, *epistemic violence*. By destroying "other" knowledges, "other" lives too become forgettable, disposable and irrelevant. In extending our registers of violence, Judith Butler (2009) argues that "if certain lives do not qualify as lives within certain [current] epistemological frames then these lives are never lived nor lost in the full sense" (1). Drawing our attention to production and politics of knowledge, Spivak and Butler compel a reimagining and reframing of violence as the key site though which peace comes to be enacted on the other. Thus, by insisting on *alternative knowledges*, I locate my pedagogical practice as *epistemic disobedience* (Mignolo 2009). Epistemic disobedience demands, that if knowledge is an instrument of imperial/settler colonization, one of the urgent tasks ahead is the decolonization of knowledge (De Lissovoy 2010, Tuck and Yang 2012).

Critical theorists, such as Butler, Mignolo, Spivak and Smith, put forward the crucial and critical questions that humble and haunt me as a professor of PJS. *Epistemic disobedience* is a commitment to question the supremacy, saliency and stability of PJS. It calls out the falsehood of goodness, civility, justice, and non-violence. It commands a recognition that PJS has been shaped by knowledges emerging out of the global north and despite its efforts to abolish "warism," the academic discipline has silenced, or failed to hear, colonized subjects/subjectivities (Azarmandi 2017).

Peace, as Arundhati Roy argues in the quote above, is in fact war. Yet, the formulation of peace as "peaceful" continues to be a central query for philosophers and practitioners of peace. Thus, I offer some theorizations of peace that have been invaluable to me in conceptualizing *an/other* peace. Frantz Fanon's (1963) theorizations of "peaceful violence"[1] are my entry point for several reasons. First, the circulation of his theories coincided with the development of PJS into a discipline; two, Fanon situates peace and violence as intersecting and interlocking "racialized" phenomena; and third, both colonialism and the process of de/colonization are central to his theorizations of peace and violence.

Fanon's theorization of peace as "peaceful violence" captures Roy's statement some fifty years later of "peace as war," whereby peace can be read as the standard for violence. Keeping Fanon's work on peace/violence as my point of departure cracks open the hypocrisies of peace, as a course of study, as nation-state practice and international policy-making: *peace as violence* and *violence as peace*. Peace, then, can be understood as the regulation and normalization of violence through the workings of *negative* (absence of direct violence) and *positive* (absence of structural violence) peace.

The work of Johan Galtung (1969; 1971; 1990; 1996), one founder of PJS, is important to note here. Galtung writes that *positive peace* is the presence of social justice and the absence of structural violence and n*egative peace* is the absence of physical and personal violence. By locating negative peace as a standalone and separate encounter even theoretically detachable from systems and structures of structural violence, he individualizes peace as something that is accessible and attainable to all equally. Galtung further theorizes violence as a triad of direct/personal, structural/systemic and cultural/symbolic. This triad of violence is helpful because it starts to provide an analytics of violence that is interconnected yet still hierarchical and restrictive. While he does reference race, gender, and colonialism in his theorizations of structural violence, he fails to recognize the structural logics of racism, sexism and colonialism that re/produces, legitimizes, and naturalizes violence and peace.

The binary breakdown of peace into an absence of personal justice (negative peace) on one hand and an amassing of collective justice (positive peace) necessitates an intersectional and decolonial analysis. The individuation of peace becomes complicit in white logics that then whiten peace and racialize violence. In his well-known Birmingham prison letter, Martin Luther King (1963) argues that *positive peace* is the presence of justice. Negative peace, conversely, is measured by the standard of moderate whiteness. King called out white moderates and white liberals who comply with the racist *law and order* structures that only afford peace to the few. I would say that negative peace is not peace at all, but rather the standard for violence, bringing me back to Fanon's theorization of peace as *peaceful violence*. It is peaceful, only insofar as it reducible and reclaimable as whiteness. *Whiteness as peace; peace as whiteness.*

Like race, gender and sexuality is also central to my understanding of war and peace. Feminist scholars in peace and justice studies have provided various important disciplinary disruptions since the 1980s; however, still through the lens of naturalizing and universalizing western (white) feminism (de Seve 1987). The two main broad feminist frames were "women as mothers" and "women as equal to men" which still reinforce sexism and militarism (Burguieres 1990). This garnered criticism among various feminist scholars that challenged "woman" as a prefixed/peaceful category of analysis, femininity as morally and naturally superior to masculinity, and women as ideal peacemakers (Boulding 1984; 1995, Rennie 1991, Reardon 1993, Caprioli 2000). However, recent interventions are beginning to call for an intersectional feminist and queer re-reading of PJS (Moolakkattu 2006, Confortini 2006, Mizzi and Bryne 2015). These interventions challenge the category of "women," particularly third world women, as passive victims and peace agents; gender as biological sex and, heteronormativity as natural. In other words, the process of categorizing and cataloguing people into binary systems (read: woman/man, masculinity/femininity; heterosexual/homosexual; victim/perpetrator) leaves the structural violence of heteropatriarchy and heteronormativity intact. In this way, race, as well as gender and sexuality, are fundamental features of peaceful violence.

Peace, then, is a site of coloniality (Azarmandi 2017). Peace, too, is entangled with whiteness, and its accompanying supremacies of ableism, anti-blackness, and heteropatriarchy. This is how I have come to know peace. If we take these critiques seriously alongside the work of decolonial feminists (Wynter 2003, Lugones 2008), we further our analysis in several ways. First, we recognize how only certain humans (read: white, middle-class, heterosexual male, able-bodied) are afforded the status of complete humans. While the other/ed (read: people of color, women, queers, disabled and poor) are seen as unfit and unworthy of peace, dignity, humanity and justice. Second, the current conceptions of peace bifurcate human/non-humans and human/nature thus creating a colonial ordering of race, gender, class and sexuality alongside the artificial hierarchy of human and non-humans (e.g. animals, land, environment, earth, ecosystem). I explain further.

The definition of the "human" remains an unstable and insecure concept in PJS. Historic and current anti-capitalist, civil rights, decolonial, indigenous, and feminist/queer rights movements, on which so much of PJS relies, question our conventional understanding of human/non-humans. One could argue, that "human" and "nature" in this reading of humanity is historically defined within a peace paradigm per se; however, this paradigm is one of expulsion (read: settler colonialism), exclusion (read: colonialism), extinction (read: genocide) as well as "economic" empowerment (read: capitalist progress).

Mahdis Azarmandi (2017) argues that peace scholars tend to advocate a "paradigm shift" in PJS without critical reflection on what it is we need shifting from and towards. The emphasis on universal rights and human progress, she argues fails to account for the hierarchies of difference that coloniality produced and continues to structure and sustain. Thus, we must be cautious that such shifting is not reliant on chronological, colonial, linear and human-centric logics.

PJS, if seen through the lens of *an/other* peace, can be a space for trans-disciplinary resistance and restoration, where human and nature are not separate realms. This means to call out the color of peace as "white" (Haunani Kay 2004) and "peaceful violence" as embedded in, what Andrea Smith has called, the three pillars of white supremacy (colonialism/genocide; slavery/capitalism and orientalism/war) (Smith 2006). Thus, as a professor of peace I am tasked with un/teaching a disciplinary dismissal of certain lands and lives as unworthy of peace.

If only a select few original "humans" can enjoy a world without war and reap the benefits of structural violence, then peace for them comes at the expense of violence directed at others. This places people of color, women, queers, disabled and the poor who work towards what King named positive peace, as "violent" disruptors of and to "peaceful violence". This leaves little room to think about violence through any other logic or formations. Thus I ask, are there other ways to imagine violence as sites of agency? Can violence be retooled to dismantle "peace?" Understanding violence this way, opens up the category of violence as pervasive and permeating but also as a site for disobedience, transformative justice and collective rehabilitation.

By positing peace as the absence of violence and violence as the absence of peace, we limit our frames for understanding how violence is mandated, measured and maintained. Violence is not an independent act/action but rather entangled in structures and systems of violence. In this way, violence as mandated by structures is so deeply sedimented that it remains invisible, unseen and unexceptional. I provide three examples for clarification.

Sexual assault is a dehumanizing act of gendered and sexualized violence (violence or coercive removal of gendered integrity). Despite this, sexual violence against feminine gendered subjects is often naturalized through hetero-masculinity (e.g. boys will be boys) and rationalized through hetero-femininity (e.g. she was asking for it). The recent #metoo movement demonstrates how common sexual violence, ranging from harassment to rape, is in the US and yet the punishment for most men are at best, mild at worst, inconsequential. Second, we can look closely at police brutality in the US, which is seen as an unfortunate yet necessary aspect of law and order. But the dynamic of who shoots (predominantly white officers) and who gets shot (predominantly men and women of color) is one that emerges out of a racist history that can be traced from slavery to Jim Crow to the prison industrial complex and the deep-seated logics that equate blackness with criminality. In order to avoid a systematic approach, the emerging rationalization for both sexual violence and police shooting rely on the narrative of the bad apple. Theorizing perpetrators of violence as "bad" apples that need disciplining and imprisonment, usually through more direct violence, and victims of violence as "weak" that need saving and protected, also usually through more direct violence, ignores how gendered, racialized and sexualized violence of sexual assault (heteropatriarchy) and police brutality (law and order) are embedded conditions of peaceful violence.

For one final example, we can look at war as the presence of direct violence (absence of negative peace), which usually impacts the most vulnerable communities, even if/when it claims to "save" them. The "war system" (Reardon 1996, Webel and Galtung 2007), as peace scholars have argued, relies on militarization, globalization, and contemporary regimes of global capital and cheap labor. If we reframe our understanding of violence as Butler suggests we see how only certain lives enjoy the privilege of peace through the systems of war. In this way, "other" lives and *an/other* peace become defiant and disposable and already and always violent. To be entitled to "modern" peace means to be powered by particular practices, productions and progressions of violence. The examples start to crack open how peace and violence are not detachable and deducible but rather coalesce in distinct and disparate ways, often with deadly consequences.

To teach *an/other* peace means to disassemble the false binaries in PJS – peace/violence, violence/non-violence, and perpetrator/victim. I suggest, in order to get at the complexities I have raised, we locate each of these vectors as interconnected assemblages and intersections that influence and inform each other. For example, theorizing peace and violence this way, not as an absence of the other but rather an entanglement and explanation of the other, we start to see them as interlocking phenomena of power. If PJS claims to go beyond normative and natural solutions to crisis and conflict, and if I, as a professor of peace, am claiming to *teach* peace, then it requires us/I to re/think histories of peace alongside and in congruence with histories and contemporaneities of violence.

My proposal here is to place peace and violence as insecure and instable locations of possibility. To me, the pedagogies of the *an/other* peace means to teach the process of peace and violence as coequals by creating a space to examine the "underbelly" of peace. This means to question what has come to be seen as legitimate, legal, and liberal. This also means to challenge what has come to be intelligible and identifiable as permissible promises of "peaceful violence". This makes room for versions of peace that for so long have been seen as deviant and disobedient often relegated to the realm of illegitimate, illegal, and illiberal forms. To study the underbelly of peace means to study the lethal and limiting fixtures of peace that fasten and discipline, rather than collectively commit us to truth.

Given the philosophical grounding and analytical refusals of this course of study, the root of peace is in fact violence, rather than benevolent and benign peace. To work towards peace means to continually engage decolonial, queer and feminist critiques of power as it renews, regulates and restructures as violence put forward by contemporary scholars (Fanton 2012, Salter 2013, Sjoberg 2014, Hagen 2016, Azarmandi 2017).

To destabilize disciplinary power within PJS means to confront what Lewis Gordon calls *disciplinary decadence* (2006, 8).[2] Thus, if peace scholars like myself proclaim to be teaching peace, then asserting a singular definition of the peace and violence is not only irresponsible, but also colonialist, racist and sexist. Adopting trans-disciplinary and anti-disciplinary methods allows us to position PJS, not simply as an intellectual project that asserts one way of learning peace but challenges us to think, do and know peace *an/other* way. It means to grasp peace as always and already present and persisting if we listen to voices and visions that have been violently invisibilized in the very search for white/western peace.

Situated Subjectivities

As feminist and queer scholarship have shown us, we come to PJS differently and disparately as *situated subjects* with fractured and fragmented subjectivities (Smith 1974, Haraway 1988, Collins 1990). By this I mean that our identities and experiences inside and outside the classroom clarify and codify our mis/understandings of peace and violence. The PJS classroom is enormously fraught with power and promise. This forces me to reflect and risk my power as the peace professor while I stay vigilant to who and where I teach. Thinking through power dynamics (social and spatial) recognizes the classroom as a microcosm of uneven and unjust power relations (Freire 1972; 1985). To construct a space with my students as co-conspirators and fellow intellectuals means to really think through several questions – who are my students? who am I as a professor? how will we engage each other? what is our relationship to the university? These questions inform this section.

Who we are and where we are informs and influences our entry points, emotions, expressions, embodiments, employments and enjoyments into systems of power and knowledge production. My classes included a range of traditional undergraduate students, some freshmen, some seniors and others in-between and across disciplines.[3] My students were studying to become activists, actors, doctors, educators, community organizers, filmmakers, finance-executives, humanitarians, and social workers. The classroom also embodied a fusion of intersectional identities across able-privilege, citizenship status, class, gender, nationality, racial, sexual, national belonging, and religious affiliations.

As a practitioner and a pedagogue, I see "peace-making" in/as many of its (false) promises – as a corporatized social enterprise, as a foreign aid (militarized) intervention, as a humanitarian exercise as well as a philanthropic endeavor. As a messy and naively whitened practice, it was usually driven by "good intentions" – intentions that were guided by an objective, neutral and universal conceptualization of peace and justice. As a feminist, queer theorist of color, I examine PJS within the university's racist and settler/colonial violent beginnings. Furthermore, as an adjunct thus contingent and precariously positioned scholar-student, the corporatization of the university becomes important to think together with my students in terms of how we all are implicated in the profiteering, production and promotion of certain forms of "real" knowledge and ideal forms of "violent" peace.

Having worked in the business of peace and justice globally for over eighteen years[4] I was processing as much as I would be professing. My goal as a professor was thus inescapable to the power dynamics of the conventional student-teacher relationship. To collectively examine peace means to call out my power and check my own authority as a "peace expert" and my students as "peace understudies". To decenter the binary relationality of student-teacher meant to challenge my authority as the professor and their depreciation as learners/students while also being mindful of my own positionality in the university as a feminist, queer woman of color professor. I alone did not have the authority to profess and proclaim knowledge while the knowledge I was offering was already *an/other* knowledge. For my students initially, I was their professor and my role was to profess peace. At first, to question the supremacy of the professor, the discipline and the university, was confusing for some and conflicting for others. This discomfort was part of a collective unlearning of how we all come to accept unequal spatial and social power dynamics in the classroom and beyond. To challenge each other and power structures of the discipline and university meant to begin to try and construct an/other relationality.

Stefano Harney and Fred Moten write – "the only possible relationship to the university today is a criminal one" (2013, 26). They, like me, are not interested in the critical academic who pursues recognition and rewards as mandated and managed by the university. Rather, they are more interested in the *subversive intellectual* who, despite being *in* the university, is not *of* the university. Subversive intellectuals are more interested in being in and of the worlds they inhabit. Thus, the only relationship to the university, they argue, is that of refusal and refuge, simultaneously. I find their theory compelling for several reasons – it destabilizes and undermines the university as the only locus of power; it refutes the binary of being for/against the university but situates power as portable and porous; it expends the university resources to communally think beyond the university; and, lastly, it shifts intellectual energies from critique to construction together with other subversive intellectuals but also communities/worlds we inhabit.

The American university has an imperial and settler colonial history. Piya Chatterjee and Sunaina Maira (2014) state that the US academy is an imperial university. Especially post 9/11, it is where much of contemporary notions of nationalism, patriotism, citizenship, and democracy are being debated and deciphered. Chatterjee and Maira state that the university is imperial because it plays a fundamental role in

> defining the racial boundaries of the nation and its 'proper' subjects and 'proper' politics. Furthermore, pedagogies of nationhood, race, gender, sexuality, class, and culture within the imperial nation are fundamentally intertwined with the interests of neoliberal capital and the possibilities of economic dominance.
>
> (8)

Along with their imperialist politics, all American universities have a settler colonial history (constructed on native land) implicating higher education in validating genocide (Gould 1992, McNeil, Wermers and Lunn 2018). If the university serves as a place of radical refuge within an imperial and settler colonial violence, PJS is not an apolitical and insipid endeavor. Rather PJS provides a complex, precarious and unsettling refuge, for my students and I alike, to think about the role of the university in the production and promotion of "peace" and "peaceful subjects." It allows us to question collectively how and why the university project may be an imperial and colonial one that perpetuates genocide, militarism, nation-building, and war. If the task of PJS is to examine power, then the social and spatial power of the universities can also not be left un-checked and the power of student intellectuals has to be understood outside a pre-prescribed peaceful politics and subjecthood, and through the lens of subversion and their own situated subjectivities.

I arrived at the American university shielded by numerous privileges and regulated by others. As my students and I started to process peace, their curiosity, courage and commitment to alternative readings of peace is when I started to see the possibilities of PJS. As we started to read texts from PJS, so much of the specters and speculations of our world became active and alive for us. Our co-studying and co-teaching peace started to be shaped by radical openness, a healthy dose of humility, and a generous suspicion of disciplinary canons. We started to hold each other accountable as we struggled to sustain and strategize alternative modes of being, knowing and doing peace.

Bearing in mind my diverse students' communities, which span from first generation college students, historically looted (often referred to as marginalized students), as well as students who are visual and different learners, I was tasked to constantly re/design the course to allow students ample and varied opportunities to reflect and express their un/learning through several modes. These included written and spoken word as well as visual illustrations and oral performances. Students wrote several short critical reflections (a practice that helps them articulate their arguments in clear and concise ways), participated as co-teachers by presenting and teaching a class with me; helped develop questions for in-class and take home assessments, and wrote papers on a topic of their choosing and passion. Their creative work was shared in the form of prose, poetry, playwriting, performance, music, or studio art, together with an artist statement/critical reflection.

Our classroom was a politically charged space of refusal and renewal. Each class would begin with us reordering the class into a circle. This process of rearranging and relocating power spatially was a minor yet important gesture to invitation (Luke and Gore 1992). However, initially the class dynamics were displayed through a defensive, distrustful and somewhat disinterested attitude. Some students remained in that space of discomfort. The difficulty with engaging an/other ways of thinking that exists within/around us necessitates that it be an intellectually arduous, emotionally laborious and spiritually awakening practice, which is not always empowering and endorsing. Over time, some of us engaged our defenses, doubts and diatribes in scripted and spoken word. Having a curriculum as our guide was helpful and permitted our classroom to slowly became an open stage of performing peace as we painfully labored together through difficult and, at times, dehumanizing themes and topics. In this co-performance of student/teacher, teacher/student, student/student and teacher/teacher, our classes became a disorderly dissonance of conversation, criticality and construction. Over the course of the semester, some of our insecurities and incongruences became less about feeling inadequate and incompetent and more about unlearning/undoing the need to be secure and intelligible.

Speculative Practice

The aspect of teaching that I find the most moving is the ability to challenge the worlds in which we understand how to be and belong to while also welcoming worlds-in-becoming. Speculative practice for me opens new epistemic and pedagogical prospects as valuable tools to profess, process and practice peace. Speculative fiction, for example, as practice of theory-making and radical practice exemplifies how to labor between/through/within identities, ideas and imagination.[5] In this section, I offer *study* as speculative practice of PJS.

Stefano Harney and Fred Moten's description of study as speculative practice is important here.[6] Building on their work, I view our classroom as an invitation to study and speculate together. Our classroom is not a chamber where knowledge is compartmentalized, consumed and commences but rather where knowledge refutes definition and becomes about dispersal, diffusion and daily practices. Studying together means to unlearn knowledge as something that is definite, discoverable and predestined. Coming together and studying together means critiquing and constructing peace as speculative practice that is not limited to the confines of our university classrooms. To study peace then means to sign up, show up, and speak back to peace. Studying peace this way is an important practice for several reasons – it dismantles the formality, functionality and futility of knowledge for knowledge's sake; the idea of study becomes a site of different (not always new) shared visions and visualizations; by communalizing and decolonizing the very notion of study is not limited to a graded exercise or disciplinary expertise but also as a shared, emotive, and endless process. Therefore, when we "study" this way, we collaborate towards decolonial and communal and ecological futures of peace and justice which have yet to be.

To study peace as speculative practice means to work, wonder, talk, labor and love together for justice. If the purpose of the class is to introduce students to peace, then my peace pedagogies necessitate that we speculate peace as economic, environmental, sexual and gender justice. Given that peace and justice are not realities, studying peace this way opens up alternative visions of peace. This retooling requires a reception of speculative knowledges that are often related to fiction, fantasy, and fantastical to a movement towards decolonization. Walidah Imarisha and Adrienne Maree Brown (2015), in extending the vision of Octavia Butler and making a case for science fiction as sites of working through what constitutes just worlds offer some guidance:

> Whenever we try to envision a world without war, without violence, without prisons, without capitalism, we are engaging in an exercise of speculative fiction. Organizers and activists struggle tirelessly to create and envision another world, or many other worlds, just as science fiction does … so what better venue for organizers to explore their work than through writing original science fiction stories?
>
> (Broomfield 2013)

In this way, speculation as voicing, visualizing and visioning helps us to write and rewrite the past/future in ways that disrupts and destabilizes contemporary power regimes and envisions alternative peace/s and systems of justice.

Over the last several years, students have expressed their frustrations and fears around the lack of solutions and remedies. In working with them, I challenge us to question why education infers empowerment. The circulating phrase "knowledge is power" supports that partial premise. However, not all education is empowering and not all empowerment is enabling. Education is not always empowering because none of us are actually free or un-free. Kevin Kumashiro (2002) reminds us – "education involves learning something that disrupts our common sense view of the world. The crisis that results from unlearning, then, is a necessary and desirable part of anti-oppressive education. Desiring to learn involves desiring difference and overcoming our resistance to discomfort" (62). Thus, disempowerment and at times disillusionment are tough discontents and discomforts of un/learning dominant knowledge. This is especially disorienting when our privileges are internalized and embedded into power structures we find emancipatory and enabling. For knowledges to be empowering/enabling means to make visible the violence that has been invisibilized in peace discourses and examine violence as a speculative practice while holding ourselves accountable to whose definitions of peace and violence we are privileging, promoting and practicing.

I share my students' anxieties and aspirations as they develop a critical consciousness surrounding their own complex and contradictory realities and subjectivities while they enter the uneven world of jobs, internships, and careers. Having worked with foundations, non-profits, corporations and governments, I am intimately aware of the painful and pathological relationship between theory and practice. Encouraging students to situate themselves within shifting regimes of desires and dichotomies, and inside complex violent economic realities, equips them to conceptualize studying not just as a moment but also as a lifelong movement towards collective freedom for dignity, humanity, peace and justice.

Teaching is a deliberate feminist and queer meditative practice of refusal and resistance, thus I value all facets and features of education as a field between emancipation and imprisonment. I welcome visibility and voice as much as I recognize the classroom as a sober/ing place for quiet study, healing, rage, anger and melancholy. We collectively question what is defined and deployed as "normal" and "natural" ways of being, learning and doing. Deborah Briztman's work is valuable here. She argues that queer pedagogy is:

> one that refuses normal practices and practices of normalcy, one that begins with an ethical concern for one's own reading practices, one that is interested in exploring what one cannot bear to know, one interested in the imaginings of a sociality unhinged from the dominant conceptual order.
>
> (Britzman 1995, 165)

Thus, rather than deny the melancholia and misery that such un/learning, denormalizing and denaturalizing inevitably brings with it, it means to experience and embrace the painful aspects of our past so we start to grasp our violent present/s, and the possibilities of our future.

Despite the production and proliferation of PJS as a restorative and reparative discipline, which advocates for rebalancing of power and reconciliation, peace has not been achieved. Peace remains an incomplete struggle for us despite the plethora of academic programs, courses, periodicals, and conferences alongside the work of peace specialists – academics, activists, humanitarian workers, human rights advocates, diplomatic corps and political leaders. Thus, the challenge that pervades so much of my pedagogical practice is to probe the overarching purpose of peace. In trying to answer this question I situate peace as a process and practice of justice by offering students *an/other* reading of peace as we speculate and study peace within/through our situated subjectivities. This reflects my desire to move beyond dichotomies and dualities of disempowered/empowered, violent/non-violent and teacher/student, which runs deep and intimate to my own trajectory as someone constantly working on/through/within and despite figurative and material borders and boundaries. I swim in these spaces with my students, often collectively gasping for air. Indeed, they are not "them", they are me. In this way, my pedagogy is committed to opening up possibilities for decolonizing, feministing and queering peace, non/violence and justice.

Conclusion

To teach peace means to sit and study together with our collective rage, our uneasiness and refusal while we process our pain and privilege, continuously. It means to share the burdens of "peaceful violence" and hold each other accountable while we speculate another world, and many worlds, of peace. This is meant to encourage us to be co-conspirators where we question, engage and challenge each other through collective and critical consciousness. To teach for me means to look inside the deepest crevices of my own being and ways of knowing while simultaneously also looking beyond into the unknown "peaceful" world that has yet to be/come.

My pedagogical practice is flawed and fluid, for which I take complete responsibility. To say that the last few years of teaching have changed me would be true, but what lies beneath this change is the practice of co-thinking with my students as we challenged academic vocabularies, formal theories, privileged knowledge and the position of a professor. I end with Toni Morrison whose work inspires so many. She has famously said "[i]f there's a book that you want to read, but it hasn't been written yet, then you must write it." I take her guidance seriously as someone who aspires to study and teach a world anew. Thus, if there is a world that we want to live in, but it hasn't been created, then we must create it. This rewriting and rebuilding is informed and indebted to archives, stories, histories, geographies of my ancestors, communities, teachers, professors, students, and mentors who along the way that have questioned me, shaken me, sustained me, decolonized my ideas, queered my analysis, and given me feminist and speculative tools. To them I owe everything. To them I owe *an/other* route to liberation.

Notes

1 While Fanon does not directly define peaceful violence the following excerpts clarify his ideas of peaceful violence – "within the framework of peaceful co-existence, all colonies are destined to disappear, and in the long run neutralism is destined to be respected by capitalism .... [b]etween the violence of the colonies and that peaceful violence that the world is steeped in, there is a kind of complicit agreement, a sort of homogeneity. The intermediary does not lighten the oppression, nor seek to hide the domination; he shows them up and puts them into practice with the clear conscience of an upholder of the peace; yet he is the bringer of violence into the home and into the mind of the native." (Fanon 1963, 79–80, 37)

2 Disciplinary decadence means that "[i]nstead of being open-ended pursuits of knowledge, many disciplines have become self-circumscribed in their aims and methods in ways that appear ontological. By this I mean that many disciplines lose sight of themselves as efforts to understand the world and have collapsed into the hubris of asserting themselves as the world."

3 The students reflected broad range of academic disciplines – biology, business management, chemistry, economics, film, international relations, marketing, peace and justice studies, non-profit studies, women and gender studies, and queer studies.

4 I worked in global philanthropy, corporate social responsibility, humanitarian aid, education policy, international development, social finance and social entrepreneurship.

5 The work of Octavia Butler, Samuel Delany and Junot Diaz inspires this type of labor and my closing section.

6 The definition of study: When I think about the way we were using the term 'study,' I think we were committed to the idea that study is what you do with other people. It's talking and walking around with other people, working, dancing, suffering, some irreducible convergence of all three, held under the name of speculative practice. The notion of a rehearsal – being in a kind of workshop, playing in a band, in a jam session, or old men sitting on a porch, or people working together in a factory – there are these various modes of activity. The point of calling it "study" is to mark that the incessant and irreversible intellectuality of these activities was already there. These activities aren't ennobled by the fact that we now say, "oh, if you did these things in a certain way, you could be said to be have been studying." To do these things is to be involved in a kind of common intellectual practice. What's important is to recognize that that has been the case – because that recognition allows you to access a whole, varied, alternative history of thought. (Harney and Moten 2012)

References

Anzaldúa, Gloria. 1987. *Borderlands/La Frontera: The New Mestiza*. San Francisco: Spinsters/Aunt Lute.

Azarmandi, Mahdis. 2017. *Colonial Continuities - A study of anti-racism in Aotearoa New Zealand and Spain*, PhD diss., University of Otago. http://hdl.handle.net/10523/7655.

Bhabha, Homi. 1994. *The Location of Culture*. London and New York: Routledge.

Boulding, Elise. 1984. "The Gender Gap." *Journal of Peace Research* 21, no. 1: 1–3.

Boulding, Elise. 1995. "Feminist Inventions in the Art of Peacemaking: A Century Overview." *Peace & Change* 20, no. 4: 408–438.

Britzman, Deborah. 1995. "Is There a Queer Pedagogy? Or, Stop Reading Straight." *Educational Theory* 45, no. 2: 151–165.

Broomfield, Matt. 2013. Interview: Octavia's Brood. *Cherwell Newspaper*, August 1. http://cherwell.org/2013/08/01/interview-octavias-brood/.

Burguieres, Mary. 1990. "Feminist Approaches to Peace: Another Step for Peace Studies." *Millenium: Journal of International Studies* 19, no. 1: 1–18.

Butler, Judith. 2009. *Frames of War: When is Life Grievable?* London: Verso Books.

Caprioli, Mary. 2000. "Gendered Conflict." *Journal of Peace Research* 37, no. 1: 51–68.

Chatterjee, Piya, and Sunaina Maira, eds. 2014. *The Imperial University: Academic Repression and Scholarly Dissent*. Minneapolis: University of Minnesota Press.

Collins, Patricia Hill. 1990. *Black Feminist Thought: Knowledge, Consciousness, and the Politics of Empowerment*. Boston: Unwin Hyman.

Confortini, Catia C. 2006. "Galtung, Violence, and Gender: The case for a Peace Studies/Feminism Alliance." *Peace and Change* 31, no. 3: 333–367.

de Lissovoy, Noah. "Decolonial Pedagogy and The Ethics of the Global." *Discourse: Studies in the Cultural Politics of Education* 31, no. 3(2010): 279–293.

de Sève, Micheline. 1987. "Feminism and Pacifism, or, The Art of Tranquilly Playing Russian Roulette." In *Women and Peace: Theoretical Historical and Practical Perspectives*, edited by Ruth Roach Pierson. London: Crom Helm, 44–49.

Fanon, Frantz. 1963. *The Wretched of The Earth*. New York: Grove Press.

Fanton, Victoria C. 2012. *Decolonizing Peace*. Lake Oswego, OR: World Dignity Press.

Freire, Paulo. 1972. *Pedagogy of the Oppressed*. New York: Herder and Herder.

Freire, Paulo. 1985. *The Politics of Education: Culture, Power, and Liberation*. Hadley, MA: Bergin & Garvey Publishers.

Galtung, Johan. 1969. "Violence, Peace, and Peace Research." *Journal of Peace Research* 6, no. 3: 167–191.

Galtung, Johan. 1971. "Structural Theory of Imperialism." *Journal of Peace Research* 8, no. 2: 81–117

Galtung, Johan. 1990. "Cultural Violence." *Journal of Peace Research* 27, no. 3: 291–305.

Galtung, Johan. 1996. *Peace by Peaceful Means: Peace and Conflict, Development and Civilization*. Oslo, Norway: International Peace Research Institute and London and Thousand Oaks, CA: Sage Publications.

Gould, Janice. 1992. "The Problem with Being "India": One Mixed-Blood's Dilemma." In *De/colonizing the Subject: The Politics of Gender in Women's Autobiography*, edited by Sidonie Smith and Julia Watson. Minneapolis: University of Minneapolis Press, 81–89.

Gordon, Lewis. 2006. *Disciplinary Decadence: Living Thought in Trying Times*. Boulder, CO andLondon: Paradigm Publishers.

Hall, Stuart. 1996. "The West and the Rest: Discourse and Power" In, *Modernity: An Introduction to Modern Societies*, edited by Stuart Hall, David Held, Don Hubert and Kenneth Thompson. Cambridge, MA and Oxford: Blackwell Publishers, 184–227.

Hagen, Jamie J. 2016. "Queering women, peace and security." *International Affairs* 92, no. 2: 313–332.

Haraway, Donna. 1988. "Situated Knowledges: The Science Question in Feminism and the Privilege of Partial Perspective." *Feminist Studies* 14, no. 3: 575–599.

Harney, Stefano and Fred Moten. 2012. "Studying Through the Undercommons," interview by Stevphen Shukaitis, *Class War University: anti-capitalist, decolonial, feminist, queer, anti-authoritarian movements on the terrain of universities and beyond.* Nov 12. https://classwaru.org/2012/11/12/studying-through-the-undercommons-stefano-harney-fred-moten-interviewed-by-stevphen-shukaitis/

Haunani-Kay, Trask. 2004. "The Color of Violence." *Social Justice* 31, no. 4 *Native Women and State Violence*: 8–16.

hooks, bell. 1994. *Teaching to Transgress.* New York: Routledge.

Imarisha, Walidah and Brown, Adrienne Maree. 2015. *Octavia's Brood: Science Fiction Stories from Social Justice Movements.* Oakland, CA: AK Press.

King, Jr, Martin Luther. 1963. *Letter from Birmingham Jail.*

Kumashiro, Kevin K. 2002. *Troubling Education: Queer Activism and Anti-Oppressive Pedagogy.* New York, NY: Routledge.

Lugones, Maria. 2008. "The Coloniality of Gender." *Worlds & Knowledges Otherwise* 2, 1–17.

Luke, Carmen and Gore, Jennifer. 1992. *Feminisms and Critical Pedagogy.* New York: Routledge Press.

McNeil, Elizabeth, James E. Wermers and Joshua Lunn, eds. 2018. *Mapping Queer Space(s) of Praxis and Pedagogy.* New York: Palgrave Macmillan.

Mignolo, Walter. 2009. "Epistemic Disobedience, Independent Thought and De-Colonial Freedom." *Theory, Culture & Society* 26, no. 7–8: 1–23.

Mizzi, Robert C., and Sean Byrne. 2015. "Queer Theory and Peace and Conflict Studies: Some Critical Reflections." In *Gender and Peacebuilding: All Hands Required*, edited by Maureen Flaherty, Sean Byrne, Hamdesa Tuso and Thomas Matyok. New York: Lexington Books, 359–374.

Moolakkattu, John. 2006. "Feminism and Peace Studies: Taking Stock of a Quarter Century of Efforts." *Indian Journal of Gender Studies* 13, no. 2: 137–162.

Moraga, Cherríe, and Gloria Anzaldúa, eds. 1981. *This Bridge Called My Back: Writings by Radical Women of Color.* Watertown, MA: Persephone Press.

Moten, Fred, and Stefano Harney. 2013. *The Undercommons: Fugitive Planning & Black Study.* New York: Minor Compositions.

Reardon, Betty. 1993. *Women and Peace: Feminist Visions of Global Security.* Albany, NY: SUNY Press.

Reardon, Betty. 1996. *Sexism and the War System.* Syracuse, NY: Syracuse University Press.

Rennie, Linda. 1991. "Women as Peacemakers." *Peace & Change* 16, no. 4: 331–354.

Roy, Arundhati. 2004. "Peace & The New Corporate Liberation Theology" The Sydney Peace Prize Lecture, Seymour Theatre Centre, University of Sydney. November 4.

Said, Edward. 1978. *Orientalism.* New York: Pantheon Books.

Salah, Trish. 2014. "Notes on the Subaltern." *TSQ: Transgender Studies Quarterly Inaugural Issue: Keywords for Trans* Studies* 1, no. 1–2: 297–305.

Salter, Colin. 2013. *Whiteness and Social Change: Remnant Colonialisms and White Civility in Australia and Canada.* Cambridge, UK: Cambridge Scholars Publishing.

Santos, Boaventura de Sousa. 2002. *Toward a New Legal Common Sense: Law, Globalization and Emancipation*. London: Butterworths.

Sjoberg, Laura. 2014. *Gender, War and Conflict*. Cambridge, UK: Polity Press.

Smith, Andrea Lee. 2006. "Heteropatriarchy and the Three Pillars of Settler Colonialism." In *The Color of Violence: The INCITE! Anthology*, edited by Andrea Lee Smith, Beth E. Richie, Julia Sudbury and Janelle White. Cambridge, MA: South End Press, 68–73.

Smith, Dorothy. 1974. "Women's Perspective as a Radical Critique of Sociology." *Sociological Inquiry* 44: 7–13.

Tuhiwai-Smith, Linda. 1999. *Decolonizing Methodologies: Research and Indigenous Peoples*. London: Zed Books.

Spivak, Gayatri Chakravorty. 1988. "Can the Subaltern Speak?" In *Marxism and the Interpretation of Culture*, edited by Cary Nelson and Lawrence Grossberg. Urbana, IL: University of Illinois Press, 271–313.

Spivak, Gayatri Chakravorty. 1999. *A Critique of Postcolonial Reason: Toward a History of the Vanishing Present*. Cambridge, MA: Harvard University Press.

Tuck, Eve and Wayne K. Yang. 2012. "Decolonization is not a metaphor." *Decolonization: Indigeneity, Education, & Society* 1, no. 1: 1–40.

Webel, Charles and Johan Galtung, eds. 2007. *Handbook of Peace and Conflict Studies*. New York: Routledge.

Wynter, Sylvia. 2003. "Unsettling the Coloniality of Being/Power/Truth/Freedom: Towards the Human, after Man, Its Overrepresentation-An Argument." *The New Centennial Review* 3, no. 3: 257–337.

12 An Irritant in the Academic Body

The Place of Peace and Justice Studies in the Modern University

Mark Lance

How should the field of Peace and Justice Studies (hereafter PJS) relate to academia more broadly? What sort of relation should we have to the modern university? I argue that attempts to assimilate to the prevailing academic structure – to become an established discipline or interdisciplinary nexus on a par with history, sociology, American Studies, etc – is in serious tension with fundamental values that should, and often do, shape our field. My argument begins with the claim that Peace and Justice studies should not pretend to neutrality. It is a field of study centered on constitutive values, values that are in stark contrast to the existing power structures of society.

Thus, PJS is committed, at the very least, to substantive challenges to the economic, gender, racial, judicial and international systems in place in the world. My second large claim is that the contemporary university is structurally complicit in deep ways with these power structures. Regardless of the intent of individual professors, there are systematic ways in which the practice and institutionalization of academia – the ways that education and research actually function – reinforce the systems that PJS is constitutively opposed to.

These claims together mean that it is part of the constitutive goal of the field to challenge institutional arrangements central to the function of the modern university. My final claim is that achieving a typical place within that institution will substantially impact our ability and inclination to engage in this critical work. Thus, if PJS is to remain true to its value-based understanding, it must seek out a different, contested place within the academy. While such a stance puts many professors in an even more precarious position than they are currently, I argue that this is simply the situation in which we find ourselves. I conclude with an examination of some concrete ways in which the field can retain a role within the modern university while still effectively challenging the broader social systems the university is complicit in.

The Nature of the Field

Many academic disciplines are based around specific normative goals, goals that shape the nature of the empirical work of that discipline. Consider nursing: the field will incorporate empirical work from anatomy, chemistry, economics, demographics, and much more, but none of this is studied purely for abstract theoretical purposes. Rather, the field is based around the constitutive goal of health. Nursing training is designed to produce competent practitioners where competence is defined as the ability to aid the health and well-being of individuals in society.[1] This is not to say that the notion of "health and well-being" is uncontested within the field. Of course there are specific cases that are hotly debated – euthanasia, abortion, certain sorts of clinical trials – and many contested issues of detail, to say nothing of competing meta-theories about the nature of health. But the general idea that there is a shared purpose of promoting health is constitutive of the field.

Similarly, I want to claim that PJS is itself organized around the constitutive goal of making the world more just and peaceful, and its pedagogy is designed to bring students to a greater competence at working for these goals. As with nursing, this does not make the field anti-empirical. Indeed, virtually every discipline in the Academy is relevant to this work. But empirical, formal, or conceptual work is centered on and relevant insofar as it contributes to the constitutive practical orientation of the field.

Though I've not conducted a systematic survey, I've been involved in the field for some 25 years and this conception is certainly standard. It is written into the bylaws of the Peace and Justice Studies Association. It is assumed in most introductory textbooks[2]. But suppose someone were to insist, on the contrary, that the field *in itself* is simply focused on understanding the social function of peace and justice along with the effects of various institutions, movements, etc. Any goal of making things better is strictly external. We scholars might, on our own time, want to make the world more just and peaceful, but that is not the goal of our research, and making students better at this not the goal of our teaching qua professional PJS academicians.

I am inclined to say that there is a very simple argument against such a self-conception: the world is very far from acceptably just or peaceful. It is, in fact, bloody, violent, and systemically unjust along numerous dimensions. Figuring out how best to change that, and developing the skills needed to do so, is hard and takes intellectual work. So some branch of academia should tackle those theoretical and pedagogical challenges. And if not Peace and Justice Studies, then who?[3]

The Entanglement of the University in an Unjust World

This premise too is, I think, fairly obvious. Universities accept contracts from the US military, the state security and intelligence apparatus, and corporations of all sorts. Students are trained for careers as soldiers, CIA operatives, leaders of corporations, political and corporate propagandists, etc. The US university – which is increasingly modeling itself on a corporation in its internal work – is, thus, deeply involved in, indeed essential to, the work of the major power centers of contemporary society. This complicity is systemic, multi-level, and multi-dimensional. If one opposes, say, militarism, then one must oppose the work of universities in making contemporary militarism possible. Similarly, for economic imperialism, the prison-industrial complex, etc. One cannot challenge the systemic aspects of police violence against African Americans, to pick just one example of hundreds, without implicitly challenging the many criminology programs that train students to work as police or prison guards and receive their funding as a result of doing so.

There is a second dimension to this connection that makes it even more significant for our work. If we are training students to be effective agents of change, one dimension of this will be to train them to be effective activists and organizers. Over my own time at Georgetown, my students have led efforts for a living wage, to unionize campus workers, for an LGBTQ center, for a right to have a gay organization and a pro-choice organization, to protest wars and university support for them, to divest from fossil fuel companies, to offer meaningful reparations for our history of slavery, and much more. In each of these cases, the students were engaging with broader societal issues, but their immediate focus was on the administration.

This has a political and a pedagogical point. One does not get good at doing activist work simply by reading books and writing papers about activist work. Just as nurses need time in a clinical setting, working with real patients, so budding social change agents need time on real campaigns, dealing with real issues. And given the realities of college life, the practical clinic is frequently going to be the most local injustice – that on campus. Thus the best way for us to train our students in the way they need to be trained in order to further our mission is to encourage them in challenging our institution.

On Not Becoming Co-opted

My claim is, then, that we can do all this more effectively if we are not established as an accepted part of the university. If PJS becomes another established department alongside English and Math, there are two dynamics that will follow. First, it means that the university has budgetary control over us. Funding of lines, tenure decisions, and yearly budgetary approval will all be conditioned upon our teaching and research in PJS and will constitute considerable leverage. The university, by and large, does not want to fund teaching and research that challenges its own practices and power. Thus, the university will use this considerable leverage to encourage a sort of leveling down of the field. Over time, we will see PJS reconceived as "peace and conflict studies" or "conflict management" or "conflict resolution". Funding will be available for lines that focus on minor tweaks to procedural matters and a field conceived around systemic change will find itself turning out the sort of practitioner who corporations find it useful to hire so as to avoid unionization.

Now of course nothing like this is necessary. But it is clear that there is strong pressure in this direction. I have been involved in this field for 25 years and have studied the evolution of programs at dozens of colleges and universities. Over and over I have seen people move in this direction simply because this was where it was possible to move a department.

And there is a second dynamic beyond direct financial pressure. As our work becomes normalized there is frequently a subtle psychological pressure not to upset those who are hiring you. This need not be fear of reprisal – though that is certainly a reality. Humans, like all animals, are more easily conditioned by positive reinforcement than by punishment. In the case of well-established peace studies, or conflict resolution scholars this can often mean a gradual erosion of radicalism, a focus on liberal reforms, and a distancing from the activist students who should be our core mission. Again, anecdotal though it may be, I have seen this over and over in the past 25 years. I say this not to condemn anyone, but it is simply a reality that when it comes to student protest, in my long experience with supporting it, one is much more likely to find a physics professor than a conflict resolution professor out on the street or locked down in the administration building.

Compare someone employed as a professor of PJS to someone, like myself, employed as a professor of philosophy. Let's suppose both want to teach courses in PJS and to train practically oriented students for effective social change work. The former professor will officially be evaluated at each stage of their career in terms of their work in this area. Tenure committees will be able to charge their work with "bias" "politicization" "lack of objectivity" and all the other tropes that serve to prioritize work that doesn't challenge the status quo. In my own case, by contrast, I went up for tenure on the basis of work in logic, philosophy of language, and philosophy of mathematics. Of course someone could have still blackballed me because of my politics, but it would be much harder. And since there was no sense that my political work – including research and teaching – was representing my department, there was much less chance of it harming future hires and future budgets.

There is no necessary progression here. It is perfectly possible to maintain a radical focus despite the financial and psychological pressure that I'm pointing to. But there is, as I said at the outset, a tension. And it is a tension we would do well not to downplay. We all like to think that we will not be subject to co-optation, or financial bullying, but the reality is that most of us are. It happens with great frequency and none of us are magically immune.

It is also obvious that there are benefits to an established program or department. Simply put, we can do more with more resources. And if folks were facing a choice between the resources of a department like Political Science balanced against the moderating control this gave to the administration, I think it would be a very hard call. But this choice is rare to non-existent. Virtually all PJS programs, no matter how many compromises they make so as to remain unthreatening, are marginalized, underfunded, staffed with adjuncts or at most full-time non-tenure line faculty, and crucially under-supported in research. Thus, it seems to me that we surrender the autonomy of outsider status, very often, at a very cheap price. Again, there are complicated factors in any such trade-off, but I think the tension is real, and needs to be taken more seriously. That our goal should be to build a department of PJS is not at all obviously correct.

Some Other Models

What other models are possible? I have already suggested one: that a PJS program be an interdisciplinary undertaking of faculty tenured in traditional departments. This has the obvious cost of meaning extra work for faculty, but the benefit that we will feel free to focus that extra work in any way we want. One can still push for things like administrative support, course buy-outs, travel, all the usual, but none of the faculty will be evaluated on the basis of this work, no line will depend on it, etc.

There is also a sort of hybrid model. At Georgetown, after 15 years of a program of the above sort that graduated some 40 minors a year, we finally succeeded in approving a major in Justice and Peace Studies. (This was the result of a brilliant activist campaign by our students, a campaign that they had learned to produce in our classes.) As part of this, the university made its first full-time appointments in JUPS. We now have two full-time non-tenure line faculty and graduate about 40 majors a year. Obviously two faculty can't teach all the courses needed for such a program. Various of us in traditional departments fill in. I teach half-time in JUPS. Several other tenured faculty teach one dedicated course per year. Others teach cross-listed courses. And we fill in with a few sections by adjuncts. We also make frequent use of *ad hoc* visitors, activists, political prisoners, community organizers, independent scholars, etc. (Being in the District of Columbia makes this easier than it would be in many locations of course.) This mixture means that those of us with greater security in the university and greater distance from the area in our official position can take certain risks. I teach the most directly activist-related courses. Our tenured participants are more likely to be the ones out and visible in protests or civil disobedience actions while our non-tenured folks specifically in the program are more likely to work behind the scenes. This works fairly well. We have more resources than we would with only department-based faculty; we protect the PJS faculty while allowing them to maintain radical content in their courses; and the university leverage over our focus is minimized. (It is also worth saying that for many reasons our administration is relatively supportive of the work we do. So everything is easier here.)

(Indecisive) Conclusion

I do not suggest that these non-departmental models, or other related models, are normatively required of everyone. For those trained in PJS, there is an obvious and fully justified goal of having the same status as anyone else in academia. And of course there is no reason in principle why the study of peace and justice should have a lesser status than anything else. But in practice, given the complicity of the university in social injustice and war, there is a very good reason to think that universities will not support a radically centered PJS department. And if the choice is between a fully funded department devoted to training in alternative dispute resolution along with a few courses in arms-reduction treaties, or a marginal constantly contested gadfly interdisciplinary program that focuses on structural violence, radical change, and mass nonviolent organizing, I would argue that the latter is a greater contribution to what the field ought to be. At the very least, again returning to my advertised conclusion, there is a tension here between our radical and practical goals, and full establishment within an institution deeply complicit in the systematic suppression of those goals.

Notes

1 Such constitutive goals are also obvious in engineering, law, public health, education and psychology, but also in the more applied areas of economics, philosophy, mathematics, etc.

2 Cf. David Barash: Approaches to Peace (Oxford: Oxford University Press, 2014); or Maia Hallward and Julie Norman: Understanding Nonviolence (Malden, MA: Polity Press, 2015); just as two examples.

3 Should one remain unconvinced, and insist on a non-normative, purely descriptive conception of the field, then take what follows as a conditional argument: if you accept that changing the world is a constitutive goal of the field, then I claim my views about the place of the field in the modern university follow. If not, then you should forthrightly accept that your work is not geared toward peace and justice, but at most interested in the abstract study of these.

Conclusion

Emily Welty

Few experiences force an academic to narrow and concretize her explanation of her field of study like talking to prospective students at a university open house. Parents and students squint at the sign "Peace and Justice Studies" amid the flurry of other departments and the overwhelming information about everything from financial aid to dorms. And they always ask the same question: "Peace and Justice Studies – what's that about?" We don't have time to unpack structural violence, the tenets of alternative dispute resolution or the complexities of peacebuilding. We don't serve our own emerging discipline by describing it as an interdisciplinary salad "a little bit of political science and a little bit of sociology". It is perhaps four habits of the heart and mind that best define what we are doing/thinking/creating/deconstructing in this field. Peace and Justice Studies is about thinking critically about power, exercising solidarity with suffering people, practicing optimism despite being aware of all of the reasons one might despair, and engaging in activism to create more just, peaceful communities on the local, national and international levels.

What emerges from this collection of essays and reflections is not a normative depiction of what a Peace and Justice Studies classroom "should" look like or feel like. Rather, these authors each provide glimpses into the ways that they have shaped particular pedagogical practices which embody particular visions of a more just, peaceful world. What is striking about this collection is not a unified vision of an idealized Peace and Justice Studies program – in fact, the chapters demonstrate both convergences and fractures when taken as a whole. While the moments of convergence are striking, it is the differences between the pieces that demonstrate the growth of the field. It is relatively easy for a single program at a particular university to create a unified vision of what peace or justice might mean in their context and to create learning outcomes, courses and extracurricular activities that embody that vision. But as a field, Peace and Justice Studies demonstrates a burgeoning maturity when there are different emphases among programs that reflect a wider, more diverse set of expressions of scholarship and practice.

In the early days of Peace Studies, the "canon" consisted of relatively few prominent scholars (mostly white, mostly men) who conveyed a message that was counter-cultural to the mainstream disciplines at the time – war was wrong, peace was achievable, injustice should be challenged and non-violence in the face of oppression was possible. These basic messages often felt like a radical spark in the midst of disciplinary canons which dictated that inequality was inevitable, political realism was a responsible security position and human nature was essentially violent. As the authors of the volume demonstrate, the field has significantly diversified and matured while not losing sight of the basic premise that another world is possible.

Nonetheless, there is more to be done. While these authors exhibit some of the best pedagogical practices of our field, none of them are content to suggest that this field has done enough to include marginalized voices, to shift the basic power structures of the university or to create classroom spaces that strike the right balance between comfort/safety and the risky space where learning occurs. Even while the field has become more intersectional and inclusive in its scholarship, there is, in the words of Geoffrey Bateman, more "queering" to be done. There are still silences around issues of ableism and disability, insufficient attention to the colonial legacies that haunt both our classrooms and our textbooks, gaps in our pedagogies that create comfort for some at the expense of others.

Convergences and Fractures

Many of the chapters demonstrate the commitment to intersectionality as a core concept for both the curriculum as well as the pedagogical practices in the classroom. Bateman recounts how a thinker like Barbara Deming provides a model for examining the intersections of gender, sexual orientation, class and race. While intersectionality has long been a standard of Women's and Gender Studies, it has not been treated as a standard value in Peace and Justice Studies. However, several authors demonstrate how this might be changing. There is an explicit embrace of feminist epistemologies in many of the chapters as well as what Sara Shroff describes as "a wayward, feminist, queer and decolonial way of teaching" which emphasizes both learning and unlearning. Byron's chapter reminds us of the importance of seeing education as attending to both the inner and outer realms of experience and the way that feminist scholarship has stressed the relationship between the personal and the political. Intersectionality goes beyond merely trying to add the voices of women or people of color into the curriculum (though that too is an important task) but demands that we also consider much deeper questions of who benefits, who profits and who is silenced in our classrooms. We seek to "diversify" the voices that are amplified in our field not simply to "expose" middle class white students to a wider range of voices but because of the fundamental truth that the difficult task of knowledge production does not have a center or a periphery. Many scholars in our field question the very basis of terms like "diversity" critiquing the way that they continue to privilege and center white voices while pretending to reach towards something wider.

Peace and Justice Studies has sometimes been caricatured as a space of soft scholarship full of students (and faculty) holding hands and talking about their feelings. Perhaps it is our aversion and even fear of such stereotypes that has fed a reticence to discuss the power of affect and emotions in the pedagogical experience. Joy Meeker and Emily Welty's chapters in this volume directly address this relative silence in the field. And Karen Ridd bravely embraces the power of love in her powerful meditation on George Lakey's injunction to teachers, "Love the students, love the material, love yourself."

Several of the authors wrestle with the difficult balance of working in a field that seems to offer pathways to either hope or despair and share their struggle of helping students to live in the paradox of both hope and despair. Randy Janzen's piece fixes our attention on the necessity of moving students in both directions – that they might fully understand and produce the critical analysis of the crisis of violence, racism, war or climate change while also maintaining a hopeful orientation which fires a commitment to working to reduce these types of violence. Welty's piece questions how to challenge the naïve optimism of many Peace and Justice Studies students without crushing them under the sense of despair that they are the problem.

Several of the authors emphasize the importance of story-telling, fiction and the humanities generally as a way to fully engage in both the act of humanizing the Other as well as imagining new possibilities for the future. Amanda Smith Byron's piece emphasizes storytelling as a practice that might "prick the consciences of readers by inviting a reexamination of the values and interests undergirding certain discourses, practices and institutional arrangements" while Michelle Collins-Sibley offers examples of the way the conscience of students might be engaged by considering the personhood of a fictional character as a way into more deeply considering the personhood of people of color in the United States. Sara Shroff's chapter reinforces this point as her emphasis on the power of speculative fiction reinforces Byron's call for stories that help us imagine new ways of being. However, Joy Meeker's chapter sounds a cautionary note about the role of stories in teaching about privilege by describing the danger of assuming that the stories of marginalized students will teach privileged students and not considering the way that this reinforces systems of oppression in the classroom.

As Peace and Justice Studies programs proliferate, these challenges of how we might dwell in the university while still making critical choices about how to oppose it become more acute. In some universities, such programs are being asked to consider whether a course such as Introduction to Peace and Justice Studies might become a mandatory, general-education requirement for all students. As scholars who believe in the value of our field and scholarship, it may be tempting to quickly agree that every student's education is enhanced by exposure to our core precepts. But several of the contributions in this book would urge us to exercise caution and to carefully examine how a mainstreaming of the field might change it in ways that we find distasteful or contrary to our own principles.

Mark Lance challenges readers to consider whether a field like Peace and Justice Studies which has maintained a critical posture of dismantling systems of oppression might be overly domesticated and weakened by becoming a mainstream discipline with all of the accoutrements of institutionalization. Sara Shroff's chapter also urges us to critically question our relationship to the university particularly given "the university's racist and settler/violent colonial beginnings" and increasing corporatization. Shroff positions herself as "not interested in the critical academic who pursues recognition and rewards as mandated and managed by the university" and expresses her desire for "the *subversive intellectual* who, despite being *in* the university, is not *of* the university". Lance's chapter reinforces Shroff's challenge as he articulates the university's desire to leverage the field to its own advantage which will mute attempts in teaching or scholarship "that challenges its own practices and power", a point echoed by Welty's examination of the importance of reflexivity as a practice within the field's core values and methodologies.

Groarke, Khoury and Pries direct our attention to specific pedagogical practices in the classroom. Groarke helps us reimagine service learning, not as a way to "help" some other group of people that we pity but as a way to practice justice by engaging in community organizing that guides students in seeing themselves as collaborators rather than helpers. Khoury similarly decenters the power relationships in the classroom by designing role plays that shift the transfer of knowledge from something to be extracted from a text and memorized to something that can be imagined and lived out in a temporary invented world of a role-playing simulation. Pries emphasizes experiential learning as a pedagogy that encourages cognitive disequilibrium which "unshackles" students from their prejudices and pre-conceived beliefs about the status quo. Pries uses one of the most difficult and intractable conflicts – the Israel/Palestine conflict – and uses a locally contextualized manifestation of the conflict to interrogate the ethics of the tactics of boycott and divestment as a nonviolent tactic.

Most of us are working in Peace and Justice Studies because we are fueled by a passion for justice and a fervent belief that the world can be a different, more peaceful, more radically just place than it currently is. We love our students and we are committed to accompanying them, learning from them and with them while guiding them into a way of being that helps them speak, write and act with confidence, grace and ambition. Perhaps because this field has been motivated by the determined imagination that human beings can be more open, more gentle, more committed to solidarity and seeking the good of one another, in our job in the classroom we are also well-positioned to question the conventional wisdom about what a university can and should be. The best wisdom of our scholarship has been that the status quo with all of its violence, greed and disregard for the dignity of human beings can and must be changed. While we teach students the radical history of those on whose shoulders we stand or we train them to critically analyze the power structures around them, we have a responsibility to mirror that wisdom and to practice those ways of being a beloved community together in the classroom. It is our hope that this collection of voices in this volume contributes to that re-imagining of the classroom as a place of joyful struggle and radical commitment to the prevention of suffering.

Index

Headings in italics indicate a publication title.

For Product Safety Concerns and Information please contact our EU representative GPSR@taylorandfrancis.com
Taylor & Francis Verlag GmbH, Kaufingerstraße 24, 80331 München, Germany

www.ingramcontent.com/pod-product-compliance
Lightning Source LLC
LaVergne TN
LVHW021129300926
849160LV00010B/925
9780815346357